Ottawa's Caribbean Community

History and Profiles – Since 1955

Rideau Canal in Ottawa, Canada. Oil painting by Shirley Van Dusen

Dave Tulloch

Ottawa's Caribbean Community: History and Profiles — since 1955
by Dave Tulloch
Copyright © 2023 Dave Tulloch
All rights reserved

First Edition
Hardcover 9781989048740
Softcover 9781989048887
Digital 9781989048894

Information about the Caribbean community has been researched and compiled by the author from public sources such as Wikipedia, the Canadian Encyclopedia, government websites, and news archives; these have been referenced throughout the book.
Font Cover map: University of Michigan
Front: Rideau Canal in Ottawa, Canada. Oil painting by Shirley Van Dusen.
Back: Caribbean Islet, north coast of Montego Bay, Jamaica. Photo by Dave Tulloch (2022)

ca. 90,000 words
8" x 10"
50 lb paper
268 p

Design and editing

Petra Books - petrabooks.ca

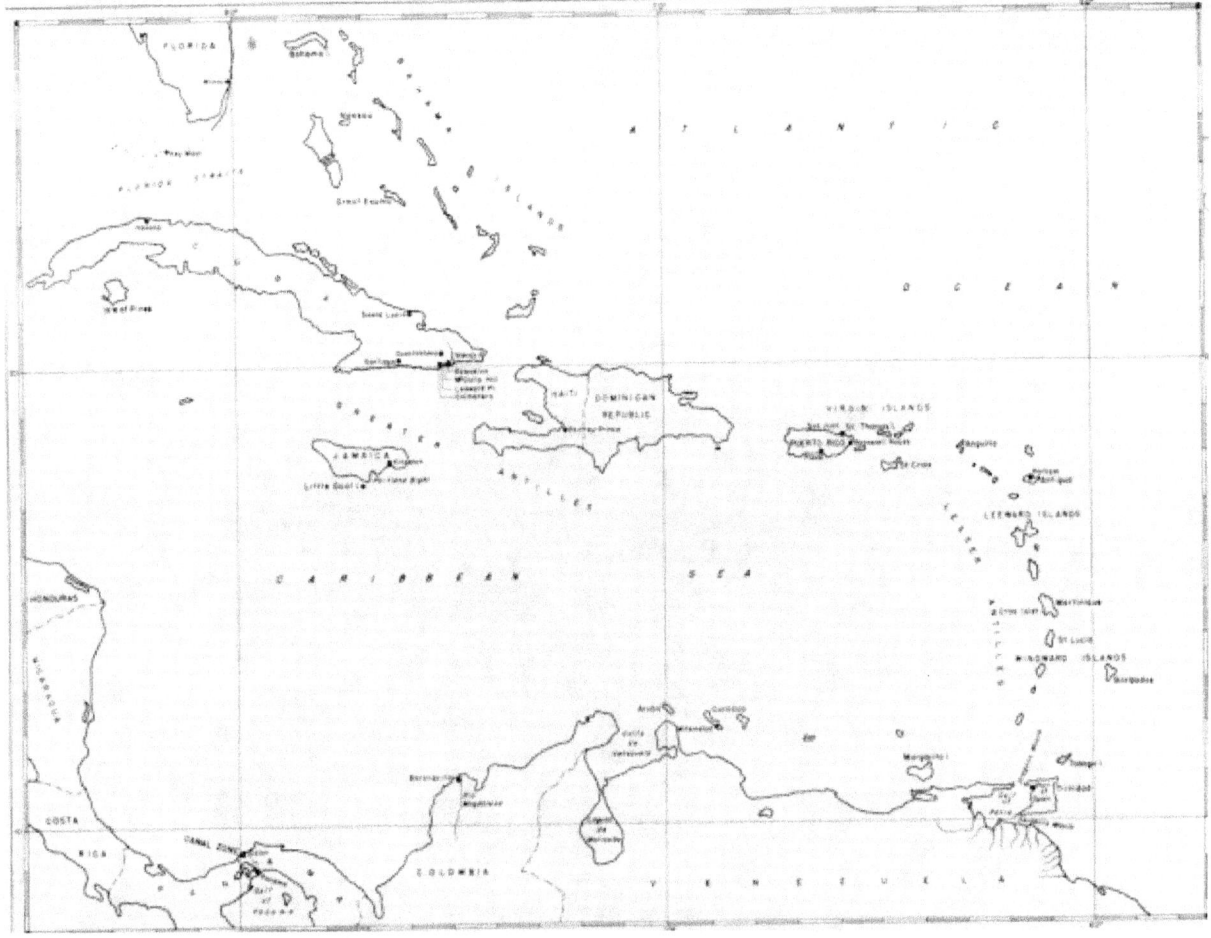

United States Bureau of Yards and Docks, 1947, Public Domain, Wikimedia Commons.
https://commons.wikimedia.org/wiki/File:Map_of_the_Caribbean_Area.jpg

Table of Contents

Foreword

Halfway through the 20th Century the Black families in Ottawa could most likely be counted on one hand. Seven decades later Ottawa's Black and Visible Minority communities account for more than 25 percent of the one million population. What is more, its members have pushed their way up through all sorts of barriers to gain recognition and respect.

It was largely a labour initiative after the Second World War that made the difference. A government-to-government Domestic Workers' Scheme, launched in the mid-fifties, resulted in hundreds of Black West Indian women coming to Canada to bring up generations of white Canadian children. Not only were these women eventually able to re-unify their own family, they also influenced the reason Canada changed its discriminatory anti-Black immigration policies, thus opening the door to thousands of their countrymen and women.

Social unrest in the Caribbean and the thirst for higher education and employment opportunities further swelled the ranks, bringing people with new cultures and colours from all walks and persuasions to this capital city. Canada benefited with an influx of teachers, nurses, bus drivers, doctors, medical technologists, athletes, scientists, journalists, agriculturalists, technicians, carpenters, electricians, builders, musicians, singers, rappers, restauranteurs, personal support workers, parsons, broadcasters, students, entrepreneurs, and others.

But all these people and their impact on Ottawa remained in a twilight zone as far as the dominant daily media was concerned. Until Dave Tulloch recognized the need to tell their stories. An Information Technology Consultant, Entrepreneur and Musician who once operated the "Take Five" jazz club in Ottawa, his life's work has been in high-tech. But none of that prevented him from seeing the need for this work and filling it so well. The people who are so painstakingly profiled in this book are the salt of the earth, many persevering through great tribulation. And this monumental work captures their life stories so well. We all owe Dave a deep debt of gratitude.

Ewart Walters, CD, BJ, MJ.

Acknowledgements

I must first pay tribute to each of the individuals who agreed to have their profiles published in this book. I thank them for taking the time to tell me their personal stories, and again later to review and approve the written work. Then I must acknowledge Naylor-Rose Ashley, an invaluable source, who through her involvement with the many Caribbean communities in Ottawa provided me with contact information for many of the people that I interviewed. I am also grateful for the counsel that I received from Ludvica Boota, who works for Crime Writers of Canada and is the Executive Director at "The Fulcrum". Ludvica's assistance was pivotal in narrowing down the appropriate publisher for this work. Ewart Walters CD, MJ, the pre-eminent Caribbean Journalist in Ottawa, provided technical guidance and mentorship along the way.

Most importantly I must thank God for allowing me the time to complete this book. It saddens me that several of the people that I interviewed over the four-year period of this project are no longer with us.

Finally, and most significantly, I must acknowledge my own family; my wife Avril, daughters; Trisha, Abigail, and Melanie and her husband Jean-Romaine Botembe who all gave me the space, continual encouragement and whose healthy and sometimes critical discussions helped me to keep pressing forward until this work was done.

D.T.

Preface

Late on the night of August 7, 1970 an Air Canada Hawker Siddeley turboprop touched down at the Ottawa Airport. Three Jamaican students, Doug Prendergast, Richard Morris, and I disembarked and headed toward the terminal to retrieve our luggage. All three of us had boarded an Air Canada jet at the Palisadoes Airport in Kingston Jamaica earlier that day. But it was not until we emerged from the Canadian customs and immigration process at the Toronto International Airport, and then stationed ourselves at the boarding area for the Ottawa flight that we each came to realize that there were no other Black people on the flight aside from us three. As we introduced ourselves to each other, we quickly understood that we were on the same mission. We were all sponsored by the Canadian International Development Agency (CIDA), and we were heading to Ottawa to study electronics technology at the Algonquin College campus on Lees Avenue. We also learned that CIDA had planned for us to spend our first few nights at the Lord Elgin Hotel, until we found suitable accommodation. CIDA had also arranged for a limo to take us from the Airport to the hotel.

We were in lockstep from the moment we disembarked. We retrieved our luggage and headed off to find our transportation contact. As soon as we emerged from the luggage area, we were approached by a big, tall, Black man, wearing a red hat and tugging a luggage cart.

"Do you boys need any help?" he asked.

We told him that help had been pre-arranged, and we headed outside the terminal in accordance with the instructions that we had been given. While it was a brief encounter, it was also a memorable one. I never expected to see a Black person and the size of the man left me with a lasting impression. Within minutes of our exit from inside the terminal building, our host's emissary had tagged us, and we were soon off to our initial destination. I never learned the identity of this Black man at the time and years went by, decades even, before I gained this insight.

By the next summer, I was the goalkeeper for the Hurricanes Soccer team, a predominantly Caribbean contingent within the Eastern Ontario District Soccer league. And I recall my first team meeting at a house in Manor Park where the team manager lived. The meeting was held just after we had played a league game. The team manager had a similar build to the man I had seen that first night at the airport, but I quickly discounted any notion that this could be the same person, because he looked much smaller wearing soccer shorts.

Decades later, after I was fully established in Ottawa, one of my daughters asked me to help her on a school project exploring the history of Blacks in Canada. We searched for references and scoured the bookshelves at the Gloucester Library looking for titles on the subject. There was nothing to be found. The experience stuck with me and became a burning catalyst for this initiative.

By that time, I had come to know many people within Ottawa's Black community, especially those with Caribbean origins. And the open question of who was the man in my initial encounter at the Ottawa Airport had just about faded from my memory. But in October of 2018, shortly after retiring from some 40 years in the Information Technology industry, one of the well-known Ottawa-Caribbean community builders passed away. I attended his funeral and, as the tributes flowed from many of his close friends and acquaintances; I was struck by the fact that a significant number of early immigrants, particularly those from Jamaica, had met the deceased at the Ottawa Airport. I then realized that it was this man, Owen (Bill) Stewart, who was in fact the first Black man that I had encountered upon my arrival in Ottawa in August 1970.

Listening to his life-story as summarized in his eulogy I became convinced that my first writing project would be to document the life stories of early Caribbean Immigrants; people like Bill Stewart, who came to Ottawa in the earliest days and who established community structures like the Hurricanes Soccer Club so that others like myself could find a welcoming and familiar environment to facilitate my transition from the native Caribbean into Canada.

It became apparent that many of us who have lived in Ottawa for decades do not have a reasonable grasp on the history of the Caribbean immigrant experience. And if this is the case, then our descendants, especially those of Caribbean immigrant parents, would lack knowledge of their history as well. It was vital that this important project be done.

The history of the Caribbean people in Ottawa, along with profiles of individuals who contributed to building the Caribbean community, while improving themselves and the lives of their families, had to be documented to provide ensuing generations with their foundation and a raison d'être. Recognizing that everyone has a life story to tell, the testimonials celebrate life's accomplishments. This publication sets out to provide the reader with a cross-section of people from Caribbean islands who came to Canada with the primary objective of making their lives better. In other words, their intention was to write for themselves a better life story than the one they envisioned in their native land. The pioneers from the Caribbean who decided to make the City of Ottawa their home did so for many different reasons. But this main objective — "a better life", appears as a common thread regardless of their island of origin. This fundamental motive of self-improvement is the catalyst that has facilitated the building of community structures that made it possible for the new immigrants to support each other, as opposed to dealing alone with the issues and obstacles that inevitably arose.

It has been my great pleasure to have researched and brought together information about our community from Wikipedia, The Canadian Encyclopedia, government websites, news archives, and many other sources; to have conducted interviews; and to have added my analysis and commentary. Anyone reading this book or perusing the contents may question why the profile of a certain person was not included. Indeed many others from the Caribbean could have been profiled as well. The initial objective was to profile twenty-five people; in the end more than fifty testimonials have been included. Furthermore, individuals profiled are mostly immigrants from Jamaica, and Barbados to a lesser extent, due to the fact that immigration from these two islands was at the very first wave of Caribbean immigration. In many cases, the information was gathered by direct interviews with interviewees and based on specific questions (See Appendix A: Interview Questionnaire); there are also several profiles of deceased individuals that were obtained from secondary sources. In general, deliberate efforts were made to seek out individuals from all the Caribbean islands, and so the representation is as wide as was feasible.

INTRODUCTION

A people without the knowledge of their past history, origin and culture are like a tree without roots.
— Marcus Garvey (1887-1940)

Most people who live in North America are either immigrants or the descendants of immigrants who came to the United States or to Canada. The immigrant's story is typically a fascinating one. It's the story of people who venture out from the familiar into the unknown, many of whom take this venture of personal risk and uncertainty because of untenable situations in which they found themselves. Others see this immigration venture as a path to improve their lives. One of these stories is portrayed in the movie "The Godfather". The story is about a young Sicilian boy who escaped assassination when the rest of his family was executed. He showed up at Ellis Island, New York, along with a shipload of migrants from Italy. He was unable to speak a word of English but ended up being one of the most powerful Italians in New York. More recent is the story of the Kenyan immigrant student who married a young woman from Kansas. Their son, Barack Obama, later became the 44th President of the United States. There are many other similar immigrant stories in biographies and other literary works. Indeed many biographies of the rich and famous have either a direct or an indirect immigrant background.

It is very difficult to find any coherent historical records on immigrants from the Caribbean who departed from their native land in search of a better life in Canada. But there are many individual success stories written about Caribbean immigrants in Canada. One such story is about an immigrant woman from Grenada who entered Canada under the West Indian Domestic Scheme. She became active in her community, later elected to the Canadian Parliament, and then appointed as the Parliamentary Secretary to Prime Minister Jean Chrétien.

> "On May 26, 2002, Jean Augustine was appointed Secretary of State for Multiculturalism and the Status of Women. In December 2003, she was re-appointed to the new Cabinet as Minister of State for Multiculturalism and the Status of Women. In 2004, she was appointed to the position of Assistant Deputy Chair of Committees of the Whole, making her the first Black Canadian to occupy the Speaker's Chair in the Canadian House of Commons."[1]

---

1 *Wikipedia.* Jean Augustine. https://en.wikipedia.org/wiki/JeanAugustine
Accessed on February 15, 2018.

Similar biographies and profiles of successful Caribbean immigrants to Canada are few and far between. This is not to say that such people do not exist. But it is my contention that, in general, the contributions and successes of the Black community in Canada have not been well documented. Therefore, knowledge of many of these trailblazers is sparse.

It is also important to note that there are a significant number of Caribbean immigrants in Canada, not all of whom are Black, who have made significant improvements in their personal lives and contributed very positively to the Canadian experience. We know this either anecdotally or directly through our own contacts and experience and by way of rare reports on a number of high achievers. Unfortunately there is very little recorded about the contributions made by many of the pioneering immigrant members of the Caribbean community in the development and evolution of our nation, and more specifically our National Capital city. In fact, the documented history of the Caribbean people who are in Ottawa is virtually non-existent. Hidden deep in the newspaper archives, one might find some articles on a few Caribbean individuals who are Black, and which are based on something newsworthy. But depending on the search criteria, there are more negative news articles than positive ones.

This book sets out to track the history of peoples from the Caribbean who arrived in the City of Ottawa beginning in the early 1950s and to profile a number of these Caribbean trailblazers, specifically those who made significant and positive contributions to the evolution of the Caribbean community in the Nation's Capital City. The publication will cover the initial 25-year phase of Caribbean immigration to Ottawa, starting in 1955 to 1980. It was during this period that Canada eased its immigration policy to move away from a racially-based approach to a more inclusive immigration system. This was also the period in which Canada discarded the racial barriers that existed in its immigration system up to 1962.

The changes to Canada's immigration policy in 1952 ushered in a flow of immigrants from Caribbean countries, many of whom made Ottawa their home. The people profiled herein may not necessarily be the earliest arrivals or even the pioneers for that matter. Nevertheless, it is of great interest to understand how these early arrivals coped with the new environment, and how they eventually integrated into Ottawa society. The book poses questions including what was their first impression upon arrival. How did they cope in their new environment? What did they do to integrate themselves into their new society? And how were they treated by their host? The answers given by the respondents profiled in this book provide interesting insights on how these early arrivals made the transition. And while a number of these people might be among the earliest to arrive in Ottawa, our primary targets are those immigrants whose actions fostered the establishment of their immigrant communities, thereby easing the integration process for those who came after them.

Our profiled individuals are trailblazers in various disciplines and practices that were beneficial to themselves and their communities. The people targeted are immigrants who ventured out in the areas of entrepreneurship, professional practices, the arts, community development, sports and other areas that fostered and facilitated the integration of their compatriots into the Ottawa society. The profiles are primarily of those who started businesses to serve their community in areas where no such services existed, those who established professional practices to provide a familiar environment for Caribbean immigrants seeking such services, others who progressed through the professional ranks of business and government institutions, thereby paving the path for others to follow, individuals who established cultural and community based initiatives to make their immigrant communities feel at home in sports, music, church organizations, and other areas that were non-existent in this new land, but part of normal life in the homeland. In some instances, the profiled person may be one of the early arrivals, or even the first of a certain group of migrants to arrive in Ottawa from the Caribbean. However, to fully appreciate the social impact, it is necessary to examine the effect of Canada's history, culture, and socio-economic trends along with Canada's policies on migrants from the Caribbean.

It is natural to assume that Caribbean Immigrants are of African origin; but the Caribbean islands are largely multi-cultural. The three largest English-speaking Caribbean Islands –Trinidad, Barbados and Jamaica—have very different populations. For instance, Trinidad is more Indian than African. The 2011 census has the Indian population at 37.6%. And in 1960 at the midpoint of the period of this subject, the Indian population was at 36.5%, indicating a slight growth. Trinidad's Black population on the other hand has seen a dramatic decline since 1960 when it was 43.3%. But in 1960 this demographic group declined by 7% down to 36.3%. This population trend in Trinidad can be explained by the increase of the mixed group from 16.3% in 1960 to 24.1% in 2011. Barbados on the other hand is 92.4% Black, with the mixed group a distant second at 3.1% and the White population at 2.7%. The Jamaican ethnic mix is similar to that of Barbados with Blacks making up 92.1% and its mixed population group making up 6.0% the Indian and White population groups are less than 1% respectively. There is a high likelihood that the immigrants from these three Caribbean islands will reflect the relationships to their respective ethnic mix. But it is also important to note that the immigrants from the white population within these nations may be overrepresented with regards to their ethnic population distribution, since these groups might have had access to more resources to finance their migration.

While the debate on the value of immigration continues, it is my belief that the migration of Caribbean peoples to Canada overwhelmingly resulted in net positive benefits to the migrants, their families, their communities and to Canada. This will be borne out by the profiles of the individuals herein. Indeed the underlying theme was their decision to emigrate in order to "better themselves"; the immigrants expected to improve their own lives as well as the lives of their families. And what's particularly interesting is that this notion to better themselves extended way beyond the individuals and their core family unit. Subsequent government policies, Multiculturalism policies, for example, were specifically aimed at augmenting immigration policies to facilitate family inclusive migration. These supplemental policies became motivating factors for those who led the way to bring others in as well.

Today, the results of the changes made to the Canadian immigration policies to become more inclusive are obvious. The face of Canada has evolved to be the face of the world. Canada is consistently rated within the top five as one of the best countries in the world. Migrants from the Caribbean, their follow-on family members, and the children born to early Caribbean immigrants are now fully functional Canadian citizens. Caribbean immigrants and/or their descendants are integrated into just about every professional discipline and socio-economic strata within Canadian society and political systems.

The Ottawa Caribbean immigrant community is a microcosm of the Canadian community at large. It has provided Canada with a contingent of teachers, lawyers, nurses, doctors, medical technologists, judges, politicians, and police personnel. They are professionals in media, technology, in business, in the service industry and in many other segments of professional activities. But most importantly, many of these same professionals find the time to contribute voluntarily to building their own communities as well as volunteering their time and their talents to effectively contribute to making Canadian society the envy of the world. It is by no accident that in 2021 Canada was ranked in the U.S. News and Report's Best Country list as "the best country in the world".

Caribbean-Canadian Immigration: A Brief History

History is not the past. It is the stories we tell about the past.
How we tell these stories - triumphantly or self-critically,
metaphysically or dialectally - has a lot to do with whether we cut
short or advance our evolution as human being
— Grace Lee Boggs (1915-2015)

In general, the population of each of the Caribbean Islands is fairly diverse racially. Most Caribbean inhabitants in just about all of the different islands are predominantly of African descent. It is estimated that approximately 73% of the people in the Caribbean is of Afro descendant. Therefore, it would be reasonable to expect that immigration of Caribbean nationals to Canada would most likely result in a greater percentage of Black immigrants as opposed to other racial groups.

It is worth noting that Black people have lived in Canada since the early 1600s. And people from the Caribbean have made Canada their homeland since the late 1700s. One of the earliest Blacks on record to have arrived in Canada was:

> "…a man named Mathieu de Costa who traveled with navigator Samuel de Champlain. Da Costa arrived in Nova Scotia sometime between 1603 and 1608 as a translator for the French explorer Pierre Dugua, Sieur de Monts. But the first known Black person to live in what would become Canada was a slave from Madagascar named Olivier Le Jeune, who may have been of partial Malay ancestry."[2]

The majority of Blacks who arrived in Canada prior to the year 1800 were brought into Canada either as slaves or those who had escaped slavery in the United States. But there was also another group of Blacks that came to Canada from Jamaica on June 26, 1796. This was a group of Jamaican Maroons: they had descended from Africans who escaped from slavery on the Colony of Jamaica and established free communities in the mountainous interior, primarily in the eastern parishes. Escaped Africans who were enslaved during Spanish rule over Jamaica (1493–1656) may have been the first to develop such refugee communities.

---

2 *Wikipedia*. Black Canadians. https://en.wikipedia.org/wiki/Black_Canadians
Accessed on February 15, 2018.

The group of

"543 men, women and children, were deported on board the three ships Dover, Mary, and Anne from Jamaica, after being defeated in an uprising against the British colonial government. Their initial destination was Lower Canada, but on July 21 and 23, their ships arrived in Nova Scotia."[3]

During that period Canada's total population was very small. In 1870, just three years after Canada's Confederation, the population of Canada was measured at 3.6 million. In addition to Indigenous peoples (about 102,000 in 1870) the two largest groups were French (one million) and British (2.1 million).[4] With such a small population and vast areas of unsettled territory, immigration was seen in the decades after Confederation as a crucial way of expanding the country and its economy.

"Between 1800 and 1920 a small number of Jamaicans and Barbadians immigrated as laborers to work in the Cape Breton and Sydney mines, but from 1920 until the early 1960s immigration was virtually nonexistent. Immigration from the Caribbean really began in the 1960s, and by 1973 accounted for almost 13 percent of all immigration to Canada."[5]

The flow of immigrants to Canada can be segmented into three major periods. The first period spans from 1900 to 1960. During this period

"Canada accepted about 21,500 immigrants from Caribbean countries, only 33 percent (approximately 9,000) of whom were placed under the ethnic-origin heading of 'Black.' … Until the immigration reforms of the 1960s, 37 per cent of Canadian Blacks lived in Nova Scotia. Today, Nova Scotia's Black population of approximately 19,200 is smaller than the numbers in each of the largest cities. But when compared to other areas in Canada, many Black communities in Nova Scotia are still living in de facto segregation. Nowhere else in Canada does the legacy of slavery remain so tangible."[6]

---

3 Jamaicans. http://jamaicans.com/historydetailed/#ixzz4y4AjIN0xG. Accessed on February 15, 2018
4 In 1871 the year that the first census was conducted in Canada, Indigenous peoples-Native and Inuit (Eskimo) was 23,037. 0.7% of the total population. Wikipedia. 1871 Canadian Census. https://en.wikipedia.org/wiki/1871_Canadian_census. Accessed on January 14, 2023.
5 *The Canadian Encyclopedia*. Caribbean Canadians. https://www.thecanadianencyclopedia.ca/en/article/caribbean-canadians Accessed on April 27, 2018.
6 Daniel Fischlin, Ajay Heble and George Lipsitz. *The Fierce Urgency of Now: Improvisation, Rights, and the Ethics of Cocreation.* (London: Duke University Press, 2013).

Chart 4
Foreign-born population in Canada, by selected regions of birth,
1951 to 2011

Population (in thousands)

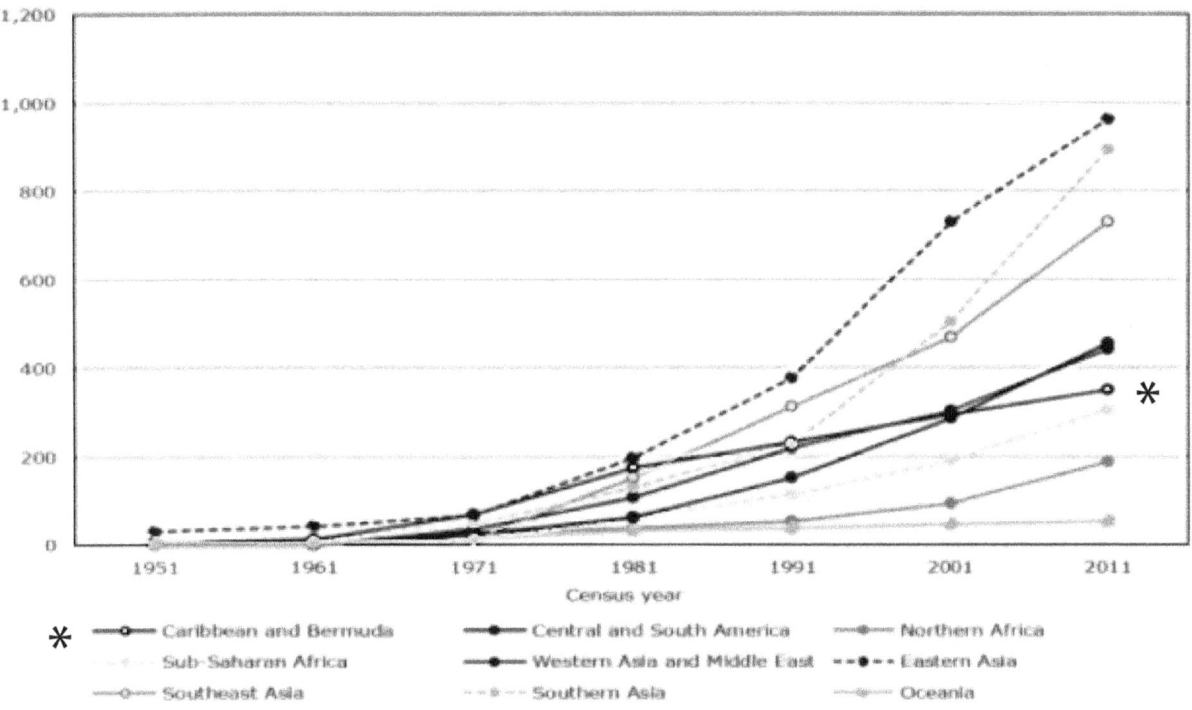

Sources: Statistics Canada, censuses of population, 1951 to 2001. National Household Survey, 2011.

Says Donald Oliver, a Nova Scotia Conservative senator and lawyer:

"We are Canada's largest indigenous Black population, and our history sets us apart and makes us unique. Nova Scotia Blacks, in fact, have been treated a lot worse…People are very afraid to talk about it, they want it buried under the carpet."[7]

The slight increase in immigration from 1945 to 1960 corresponded with postwar economic expansion and the West Indian Domestic Scheme (1955–60) which was initially established, almost exclusively, to secure childcare workers from Jamaica and Barbados. In subsequent years this program was extended to include women from other Caribbean Islands, allowing them to migrate to Canada as domestic workers.

---

7 Racism's Long History in Quiet East Coast towns. The Globe and Mail. https://www.theglobeandmail.com/news/national/racisms-long-history-in-quiet-east-coast-towns/article1241300/ Accessed on October 12, 2018.

"The second period, from 1960 to 1971, corresponded with the 'liberalization' of the Canadian Immigration Act. During this period Canada accepted about 64,000 people from the Caribbean."[8]

Furthermore,

"It is noteworthy to recognize that there were earlier attempts to enact laws that would prevent Blacks from entering Canada, based on the notion that they were "unsuitable to the climate and requirements of Canada."[9]

In 1911, Frank Oliver — the Minister of the Interior of Canada and an MP in Edmonton at the time — recommended an Order-in-Council that banned "any immigrant belonging to the Negro race." According to an archived document obtained by the Canadian Museum of Immigration, Order-in-Council P.C. 1324 states:

"His Excellency in Council, in virtue of the provisions of Sub-Section (c) of Section 38 of the Immigration Act, is pleased to Order and it is hereby Ordered as follows: For a period of one year from and after the date thereof the landing in Canada shall be and the same is prohibited of any immigrant belonging to the Negro race, which race is deemed unsuitable to the climate and requirements of Canada."

The Order was adopted on August 12, 1911 and signed by then Prime Minister Wilfred Laurier. It was not officially legislated or included in the Immigration Act and was cancelled on October 5, 1911, the order being cancelled after "having been inadvertently passed in the absence of the Minister of the Interior."[10]

---

8 *The Canadian Encyclopedia*. History of Caribbean Immigration to Canada. https://www.thecanadianencyclopedia.ca/en/article/caribbean-canadians. Accessed on February 9, 2023.

9 Gregory P. Marchildon. *Immigration and Settlement, 1870-1939* (Regina: University of Regina Press, 2009) 500 ·

10 *The Canadian Encyclopedia*. Order in Council PC1911-1324. https://www.thecanadianencyclopedia.ca/en/article/order-in-council-pc-1911-1324-the-proposed-ban-on-black-immigration-to-canada Accessed on February 9, 2023.

Canadian Immigration Policy Changes – Timeline

Canadian Council for Refugees. *A hundred years of immigration to Canada 1900 – 1999 (Part 2)*.
https://ccrweb.ca/en/hundred-years-immigration-canada-part-2 Accessed on February 9, 2023.

1952	A new Immigration Act was passed, less than a month after it was introduced in the House (it came into effect 1 June 1953). This Act, which did not make substantial changes to immigration policy, gave the Minister and officials substantial powers over selection, admission, and deportation. It provided for the refusal of admission on the grounds of nationality, ethnic group, geographical area of origin, peculiar customs, habits and modes of life, unsuitability with regard to the climate, probable inability to become readily assimilated, etc. Homosexuals, drug addicts and drug traffickers were added to the prohibited classes. The Act provided for immigration appeal boards, made up of department officials, to hear appeals from deportation.
1957	In the federal election campaign, John Diefenbaker promised his government would develop a vigorous immigration policy and overhaul the Immigration Act.
Feb. 1962	Minister of Citizenship and Immigration Ellen Fairclough implemented new Immigration Regulations that removed most racial discrimination, although Europeans retained the right to sponsor a wider range of relatives than others.
Nov. 1962	Minister of Citizenship and Immigration Richard Bell suggested that immigration should be at the rate of 1% of the population. Despite high levels of unemployment, immigration was increased.
Oct. 1966	A white paper was tabled, recommending an immigration policy that was "expansionist, non-discriminatory, and balanced in reconciling the claims of family relationship with the economic interest of Canada". The paper began: "There is a general awareness among Canadians that the present Immigration Act no longer serves national needs adequately, but there is no consensus on the remedy". Evidently no consensus was found, since the white paper did not lead to a new Act.
Oct. 1967	The points system was incorporated into the Immigration Regulations. The last element of racial discrimination was eliminated. The sponsored family class was reduced. Visitors were given the right to apply for immigrant status while in Canada.
1970	Immigration from Asia and the Caribbean represented over 23% of the total, compared with 10% four years previously.
1970	Following Canada's signing of the Refugee Convention, refugee selection became an issue. According the immigration department's annual report: "under our resettlement program, refugees considered capable of successful establishment may be selected regardless of their inability to meet immigration assessment norms". Visa officers took into account resources available from the department and from Canadian organizations and citizens.
1970	First 92 of a group of Tibetan refugees settled in Alberta, Ontario and Québec.
1971	The federal government announced its policy of multiculturalism. (But did not enact it until the "Canadian Multiculturalism Act (R.S.C., 1985))
1972	The 10 millionth immigrant since Confederation was celebrated. It was reportedly British psychiatrist Dr. Richard Swinson "and his family".
1974	The federal government launched the Immigrant Settlement and Adaptation Program (ISAP) through which funding for settlement services are provided.
Apr. 1978	The new Immigration Act came into effect. It identified objectives for the immigration program and forced the government to plan for the future, in consultation with the provinces. Immigrants were divided into four categories: independents, family, assisted relatives and humanitarian. The Refugee Status Advisory Committee was created. The "prohibited" categories were replaced with "inadmissible" categories, among which were no longer to be found epileptics, imbeciles, persons guilty of crimes of moral turpitude, homosexuals, and people with tuberculosis. Deputy Minister Allan Gotlieb described the legislation as "a beautiful piece of work - logical, well-constructed, liberal, and workable". The accompanying Immigration Regulations revised the points system and created the Private Sponsorship of Refugees Program.

Immigration policies since 1910-1911

Various governments re-framed immigration policies over the years, including amending the Immigration Act in 1919. However, Canada continued to enact policies such as the Chinese Immigration Act of 1923 and the Canadian Citizenship Act of 1947 that continued to discriminate people based on their ethnicity or occupation.

> "The Immigration Act of 1976 was viewed as a turning point in immigration policy, because it allowed for family reunions and classified refugees as immigrants."[11]

The third wave of period, post-1970, continued with more rapid growth in immigration primarily from the continent of Africa. Many of these new arrivals were of the refugee class,

> "In 1978, Canada enacted a new Immigration Act that, for the first time, affirmed Canada's commitment to the resettlement of refugees from oppression; that is, persons who have a well-founded fear of persecution in their country of citizenship. Accordingly, refugees would no longer be admitted to Canada as an exception to immigration regulations. Admission of refugees was now part of Canadian immigration law and regulations."[12]

Throughout all these periods of immigrant inflows into Canada, there were steady inflows of students. These students were primarily registered at post-secondary institutions. Most were financed through scholarships, but a smaller proportion was self-financed. And so, the higher learning institutions in Ottawa, predominantly Carleton University, Ottawa University and Algonquin College (formerly Eastern Ontario Institute of Technology) were all recipients of small contingents of Black students, Caribbean, and African domiciles at the beginning of each successive school year. A similar pattern was replicated across Canada in most of the major cities where post-secondary institutions were located.

In any case the Black population in Canada was relatively small through the 1950s and 1960s. And up to 1970 the population of Blacks in Canada was still well below 100,000.

---

11 Anti-Black racist history in Canada: 1911 order sought to stop Blacks from immigrating. Toronto City News. https://toronto.citynews.ca/2020/07/01/anti-black-racism-canada-immigration/ Accessed on October 12, 2018.
12 *The Canadian Encyclopedia.* Immigration to Canada. https://www.thecanadianencyclopedia.ca/en/article/immigration Accessed on October 12, 2018.

Canadian Immigration Policies

In Canada the province of Ontario was the pioneering province for social change in relation to Racial Discrimination. On the 14th of March 1944, the Province of Ontario passed the Racial Discrimination Act. This landmark legislation effectively "prohibited displaying or publishing symbols that expressed racial or religious discrimination"[13] including any symbol, sign, or notice that expressed ethnic, racial, or religious discrimination. It was followed by other sweeping legislation.

> "Even then, many restaurants, hotels, barbershops and stores kept refusing service to Black people in the 1950s. Fortunately by this time, many tireless campaigns were led by individuals and groups pushed for equality, change and dissolve discrimination."[14]

But it was not until the early 1950s that the Canadian immigration policies began to ease historic restrictions on admitting Blacks to Canada. Even towards the late 1940s Canada was not favourable to allow Blacks to enter the country, as reflected in the following statement made by Prime Minister Mackenzie King on May 1, 1947 in the House outlining Canada's immigration policy.

> "The policy of the government is to foster the growth of the population of Canada by the encouragement of immigration. The government will seek by legislation, regulation, and vigorous administration, to ensure the careful selection and permanent settlement of such numbers of immigrants as can advantageously be absorbed in our national economy."[15]

In terms of discrimination, King made it clear that Canada is "perfectly within her rights in selecting the persons whom we regard as desirable future citizens".[16] Still, he allowed that it might be as well to remove "objectionable discrimination".[17] On the other hand,

> "the people of Canada do not wish, as a result of mass immigration, to make a fundamental alteration in the character of our population. Large-

13 Course Hero Seneca College. In Canada in Ontario Racial Discrimination Act was declared in 1944. https://www.coursehero.com/file/p2sthl/In-Ontario-Racial-Discrimination-Act-was-declared-in-1944-which-prohibited/ Accessed on May 5, 2019.
14 Ibid
15 Canadian Council for Refugees. Hundred Years Immigration Canada 1900-1999. https://ccrweb.ca/en/hundred-years-immigration-canada-1900-1999] Accessed on November 21, 2017.
16 *Alberta Online Encyclopedia*. Canada's Postwar Immigration Policy. http://wayback.archive-it.org/2217/20101208165211/ http://www.abheritage.ca/albertans/speeches/king_1.html Accessed on February 9, 2023.
17 Ibid.

scale immigration from the orient would change the fundamental composition of the Canadian population".[18]

This meant that the melting pot theory of immigration would be expected to absorb these new arrivals into mainstream Canada and that the fundamental makeup of the country would remain relatively unchanged.[19]

"The main source of the new immigrants was targeted as U.S., British, and North-western Europeans. These immigrants would not upset the balance across Canada and were actively recruited. One of the main groups to be accepted were the Dutch who were faced with overcrowding in the Netherlands, and with the loss of so much farmland during the later stages of World War II, they also faced food shortages. The Government through an imitative known as the Netherland Farm Families Movement. Germans were welcome due to the Canadian populations view of them as being ethnically similar to the rest of Canada, as well as many British wives of soldiers who had served overseas."[20]

Most Canadians in the 1950s continued to accept the essentials of the principles contained in the Immigration Act of 1910, as these principles came to be expressed by Mackenzie King in his speech of 1947, without any words about "less civilized races" and about Canada being a "white man's country".[21]

Notwithstanding the Federal Government's position, the Province of Ontario followed up with its progressive positions on anti-discrimination practices and

"eventually, a number of individual laws such as Fair Employment Practices Act (1951), Fair Accommodation Practices Act (1954), and Ontario Anti-Discrimination Commission Act (1958) were passed in Ontario to protect the rights of the individuals. Fair Employment Practices Act prohibited any discriminatory actions in employment that were based on race and religion. Whereas Accommodation Practices Act banned any public places discrimination based on religious, racial, and ethnic backgrounds. Additionally, an amendment was made to this act to make sure that rental accommodation is also not subjected to any discrimination."[22]

18 Canada First Immigration Reform Committee. Immigration Act of 1910.
http://canadafirst.nfshost.com/?tag=immigration-act-of-1910 Accessed on February 9, 2023.
19 The Canada History Society. Immigration.
https://www.canadahistory.com/sections/periods/Later_Canada/The_Peace/Immigration.html
Accessed on November 21, 2017.
20 Ibid.
21 Canada First Immigration Reform Committee. Immigration Act of 1910.
22 Course Hero Seneca College. In Ontario Racial Discrimination Act was declared in 1944.

After the Second World War, Canada began to re-build its economy. The country continued to maintain a strong rural agricultural base, but its economy gradually transitioned towards industrialization and urbanization. This opened many opportunities for better educated and skilled workers, placing acute constraints on the country's ability to source the types of workers needed to fill industrial jobs. Canada soon came to the realization that there was an acute shortage of the labour resources that were needed to achieve its industrialization objectives, labour resources that were available in abundance in other countries, especially in the non-industrialized nations. However Europe, and other industrialized countries, was also experiencing similar labour resource shortages and hence these countries looked to find appropriate sources from where they could recruit people to help them meet their re-construction objectives.

Under the current immigration policies which restricted immigration from non-European countries, Canada was forced to compete for European labour resources with Great Britain and other European countries. The country was at a disadvantage in this labour market, given its distance away from the labour resources. Canada had to find a solution for this problem if it was to achieve its domestic objectives. The industrial job opportunities were opening quite rapidly and Canadian families adapted to the changing work environment. Women, who would have normally remained at home as traditional housewives, entered the paid workforce in greater numbers. This new trend placed constraints on parents' ability to provide childcare which in turn created a new category of labour resources. Child-care service workers were now required to fill the child-care role for working mothers. Facing constraints on sourcing industrial labour from Euro-centric countries and a growing need for childcare labour at home, Canada found it much easier to solve the child-care problem by sourcing domestic (child-care) workers from the UK and other European countries.[23] But this approach turned out to be a very short-term fix.

While it was relatively easy to recruit child-care workers from Europe, keeping them in the job for any extended period proved to be very difficult. Since these workers were predominantly young women, many would marry Canadian men shortly after their arrival in Canada and abandon their jobs. It was at this juncture that Canada sought other methods to remedy this situation. Up until this time Canada had placed severe restrictions on immigration from non-Euro-centric countries. But faced with these labour constraints,

---

23 Canada First Immigration Reform Committee. Immigration Act of 1910.

"Canada's restrictive immigration policies began to ease after the Second World War slowly and gradually, partly thanks to booming economic growth (and demand for labor) and partly due to changing social attitudes."[24]

Canada solved the childcare labour problems by sourcing domestic labour resources from the Caribbean. And in 1955 the Canadian Government introduced the 'Domestic Scheme', a program designed to source Caribbean domestic help for Canadian families.[25] Shortly thereafter, a relatively small number of Caribbean immigrants began to flow into Canada. Some of these new Caribbean immigrants would be assigned to work with families who lived in Ottawa.

Further modifications to the Canadian immigration policies, specifically the elimination of racially-based admittance criteria and the establishment of the Canadian International Development Agency, increased the flow of Caribbean immigrants to Canada during the 1960s. In January 1962 Canada dismantled its discriminatory 'White Canada' immigration policy.

"During her term as Minister of Citizenship and Immigration, Ellen Fairclough oversaw improvements to the Canadian Immigration Service, but her most significant accomplishment was the radical reform of the government's "White Canada" immigration policy. Regulations tabled in 1962 helped to eliminate racial discrimination in Canada's immigration policy."[26]

Canadian Immigration polices continued the path of liberalization. And

"in October 1967 the points system was incorporated in the Immigration Regulations. The sponsored family class was reduced. Visitors were given the right to apply for immigrant status while in Canada."[27]

The major immigration policies that facilitated immigration from the Caribbean were the Domestic Scheme, the introduction of the Points System and the establishment of the Canadian International Development Agency (CIDA). The people profiled here would most likely have entered Canada under one of these three programs. And from 1970 onwards, Caribbean immigration continued

---

24 The Canada History Society. Immigration.
25 *The Canadian Encyclopedia.* West Indian Domestic Scheme: Nurturing a Nation. https://www.thecanadianencyclopedia.ca/en/article/west-indian-domestic-scheme-nurturing-a-nation Accessed on February 9, 2023.
26 *The Canadian Encyclopedia.* Immigration. https://www.thecanadianencyclopedia.ca/en/timeline/immigration Accessed on March 26, 2019.
27 *A hundred years of immigration to Canada 1900 - 1999 (Part 2)* Janet Dench, Executive Director, Canadian Council for Refugees.

to increase at an even pace. By 1980 the number of immigrants who entered Canada from the Caribbean was about 175,000.

"According to data from the 2016 census by Statistics Canada, 21.9% of the Canadian population reported they were or had been a Landed Immigrant or permanent resident in Canada – nearly the 22.3% recorded during the 1921 Census, which was the highest level since the 1867 Confederation of Canada. More than one in five Canadians were born abroad, and 22.3% of the population belonged to visible minorities, three in 10 were born in Canada."[28]

28 *Wikipedia*. Immigration to Canada. https://en.wikipedia.org/wiki/Immigration_to_Canada Accessed on July 17, 2019.

Era of Slavery in Canada [29]

Canada is not normally viewed as a country with a history of slavery, nevertheless slavery in Canada "predates the arrival of Europeans with some Indigenous peoples enslaving prisoners taken in war".[30] When the Europeans arrived, they introduced a different kind of slavery to North America. Unlike the Indigenous people, Europeans saw enslaved people more as property that could be bought and sold, and less as human beings. In addition, Europeans viewed slavery in racial terms, with Indigenous and Black people serving, and white people ruling as masters. This European form of slavery was not unique to the United States. Canada certainly had its fair share of slave owners. Slavery was a common practice in the colony of New France, founded in the early 1600s as the first major settlement in what is now Canada. When New France was conquered by the British in 1759, records revealed that approximately 3,600 enslaved people had lived in the settlement since its beginnings.[31] The vast majority of them were Indigenous (often called Panis)[32], but Black enslaved people were also present because of the transatlantic slave trade.

The transatlantic slave trade helped shape the presence and role of slavery in Canadian history. With the increasing use of African enslaved people in North America, a pattern of trade emerged that has since been called the 'trade triangle'. European merchants would leave Europe for Africa, travelling in ships laden with goods. In Africa, they would exchange their goods for enslaved people and then transport the people to the Americas, often in cramped and inhumane conditions. In the Americas, the surviving enslaved people would be sold and then goods produced by slaves would be carried back to Europe for sale. Slavers saw their trade from a purely economic standpoint and viewed enslaved people as just another set of 'goods' they could transport and sell. With this mentality, slavers denied the fundamental human rights of millions of African men and women.[33]

---

29 Canadian Museum for Human Rights. Slavery in Canadian History.
https://humanrights.ca/story/story-slavery-canadian-history Accessed on July 17, 2019.
30 Charles G. Roland. *Slavery*. Oxford Companion to Canadian History, 585.
31 Robin Winks. *The Blacks in Canada: A History, second edition* (Montreal and Kingston: McGill-Queen's University Press, 1997), 9.
32 Refers to 'Pawnee', an Indigenous nation which inhabited the basin of the Missouri River.
Canadian Museum of History, Virtual Museum of New France, Population, Slavery
https://www.historymuseum.ca/virtual-museum-of-new-france/population/sl Accessed 22 Aug. 2018
33 James A. Rawley, *The Transatlantic Slave Trade: A History, revised edition* (Dexter, MI: Thomson-Shore Inc., 2005), 7.

Slavery continued after the British conquest of New France in 1763. The territory was eventually renamed British North America, and Black enslaved people came to replace Indigenous enslaved people. Compared to the United States, enslaved people made up a much smaller proportion of the population in British North America, implying that some of the worst traits of slavery in America, such as the employment of overseers and the horrible practice of forcing enslaved people to reproduce, did not happen in what is now Canada. It would be wrong, however, to suggest that enslaved people in British North America were treated well. The very nature of slavery meant that its victims were stripped of their basic human rights and exploited. Most wills from that era treated

Cover page of the Code Noir (Black Code), a slavery rulebook from 1743 brought from France to Canada. Although there is no evidence the Code Noir was formally proclaimed in New France, it appears to have been used as customary law. — Bibliothèque nationale de France

enslaved people as nothing more than property, passing on ownership of human beings the same as they would furniture, cattle, or land.[34] Defiant or troublesome enslaved people were often severely punished. Physical and sexual abuses were always a very real threat.

General James Murray, British governor of Quebec stated in 1763:

"Had I the inclination to employ soldiers which is not the case, they would disappoint me, and Canadians will work for nobody but themselves. Black slaves are certainly the only people to be depended upon."[35]

---

34 Winks, *The Blacks in Canada*, 53.
35 Canadian Museum for Human Rights. Slavery in Canadian History.
https://humanrights.ca/story/story-slavery-canadian-history Accessed on July 17, 2019.

However Black slaves resented their position in society:

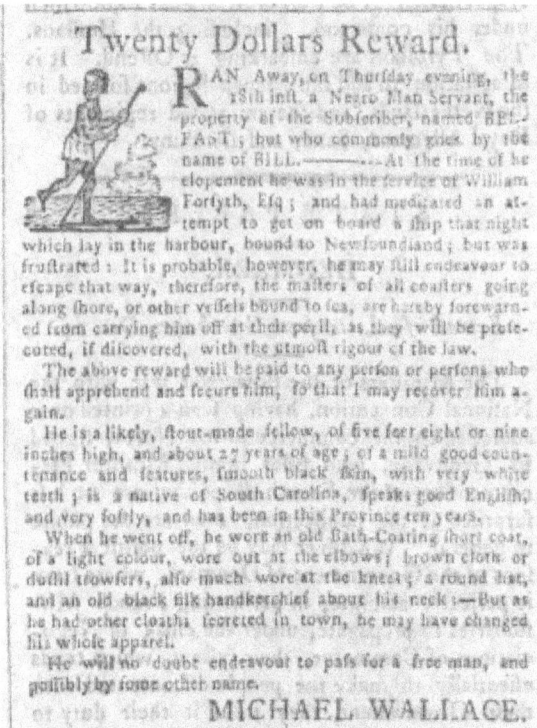

An advertisement offering twenty dollars for the capture of a runaway enslaved person in Nova Scotia, dating from March 1794. Many enslaved people made similar attempts to escape. — Quebec Gazette

"Enslaved people often resisted the institution of slavery. They fought back in many ways: by asserting their humanity in the face of a system that wished to deny it to them, by running away from masters or by assisting other runaways. In fact, in 1777, several enslaved people escaped from British North America into the state of Vermont, which had abolished slavery in that same year."[36]

For many years, the practice of indentured servitude existed alongside slavery in what is now Canada. Under the system of indentured servitude, individuals signed a contract committing them to perform unpaid labour for a set number of years in exchange for transport, shelter and food.

Indentured servitude was cruel and exploitative but was different from the slavery that was practiced in New France and British North America. At the end of their contracts, indentured servants were free to go, and sometimes received a payment of land and goods. In contrast, slavery defined humans as property and involved lifelong forced labour. The children of enslaved people also became property, making slavery intergenerational.

In British North America, if Black enslaved people were freed, they often still had to work as indentured servants for several years. On Prince Edward Island in 1796, an enslaved man named Dimbo Suckles was freed, but only on the condition that he work for his former master as an indentured servant for seven years, from

---

36 Ken Alexander and Avis Glaze, *Towards Freedom: The African-Canadian Experience* (Toronto: Umbrella Press, 1996), 29.

1796 until 1803. Historian Jim Hornby notes that such indentured servitude contracts were the "then-standard rate" for freedom.[37]

By the late 1700s, the free population of British North America was beginning to change its attitudes toward slavery. On March 25, 1807, the slave trade was abolished throughout the British Empire – of which British North America was a part – making it illegal to buy or sell human beings, and ending much of the transatlantic trade. In 1834 slavery itself was abolished everywhere in the British Empire. Some Canadian jurisdictions had already taken measures to restrict or end slavery by that time. In 1793 Upper Canada (now Ontario) passed the Anti-slavery Act. The law freed enslaved people aged 25 and over, and made it illegal to bring enslaved people into Upper Canada[38] or Prince Edward Island. The complete abolition of slavery was pronounced by the legislature in 1825, nine years before the Imperial abolition of 1834.[39]

An announcement of the sale of enslaved people. It appeared in the Quebec Gazette in May 1785. One of the horrors of slavery was that enslaved people were treated as property rather than as human beings. — Quebec Gazette

> "The abolition of slavery allowed the British colonies in North America to become a safe haven for escaped enslaved people in the United States, with many making their way North via the famous Underground Railroad. The story of the Underground Railroad is a positive moment in Canadian history, worthy of commemoration. We must also recall, however, that for more than two hundred years, slavery happened here, too."[40]

---

37 Jim Hornby, *Black Islanders: Prince Edward Island's Historical Black Community* (Charlottetown: Institute of Island Studies, 1991), 30.
38 Canadian Heritage, Historic Black Communities, Black History Month: https://www.canada.ca/en/canadian-heritage/campaigns/black-history-mont ... Accessed on August 22, 2018.
39 Hornby, *Black Islanders*, 8.
40 Matthew McCrae, Canadian Museum for Human Rights. *The story of slavery in Canadian history, It happened here, too.* https://humanrights.ca/story/the-story-of-slavery-in-canadian-history Accessed on July 17, 2019.

Canada's Black History – A Timeline

The Canadian Encyclopedia has provided the following timeline[41] that annotates selected key milestones of historic events relating to Blacks in Canada. Another important historical source is Historica Canada[42], an organization whose mission is to "build awareness of Canadian history and citizenship".

January 1911: Oliver's Immigration Policy

Alberta's Frank Oliver wanted tighter controls on immigration. He became the Liberal government's Minister of the Interior in 1905. Oliver was staunchly British, and his policies favoured nationality over occupation. By 1911, he was able to assert that his immigration policy was more "restrictive, exclusive and selective" than his predecessor's.

February 1911: Anti-Black Campaign

By 1909, hundreds of Oklahoma Blacks had moved to the Canadian Prairies, where they met the same wariness and discrimination that had allowed slavery to exist in an earlier time. In February 1911, a few newspapers in Winnipeg even predicted that the Dominion government would move to exclude "Negro immigrants."

March 10, 1913: Heroine of the Underground Railroad Dies

Harriet Tubman, ardent abolitionist, and heroine of the Underground Railroad, died in New York in 1913. As a conductor with the Underground Railroad, she made 19 secret trips to the American South and guided more than 300 slaves to freedom in Canada.

1914-1918: Black Canadians on the Home Front in WWI

Between 1914 and 1918, Black Canadians at home became actively involved in the war effort. Black associations—on their own and in cooperation with White groups—raised funds, worked in factories, and volunteered in hospitals.

---

41 *The Canadian Encyclopedia*. Black History Timeline.
https://www.thecanadianencyclopedia.ca/en/timeline/black-history Accessed on July 20, 2019.
42 *Historica Canada*. historicacanaada.ca

July 5, 1916: WWI All-Black Battalion

In 1916, Canadian enlistment figures fell from 30,000 to 6,000 per month, while the year-end goal was a force of 500,000. When Reverend C.W. Washington of Edmonton offered to raise an all-Black battalion, military officials authorized the creation of the No. 2 Construction Battalion. The battalion served in France with the Canadian Forestry Corps.

1939-1945: Blacks Accepted into Canadian Services in WWII

Initially, the Canadian military rejected Black volunteers, but as the war continued, many Blacks were accepted into the Regular Army and officer corps. While there was still some segregation in the Canadian forces until the end of the war, hundreds of Black Canadians served alongside Whites in Canada and Europe.

1939-1945: Conditions on the Home Front in WWII

Blacks at home assumed the responsibilities of the men and women serving overseas, working alongside Whites in jobs across the country. During World War II, hundreds of Black workers joined unions for the first time. The all-Black Brotherhood of Sleeping Car Porters was one of the greatest success stories of the war years.

March 14, 1944: Ontario Passes Racial Discrimination Act

Ontario was the first province to respond to social change when it passed the Racial Discrimination Act of 1944. This landmark legislation effectively prohibited the publication and display of any symbol, sign, or notice that expressed ethnic, racial, or religious discrimination. It was followed by other sweeping legislation.

8 November 1946: Black Woman Sits in Theatre's "White Section"[43]

The Nova Scotia Association for the Advancement of Coloured People (NSAACP) united civil rights forces. The NSAACP supported Viola Desmond, a Black woman from Halifax, in her case against a New Glasgow theatre where she was arrested for sitting in the "White-only" section, even though she was willing to buy the more expensive ticket.

---

43 *The Canadian Encyclopedia.* Viola Desmond.
https://www.thecanadianencyclopedia.ca/en/article/viola-desmond Accessed on July 7, 2020.

September 2, 1954: *Toronto Telegram* Covers the Dresden Story

Black discrimination continued in the 1950s, despite legislation prohibiting it. In 1954, two Blacks visited rural Dresden, Ont. and were refused service in two restaurants. The *Toronto Telegram* sent Black "testers" to investigate, who were also refused. When the *Telegram* ran the story, it confirmed what many Blacks suspected, that Canada's laws and regulations were ineffective.

January 19, 1962: Fairclough Dismantles Discriminatory Policy

During her term as Minister of Citizenship and Immigration, Ellen Fairclough oversaw improvements to the Canadian Immigration Service. But her most significant accomplishment was the radical reform of the government's "White Canada" immigration policy. Regulations tabled in 1962 helped to eliminate racial discrimination in Canada's immigration policy.

September 25, 1963: First Black Elected to a Canadian Parliament

Leonard Braithwaite became the first African-Canadian in a provincial legislature when he was elected as the Liberal member for Etobicoke, Ontario in 1963.

January 1, 1964: Africville Demolished

"Africville was a small community of predominantly Black Canadians located in Halifax, Nova Scotia, Canada. It developed on the southern shore of Bedford Basin and existed from the early 1800s to the 1960s."[44]

Encouraged by media attention to Africville's so-called "American-style ghetto," the Halifax City Planning Commission expropriated the land. Residents resisted, citing the community's proud traditions, although Africville lacked basic services such as water, sewage, and good roads. Between 1964 and 1970, residents were relocated and the community razed.[45]

---

44 *Wikipedia*. Africville. https://en.wikipedia.org/wiki/Africville Accessed on July 7, 2019.
45 *The Canadian Encyclopedia*. Black History Timeline.

January 01, 1965: Last Racially Segregated School in Ontario Closes

Thanks to the activism of Black parents, racially segregated schools in Ontario were gradually phased out. The last racially segregated school in Ontario, School Section No. 11 in Colchester, closed in 1965. This was accomplished after newly elected MPP Leonard Braithwaite pushed for the clause on segregated schools for Blacks to be officially removed from provincial education policy. Ontario and Nova Scotia were the only provinces to legislate racially segregated schools. The last one in Nova Scotia, in Guysborough County, closed in 1983. However, informal segregation was present in other provinces including Alberta, Saskatchewan, New Brunswick and Prince Edward Island.

August 11, 1965: Klan Activity in Amherstburg

In 1965, racial tension ran high in Amherstburg, Ont. A cross-burning set the tone; the Black Baptist Church was defaced and the town sign was spray-painted "Amherstburg Home of the KKK." Five days of racial incidents threatened to escalate but the situation was saved by an investigation by the Ontario Human Rights Commission. No arrests were made.

July 28, 1967: Toronto's Caribana Festival Founded

Approximately two-thirds of Canada's West Indian population resides in the greater Toronto area. On 28 July 1967, ten Torontonians with a common West Indian heritage founded the Caribana cultural festival to display their rich cultural traditions. The Caribana festival continues to promote cultural pride, mutual respect, and social unity.

September 18, 1967: African-Canadian Wins Middleweight Championship

In 1967 David Downey won his first Canadian Middleweight Boxing Championship, which he retained until August 1970. Downey's boxing career coincided with one of the most dynamic periods in Halifax's history, which saw the emergence of the city's Black population as a social and political force.

October 1, 1967: Immigration "Points System"

Prior to 1967, the immigration system relied largely on immigration officers' judgment to determine who should be eligible to enter Canada. Deputy Minister of Immigration Tom Kent established a points system, which assigned points in nine categories, to determine eligibility. Ethnic groups all across Canada endorsed the new selection process.

January 1, 1971: African-Canadian Sprinter Receives Order of Canada

In 1971, sprinter Harry Jerome was awarded the Order of Canada medal for "excellence in all fields of Canadian life." Jerome proudly represented Canada in three Olympic Games, winning bronze at Tokyo in 1964.

October 1, 1971: Trudeau Introduces Canada's Multicultural Policy

Canada's multiculturalism policy grew partly in reaction to the Royal Commission on Bilingualism and Biculturalism, which endorsed a "bicultural Canada," barely recognizing "other ethnic groups." This dilemma was partially resolved in 1971 by Prime Minister Trudeau's assertion that Canada was a "*multicultural* country with two official languages."

1974: West Indian Immigration Overwhelms Black Communities.[46]

With the Immigration Act of 1962 and 1967 reforms, Black West Indians flocked to Canada. Indigenous Blacks and their established communities were overwhelmed by the influx and felt threatened by cultural differences. At first some thought skin colour was their only connection. In the early 1980s, Black Canadians of all backgrounds began uniting around common causes.

January 1, 1975: Head Founds Urban Alliance on Race Relations

Black reformer Wilson Head brought a lifetime of experience in civil rights activism with him when he moved from the US to Canada in 1959. Among his numerous accomplishments was the creation, in 1975, of the Urban Alliance on Race Relations. The organization is still dedicated to fighting discrimination against all ethno-racial communities.

---

46 *The Canadian Encyclopedia.* Timeline - Black History.
https://www.thecanadianencyclopedia.ca/en/timeline/black-history Accessed on July 21, 2020.

Harriet Tubman, abolitionist, and heroine of the Underground Railroad.

A musical band from the No.2 Construction Battalion, c. 1917.

Viola Desmond sits in 'whites' section of New Glasgow theatre.

Ellen Fairclough, former Minister of Citizenship and Immigration (photograph by D. Cameron, courtesy Library and Archives Canada / PA-12 9254).

Dr. Wilson A. Head (courtesy Quebec English Schools Network).

A performer at Toronto's Caribana Festival (photograph by Jeffrey Gunawan).

Black Railway Porters in Montréal, Québec. Railway porters played an important role in the struggle for Black rights in Canada (courtesy Africville Genealogical Society).

History of Blacks in Ottawa

History is not the past. History is the present. We carry our
history with us. To think otherwise is criminal.
— James Baldwin (1924-1987)

Canada's capital, the City of Ottawa, has a well-established Caribbean Community. There is evidence of Caribbean culture throughout the city. Rather than having pockets of ethnic concentration, the City of Ottawa integrates its populous in such a way that there are Caribbean residents in just about every residential area, as well as in the city core. Caribbean immigrants or their descendants are now in every tier of the economic strata, from the low income to the affluent. Wherever the people of Caribbean origin reside, the culture of the Caribbean exists as well. Indeed specific Caribbean retail outlets and dining establishments are easily found in Ottawa; and by the year 2000, Caribbean products were already widely distributed through mainstream retail establishments. In fact, the specialty Caribbean establishments — the initial owners of the Caribbean-products market in Ottawa — had begun to face formidable competition from well-established and large-scale retail chains. Nonetheless new Caribbean businesses continued to enter the marketplace and early entrants continued to thrive.

But this was not always the case. In 1970 there were absolutely no Caribbean stores to be found in Ottawa; virtually nothing Caribbean could be purchased anywhere in Ottawa, simply because there was no market for Caribbean products.

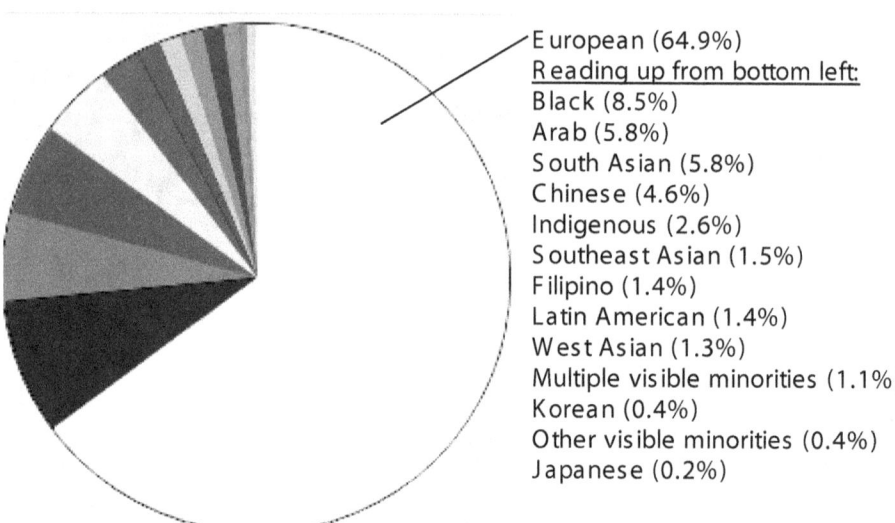

European (64.9%)
Reading up from bottom left:
Black (8.5%)
Arab (5.8%)
South Asian (5.8%)
Chinese (4.6%)
Indigenous (2.6%)
Southeast Asian (1.5%)
Filipino (1.4%)
Latin American (1.4%)
West Asian (1.3%)
Multiple visible minorities (1.1%)
Korean (0.4%)
Other visible minorities (0.4%)
Japanese (0.2%)

Pie chart of the ethnic breakdown of Ottawa based on the 2021 census,
Wikipedia. Demographics of Ottawa. https://en.wikipedia.org/wiki/Demographics_of_Ottawa
Accessed on January 19, 2023.

At that time the Caribbean people were few in numbers. But this demographic would experience rapid changes in the ensuing decades. By the 1990s specialized Caribbean outlets ruled the City of Ottawa vis-à-vis the sale of Caribbean products.

Currently the population of Caribbean immigrants and their descendants living in Ottawa is in the thousands. And although the exact number is uncertain, the growth in this demographic sub-group over the past five decades is unmistakable. Caribbean Immigrants

Paul Barber: One of the first African-Americans to be a Canadian permanent resident in Ottawa.

started their inflow into the Ottawa area during the mid-1950s and during the ensuing decades, this group has seen near exponential growth.

Based on the 2011 Census data, the population of Blacks in Ottawa numbered 49,650, 5.7% of Ottawa's population. This was the largest group within the "visible minorities" demographic segment. And while the Blacks from the Caribbean are a sub-set of the Black population of Ottawa, it is a significant proportion of this demographic.

> "Ottawa has Canada's third-largest Caribbean community, and the second-fastest growing behind Montréal. As of 2011, there were 22,730 people of Caribbean origin living here."[47]

Partly due to the immigration process, the growth is also the result of the subsequent generations of Canadian citizens who are born to parents and re-unified family members of Caribbean immigrants.

> "The first Black person (on record) to have been sighted in *the Ottawa* area was a man named London Oxford, a free black man who was part of the original pioneer group which came with Philemon Wright in the year 1800. London Oxford was a free Negro who had married in Woburn. He probably brought his family with him when he came in 1800, for he had children born in Hull before the family left the area sometime after 1809."[48]

47 City of Ottawa. Ottawa's Population https://ottawa.ca/en/city-hall/get-know-your-city/statistics-and-economic-profile/statistics/ottawas-population and https://ottawa.ca/en/living-ottawa/statistics-and-demographics/2011-census Accessed on July 7, 2019.
48 Bruce S. Elliott. *The Famous Township of Hull: Image and Aspirations of a Pioneer Quebec Community.* Carleton University Social History Seminar. https://hssh.journals.yorku.ca/index.php/hssh/article/view/39013/35395 Accessed on July 20, 2019

Tom Barber says renaming the street is symbolic of the fair treatment his grandfather received when he moved to Ottawa. (Alan Neal, CBC) [51]

Later on in 1844 another Black man named Perry Adams and his wife, Henrietta Joyce moved into Bytown (Ottawa's original name).

"They were in Bytown in the year 1844. On March 10th of 1844, they baptized their child, Frances, at Notre Dame Cathedral on Sussex Drive, in downtown Ottawa. The Godmother at this baptism was Mary McHale, an Irish immigrant, who with her husband and family, farmed on the Manotick Station Road in Osgoode Township. The McHale family were friends and neighbours of my great great grandparents, Lawrence Burns and Margaret Doyle."[49]

But the most detailed record of a Black resident tells the story of a horse trainer named Paul Barber.[50]

"Born into slavery, he was sold to the Barber family in 1853 when he was four years old, and assumed the name of his owners. The Barbers were well-known horse breeders in Kentucky, and he learned how to ride, train, and care for the animals. He also helped sell the family's horses, and his sales trips to Canada led him to believe that he could live and raise a family in the northern country, according to his descendants. After he became a free man, he eventually made his way to Ottawa in 1885. The Barbers lived in Ottawa's Lowertown, and their interracial family was believed to be one of the first in the city."

In 2019, the City of Ottawa ultimately recognized Barber's pioneering and historic contribution to Ottawa. "Part of a street in Lowertown has been renamed to honour a man who overcame slavery and eventually made Ottawa his home as a renowned horse trainer." [51]

49 Drouin Records for Notre Dame Cathedral at ancestry.ca Accessed on

50 Olivia Bowden, *Capital Builders: The Remarkable People Who Shaped Ottawa* (Ottawa: Magic Light Publishing, 2017)

51 Ottawa street renamed in honour of former slave who became famed horse trainer. CBC News, August 15, 2016. https://www.cbc.ca/news/canada/ottawa/barber-street-ottawa-slave-clarence-renamed-1.3721409 and https://twitter.com/CdnHeritage/status/827532535337013248/photo/1

The City of Ottawa was almost void of additional Black residents for the ensuing 50 years, until Herbert "Pops" Brown[52] a Jamaican immigrant, who first settled in Montreal, moved his family into the Ottawa area. Brown originally worked on a cruise ship that was docked in Montreal when the Second World War began. Although he was a Jamaican citizen, he was also a member of the British Commonwealth. So he joined the Canadian Army and fought alongside other Canadians during the war. In 1942 after the end of World War II, Brown returned to Montreal. He secured work in a dry-cleaning business, learned the trade, and continued working in Montreal until 1951. He then moved to Hull (Quebec) to work at the EB Eddy paper mill. Brown would soon transition over to his entrepreneur role with the opening of his first Dry Cleaning & Tailoring store on Murray Street in downtown Ottawa. Brown then began the reunification of his family, whom he had left behind in Jamaica. He then expanded his Dry Cleaning business with the opening of a Bank Street location that included a bridal gown business.

Nessa (Brown) Bedward was one of the Brown's family members who immigrated to Canada in 1953, along with her mother Estelle, her brother Herbert and her sister Velma. The four family members reunified in Hull. Shortly after this re-unification, the family moved across the river to take up residence in Ottawa. Nessa Brown provides the account of the Brown family history in Ottawa as outlined in the profiles section of this publication along with her own personal story on her life experiences in the City of Ottawa. Today, Brown's Cleaning outlets dot the city although no longer owned by the Brown family.

---

52 *Wikipedia*. History of Ottawa. https://en.wikipedia.org/wiki/historyofottawa
Accessed on July 22, 2019.

The City of Ottawa
Population Demographics

The history of Ottawa, the capital of Canada, has been shaped by several significant events. One of the most noteworthy was the construction of the Rideau Canal. Historically, Ottawa was one of the centers for the lumber industry.

"The Ottawa River timber trade, also known as the Ottawa Valley timber trade or Ottawa River lumber trade, was the nineteenth century production of wood products by Canada on areas of the Ottawa River destined for British and American markets. It was the major industry of the historical colonies of Upper Canada and Lower Canada and it created an entrepreneur known as a lumber baron. The trade in squared timber and later sawed lumber led to population growth and prosperity to communities in the Ottawa Valley, especially the city of Bytown (now Ottawa, the capital of Canada). The product was chiefly red and white pine. The Ottawa River being conveniently located with access via the St. Lawrence River was a valuable region due to its great pine forests surpassing any others nearby. The industry lasted until around 1900 as both markets and supplies decreased."[53]

The choice of Ottawa as the location of Canada's capital, as well as American and European influences and interactions enabled the city's growth. By 1914, Ottawa's population had surpassed 100,000; today it is the capital of a G7 country and whose metropolitan population exceeds one million.

"The name 'Ottawa' is derived from the Algonquin word *Adawe*, meaning 'to trade'. The word refers to the indigenous peoples who used the river to trade, hunt, fish, camp, harvest plants, ceremonies, and for other traditional uses. The first maps made of the area started to name the major river after these peoples. For centuries, Algonquin people have portaged through the waterways of both the Ottawa River and the Rideau River while passing through the area. French explorer Étienne Brûlé was credited as the first European to see the Chaudière Falls in 1610, and he too had to portage past them to get further inland. No permanent

---

53 *Wikipedia.* Ottawa River timber trade. Updated 2021.
https://en.wikipedia.org/wiki/Ottawa_River_timber_trade Accessed on July 20, 2019.

settlement occurred in the area until 1800 when Philemon Wright founded his village near the falls, on the north shore of the Ottawa River."[54]

Table 1: Panethnic groups in Metro Ottawa (2001–2021)		
Panethnic Group	2021 Pop.	%
European	1036525	70.78
African	114225	7.80
Middle Eastern	83730	5.72
South Asian	60780	4.15
East Asian	57460	3.92
Indigenous	46540	3.18
Southeast Asian	32995	2.25
Latin American	20625	1.41
Other	17095	1.17
Total responses	1464495	98.40
Total population	1488307	100.00

The City of Ottawa was first an Irish and French Christian settlement, but it now has a very diverse population. The inception of the city was directly related to the construction of the Rideau Canal, a mega-Project led by Lt.-Col. John By, a British Engineer.[55] The Canal project started in 1826 and by its completion some six years later the settlement that was to become Ottawa, was called Bytown with approximately 1,000 residents. By 1855, Bytown's population had grown to 11,000 and with a name change it became the city of Ottawa.

The 2021 census data showed that approximately 30% of Ottawa's population was of non-European origin (Table 1) [56] . This included immigrants from African and Caribbean countries. The population of the City of Ottawa has steadily increased over the last five decades. And whereas, the Black population in Ottawa was almost non-existent 50 years ago, this segment had grown to 8.5% and accounted for the second largest ethnic group in Metro Ottawa in the 2021 census. By this time the metro Ottawa population had grown to approximately 1.5 million, with blacks the black population at about 126,500.

---

54 Wikipedia. History of Ottawa https://en.wikipedia.org/wiki/History_of_Ottawa , Accessed on January 19, 2023.
55 Olivia Bowden, Capital Builders
56 Government of Canada, Statistics Canada. "Census Profile, 2021 Census of Population". Accessed on October 26, 2022

Table 2 Ottawa's Population Growth		
Year	Pop.	% increase
1951	246,298	19.30%
1956	287,244	16.60%
1961	358,410	24.80%
1966	413,695	15.40%
1971	471,931	14.10%
1976	520,533	10.30%
1981	546,849	5.10%

Between 1950 and 1980, Ottawa's population grew from approximately 246,000 to over 500,000, doubling in size in a thirty-year period (Table 2) [57]. The Caribbean immigrant population remained relatively small. At the time of the 2016 census, the population of immigrants from the Caribbean who lived in Ottawa was 6.6%. This ratio does not reflect the percentage of the Ottawa population who are children or grandchildren born to immigrants from the Caribbean, and considered to be Canadian citizens. [58]

"Ottawa's industrial appearance was vastly changed due to the 1940s Greber Plan. Later powers were given by an Act of Parliament to the newly formed National Capital Commission (NCC) to attain ownership of lands, and effect vast changes. Some of the results of these were the National Capital Greenbelt, expropriation of areas in downtown, the removal of large industrial areas, the removal of downtown railway tracks, the relocation of the train station out of downtown, and the creation and maintenance of areas that would provide the nation's capital with a more attractive appearance. In the 1960s and 1970s, a building boom vastly changed Ottawa's skyline. Ottawa became one of Canada's largest high-tech cities and was nicknamed Silicon Valley North."[59]

---

57 *Wikipedia*. Demographics of Ottawa https://en.wikipedia.org/wiki/Demographics of Ottawa Accessed on July 22, 2019.
58 Statistics Canada. 2016 Census. https://www150.statcan.gc.ca/n1/daily-quotidien/171025/dq171025b-eng.htm Accessed on September 20, 2019.
59 *Wikipedia*. History of Ottawa. https://en.wikipedia.org/wiki/History_of_Ottawa Accessed on July 22, 2019.

Caribbean Canadian Connection

Canada and the majority of the Caribbean Islands are members of the British Commonwealth; in general the remaining islands are mainly connected to France. Therefore, the languages spoken by the people of the Caribbean are directly aligned with Canada's two official Languages. Because of this affiliation Canada has had a very long history with the Caribbean nations.

> "The Commonwealth of Nations, normally known as the Commonwealth, is a unique political association of 56 member states, the vast majority of which are former territories of the British Empire."[60]

Those Caribbean Islands that have been members of the British Commonwealth are English-speaking nations. Hence the influence of the British political and economic system was evident in the government institutions, the legal systems and even in certain aspects of culture in both the Caribbean nation states and in Canada.

The Caribbean is also an economically and culturally diverse group of 27 countries and territories including Antigua and Barbuda, the Bahamas, Barbados, Belize, Dominica, Grenada, Guyana, Haiti, Jamaica, Montserrat, Saint Lucia, St. Kitts and Nevis, St. Vincent and the Grenadines, Suriname, and Trinidad and Tobago. In the 2006 census, 578,695 Canadians reported that they originated from the Caribbean, and the overwhelming majority of these people have immigrated to Canada since the 1970s.

Canadians of Caribbean origin belong to one of the largest non-European ethnic groups in Canada. A group of 556 Jamaicans arrived in Canada in 1796 after an unsuccessful British attempt to enslave them in Jamaica (see Black Canadians), but early contact between Canada and West Indians were few. Between 1800 and 1920 a small number of Jamaicans and Barbadians immigrated as labourers to work in the Cape Breton and Sydney mines, but from 1920 until the early 1960s immigration was virtually nonexistent. Immigration from the Caribbean really began in the 1950s, and by 1973 accounted for almost 13 per cent of all immigration to Canada.[61] (See Appendix B: 10 Fast Facts About Caribbean Immigrants in Canada.)

---

60 *Wikipedia.* Commonwealth of Nations.
https://en.wikipedia.org/wiki/Commonwealth_of_Nations Accessed on February 10, 2023.
61 *The Canadian Encyclopedia.* Caribbean Canadians.
https://www.thecanadianencyclopedia.ca/en/article/caribbean-canadians Accessed July 21, 2019.

There have been three major periods of immigration from the Caribbean. From 1900 to 1960, Canada accepted about 21,500 immigrants from Caribbean countries, only 33 per cent of whom were placed under the ethnic origin heading of "Black". The slight increase in immigration from 1945 to 1960 corresponded with postwar economic expansion and the West Indian Domestic Scheme (1955–60) which was established, almost exclusively, for the immigration of women from Jamaica and Barbados who immigrated as domestic workers. The second period, from 1960 to 1971, corresponded with the "liberalization" of the Canadian Immigration Act. During this period Canada accepted about 64,000 people from the Caribbean. [62]

Since the 1970s Canada saw increased migration as part of an international movement to slow European emigration, and Canada began to depend increasingly on the developing nations. The last period, which began in the early 1970s, coincided with the economic recession. Except for 1973 and 1974 (unusual years because of the Addressment of Status Program that helped many persons regularize their status), immigration from the Caribbean declined. Caribbean immigration fell from 10 per cent of total immigration in 1975 to six per cent in 1979 and remained at six per cent until 1996. Before 1960, most immigrants came from the British colonies, especially from Barbados, Jamaica, Trinidad, and Bermuda.[63]

The population of Canadians of Caribbean origin has grown more quickly than the Canadian population as a whole. Between 1996 and 2001, the Canadian population grew by four per cent but the Canadian-Caribbean population rose by 11 per cent. Caribbean-Canadians are concentrated overwhelmingly in the major urban centres of Québec and Ontario; in 2001, 91 per cent of Caribbean-Canadians lived in one of these two provinces. Between 1973 and 1980, 96 per cent of Haitian immigrants to Canada settled in Québec, and in 2001, 90 per cent of Haitians lived in Québec, eight per cent in Ontario, and one per cent in each of British Columbia and Alberta. At that time, most Haitians in Québec lived in Montréal (83 per cent). [64] In 2006, the largest populations of Canadians of Caribbean origin were from Jamaica (231,110) followed by those from Haiti (102,430), Guyana (61,085) and Trinidad and Tobago (58,415).[65]

---

62 Ibid. The Canadian Encyclopedia. Caribbean Canadians.
63 *The Canadian Encyclopedia*. Caribbean Canadians.
https://www.thecanadianencyclopedia.ca/en/article/caribbean-canadians Accessed July 21, 2019.
64 *The Canadian Encyclopedia*. Haitian Diaspora in Quebec.
https://www.thecanadianencyclopedia.ca/en/article/haitian-diaspora-in-quebec
Accessed on July 21, 2019.
65 *The Canadian Encyclopedia*. Caribbean Canadians.

Reasons for Immigrating to Canada

The life stories presented by approximately 60 people who were interviewed for this publication are as varied as the individuals themselves. Nonetheless, a common theme emerged with regards to the central reason for coming to Canada. Each person wanted to improve their life. Just about everyone had the same reason for immigrating to Canada at the time that they chose to leave their homeland. For the domestic worker, in particular, this objective also extended to improving the lives of the families that they left behind — parents, siblings, and extended family members. They were encouraged by the fact that they could become Landed Immigrants after their contracted period of service ended which gave them reasons to believe that this objective could be achieved. It should be noted that many of the Domestic Services immigrants were professionals in their home countries. Many of this group had successfully completed secondary education and a number had also attained post-secondary educational status becoming teachers, nurses, secretaries, and office administrators.

The student immigrants saw themselves attaining higher levels of education that would propel their careers in the future. And most, if not all, had the intention of returning to their homeland when this education objective was realized. But as it turned out, the majority of student immigrants remained in Canada. And even a few who returned to their country came back to take up residence in Canada not long thereafter. For the professional class this objective was obvious. Despite the fact that all of this group had been gainfully employed and had attained the appropriate levels of education for their chosen profession, they elected to leave their homeland in order "to better themselves".

While the Canadian Government had specific reasons for admitting immigrants, the immigrants themselves had their own reasons for wanting to migrate to Canada. And those who intended to return after their goals were accomplished recognized that they then had other reasons to remain in Canada. By the time they had completed their set goals, they had established themselves inside new communities, made new friends, established new families and had been assimilated into the Canadian culture. Their decision to remain in Canada was in most cases a simple one. Still, many struggled with their loyalty to their homeland, which was in conflict with the loyalty that they had since developed for Canada. Some elected to return to their Caribbean homeland; but in many of these instances the return experience turned out to be unsuccessful. In quite a number of these cases, individuals returned to Canada as Landed Immigrants and ultimately became Canadian citizens.

Caribbean Peoples in Ottawa

Historical data from the 1951 Canadian Census indicates that there were no Black residents in the City of Ottawa. This suggests that there may be a baseline threshold for population data by sub-groups to be significant, because historical records do document the presence of a number of Blacks, though very miniscule in numbers who lived in the City of Ottawa in 1951. The numbers were so insignificant that Ottawa's Black population count did not register in Statistics Canada's population numbers.

The total Canadian Black population count as recorded in 1951 was approximately 18,020 and this turned out to be 4,000 less than the count that was recorded in the census taken ten years earlier in 1941 when Canada's Black population was 22,174.[66] But imminent changes to Ottawa's Black population was about to happen starting in the mid-50s. The catalyst for the pending changes would be a liberalization of the Canadian Immigration policies to make Canada more racially inclusive which changed the trajectory and led to the onset of an initial influx of immigrants from the Caribbean arriving in Ottawa.

The earliest groups of new immigrants were predominantly Black, starting the trend that would over the ensuing decades result in the multi-racial National Capital Region of today. Prior to Canada's change in its immigration policy, the historical records indicated that the few number of Blacks from the Caribbean or elsewhere who were living in Ottawa, arrived in the city shortly after World War II. At that time there was "a great demand for unskilled workers" which resulted in the National Act of 1948.[67] This Act was designed to attract cheap labourers from British colonies overseas, and resulted in many West Indians, including Jamaicans coming to Canada. The Jamaicans who entered Canada after World War II did so because they still believed it was an opportunity to escape poverty and seek a new start in a world where personal advancement and success seemed to be encouraged. Wanting to stop the inflow of Black West Indians, the Walter Act of 1952 was passed to impose a "severely restricted quota"[68] on Black West Indians entering the country. It is fair to assume that a number of these post-war

---

66 Jamaicans.com. Jamaicans in Canada: A Detailed History. Jamaicans Living In Toronto Jamaicans In Canada: A Detailed History by Evon Smith.
http://jamaicans.com/historydetailed/#ixzz4yAj1N0xG Accessed on July 17, 2019.
67 *Wikipedia*. Jamaican Canadians. https://en.wikipedia.org/wiki/Jamaican_Canadians
Accessed on April 27, 2018.
68 James & Walker, 1984

immigrants would have landed in Ottawa. There were a few students who attended universities as well as nursing students who had migrated to Ottawa in the post-war period leading up to the mid-1950s.

The initial inflow of Caribbean immigrants, starting with the first group of domestic workers, began in earnest during the latter part of the 1950s. This was followed by a second wave of Caribbean immigrants who were admitted into Canada with the introduction of the points system in 1967. Potential immigrants were evaluated and assigned a number of points based on their educational skills, the potential for self-sufficiency, and their ability to contribute to Canadian society. Many of these newcomers settled in Toronto, while others headed to Ottawa to reunite with family members who had obtained their Landed Immigrant Status and had made Ottawa their permanent home.

The 'points system' policy initiative was immediately followed by the formation of the Canadian International Development Agency (CIDA) in 1968 out of a Foreign Aid Office in the External Affairs Ministry. CIDA's mandate was

> "to support sustainable development in developing countries in order to reduce poverty and to contribute to a more secure, equitable and prosperous world."[69]

The CIDA mandate initiated the flow of students from the Caribbean under its sponsorship program. Furthermore, prior to CIDA's existence, the Canadian Government sponsored students in the 1960s to pursue advanced studies in Canada under the Commonwealth Scholarship scheme. While some of these students came directly to Ottawa, a few others made Ottawa their permanent home later after their arrival in Canada. There were also other self-sponsored students who came to study in Ottawa during the early 1960s.

---

69 *Wikipedia*. Canadian International Development Agency.
https://en.wikipedia.org/wiki/Canadian_International_Development_Agency
Accessed on July 21, 2019.

Cultural Assimilation

New immigrants to Canada or to any other country for that matter can expect to encounter a much different society from whence they came. Their new country usually differs in many ways. People are different. They look different and they speak differently, even if the language is the same. The food is not the same as back home. And just about every aspect of the new environment is different from that which the new immigrant has been familiar in their motherland. There are the multitude of social norms, some obvious and others rather subtle. Every new immigrant must navigate through innumerable scenarios, resulting in a state of unease which may create anxieties for the newly arrived. The typical new immigrant's initial reaction is to seek out anyone, anything familiar, to ease their anxiety.

An extensive body of research studies has been amassed on the topic of how immigrants are assimilated into their adopted country.

> "Assimilation, sometimes known as integration or incorporation, is the process by which the characteristics of members of immigrant groups and host societies come to resemble one another. That process, which has both economic and socio-cultural dimensions, begins with the immigrant generation and continues through the second generation and beyond."[70]

The process by which a new immigrant is integrated into their new society is long-term and multi-generational. At the initial stage, some new immigrant may face a series of obstacles and assimilation barriers that potentially extend this process for longer periods than others. These obstacles are contingent on the levels of similarities between the immigrant and the people of the new country, and between the new host-land and the immigrant's homeland.

Evidently a new immigrant from Great Britain would find it much easier to integrate into Canadian society than an immigrant from Brazil. Most Canadians are in fact British immigrants, and therefore a new British immigrant would be not have language barriers. Most British immigrants are Caucasians, and hence their physical features immediately blend with the majority of the Canadian populous. There are many other potential assimilation barriers that are minimized or even eliminated if you are a British immigrant as opposed to a Brazilian who speaks Portuguese. Indeed, similar diets, cultural practices, and most importantly

---

70 Susan K. Brown and Frank D. Bean. *Assimilation Models, Old and New: Explaining a Long-Term Process*; October 1, 2006.

already established and familiar institutions welcome British immigrants to Canada. Integration infrastructure that is in place to assimilate the British immigrant is normally not in place for immigrants from many other nations.

Since the liberalization of Canada's immigration policies in the early 1950s, Canada had made other structural changes aimed at facilitating the integration of new immigrants into the Canadian social fabric.

> "On 8 October 1971, Prime Minister Pierre Elliott Trudeau declared in the House of Commons of Canada that, after much deliberation, the policies of bilingualism and multiculturalism would be implemented in Canada. In other words, the Government of Canada would recognize and respect its society including its diversity in languages, customs, religions, and so on. According to Immigration, Refugees and Citizenship Canada (IRCC): *In 1971, Canada was the first country in the world to adopt multiculturalism as an official policy.*"[71]

The Canadian Government has also established additional policies to facilitate the assimilation process for specific new immigrant groups. A number of these policies have been targeted towards the integration of Refugees into the Canadian society. Although it was

> "only since the early 1970s that refugees have been a constant component of the immigration program. Canada formally organized its refugee policies and management structures in the 1976 act, thereby institutionalizing an ongoing commitment to fulfill legal obligations toward refugees."[72]

Many of the day-to-day experiences that help new immigrants adapt to their new country result from the structures that were established by other precedent immigrants. New immigrants find comfort in numbers. So those of similar homelands tend to reach out to each other, and soon, communities of the similar evolve. Once again, the Canadian Government fosters the establishment of these communities. The evidence is seen in just about every major Canadian city. The Italian and Chinese communities are visible examples. However the Government did not establish the infrastructure for these communities; this was accomplished by the immigrants themselves.

---

71 *Wikipedia.* Canadian Multiculturalism Act.
https://en.wikipedia.org/wiki/Canadian_Multiculturalism_Act Accessed on Aril 27, 2018.
72 Migration Policy Institute. Canada's Immigration Policy: a Focus on Human Capital.
https://www.migrationpolicy.org/article/canadas-immigration-policy-focus-human-capital Accessed on February 15, 2018.

When the initial group of Caribbean immigrants arrived in Ottawa during the mid-1950s they had very little choice other than to adapt to the culture of the Canadian society. Their most fundamental needs, food, shelter and clothing were essentially the same as those available to the native consumer. There were no Jamaican patties, no *Roti* from Trinidad, no yams, plantains or chayotes. None of the authentic Caribbean foods could be purchased anywhere in Ottawa. Caribbean music was a rare airing of Harry Belafonte. Anything authentic to the Caribbean was to be found only in the hearts and minds of the early immigrants to the City of Ottawa.

However cultural forces are dominant forces, as if culture is embedded in our DNA. The early Caribbean immigrants soon began to recreate whatever aspects of their cultural environment that they had left behind. Immigrants from the Caribbean integrated into the Canadian social fabric in a manner similar to other immigrant ethnic groups since cultural assimilation began almost immediately after their arrival. Their initial food choices and other social behaviours comported with existing Canadian norms.

But as their numbers grew, Caribbean immigrants to Ottawa recognized that their island compatriots, who had settled in either Montreal or Toronto, were exposed to a much broader spectrum of the Caribbean cultural experiences. Being much larger cities, Montreal and Toronto had much larger Caribbean immigrant populations than Ottawa. Montreal was the de facto port of landing for Haitian immigrants and for many others from the Caribbean. Toronto, on the other hand was the primary port of landing for the majority of English-speaking Caribbean immigrants. Montreal and Toronto soon became the week-end entertainment and cultural exposure destination for many Caribbean immigrants who lived in Ottawa. And on their return to Ottawa, they would bring back anything that was relative to their Caribbean culture that they needed: food items, recorded music, reading material, hair care products and many other Caribbean items that were unavailable in Ottawa.

These factors contributed to the establishment of a number of the earliest Caribbean businesses in Ottawa. By the late 1960s to the early 1970s the Ottawa Caribbean population had grown to the point where Caribbean entrepreneurs saw opportunities in a number of areas; products and services that were available in Montreal and Toronto could be marketed directly to the Caribbean consumers in Ottawa. This would be beneficial to the consumers in that they would no longer have to leave Ottawa to purchase the products that they needed. Despite the cost being a small premium above Montreal and Toronto, it was still a good deal.

The emergence of Caribbean-focussed products and services outlets in Ottawa also exposed other Canadians to aspects of Caribbean culture. One of the earliest Caribbean restaurants, Spicy Luke's, exposed many Canadians to Jamaican patties and other Caribbean dishes. Meanwhile a hybrid Canadian-Caribbean culture emerged in Ottawa similar to that established in Montreal and more so in Toronto. Canada has since emerged as a model country because of its approach to ethnic and cultural difference. This is articulated quite clearly in the preamble of the Canadian Multiculturalism Act (See Appendix C: Canadian Multiculturalism Act).

Racial Attitudes

The subject of race specifically as it relates to the attitudes held by the white Canadian population towards Blacks is a common discussion among Blacks in Canada. It is quite normal for this issue to get an impromptu airing whenever a group of Black people find themselves together in just about any forum. However should a white person draw near while a discussion is in progress, the Black voices will immediately become muted, and the subject most likely changed to a topic in which the approaching white counterpart could participate without feeling awkward and uneasy. For the most part Blacks tend to keep racial discussion to themselves. Equally, it is not evident how white people deal with this topic when they are together. What became clear from participant interviews is that the early immigrants to Ottawa were also uncomfortable addressing the topic of race with their white counterparts. Many of the interviewees reported incidences of racial problems both in their work environments and in the social sphere. They immediately understood that they needed to hone appropriate strategies to deal with these issues if they were to make progress towards achieving objectives that they had established for themselves.

Two of the twenty questions posed to each participant focused indirectly on evoking a response to uncover their respective experiences with the obstacles that they encountered. Without mentioning race, participants were asked the following two questions: first, what obstacles did you encounter? And second, how did you deal with these obstacles?

The questions were staged within the context related to their job as well as in their social interactions within their community. A small number responded with no reference to issues or obstacles relating to their race. But most of the respondents immediately reflected on one or more issues that they considered to be directly related to the fact that they were Black. The responses to these questions covered the full spectrum from the absurd to the unbelievable. For example, one of the earliest nurses who came to Ottawa from the Caribbean during the mid-1960s encountered a mother and a child who appeared to be her daughter near her hospital in what is now mid-town Ottawa. Upon seeing her, the daughter commented to her mother that this woman was dirty (referring to her black skin) and needed to go take a bath. At the other extreme was a Black lawyer, who showed for an interview, and was kept waiting in the reception area for near to three hours, while office doors would open from time to time and the office occupant would peek out to see if the potential interviewee was still there. This interview did not happen; incidentally, this prospect had earlier represented Canada in the Olympic Games.

Evolution of the Ottawa Caribbean Culture

One of Ottawa's earliest Caribbean Cultural forms is the Steel Band.

> "The Steel Band originated on the Caribbean Island of Trinidad about 1940, an invention of poor people in Port of Spain who played music during Carnival to represent their neighborhoods and to compete with rival bands. Initially, metal buckets, cans, and other containers were integrated into ensembles of bamboo stamping tubes, called tamboo bamboo, which provided percussion accompaniment for masquerading and singing. By the late 1940s steel bands had become a prominent feature of Carnival in Trinidad, and by the early 1950s the tradition had spread to other islands of the Caribbean, most notably Antigua and St. Thomas."[73]

Trinidad began to export its 'Pan' culture in the late 1940s. Rudolph Carter, better known as Rudy King, is widely thought to have been the first person to bring steel pan to the United States from Trinidad. He migrated from Trinidad to New York City in 1949 and established a career as a pan builder, tuner, and performer. King's contributions to the U.S. pan movement mainly affected the New York City area: he competed and performed on pan at Harlem's Apollo theatre.[74] Later on:

> "The Trinidad All-Steel Pan Percussion Orchestra (TASPO) was formed to participate in the Festival of Britain in 1951. The group was the first steelband to travel abroad from Trinidad and Tobago, presenting the newly invented steelpan to an international audience."[75]

In 1959 Ottawa ushered in its first Caribbean nightclub, the Coral Reef located on Sparks Street near Kent. Its resident band was a Steel Band composed of a core group of Trinidadian immigrants, and was the first steel band to appear in Ottawa. The individuals credited with establishing this form of Caribbean culture are discussed in the 'Profiles' of this publication.

---

73 Britannica. Steel Band. http://www.britannica.com/art/steel-band Accessed on July 3, 2019.
74 Janine Tiffe. *Tropicalism and the Struggle for Legitimacy: A History of the Steel Band Movement in American Universities*. Doctor of Philosophy Thesis. Florida State University Libraries; Electronic Theses, Treatises and Dissertations: The Graduate School, 2015.
75 *Wikipedia*. Trinidad All-Steel Pan Percussion Orchestra.
https://en.wikipedia.org/wiki/Trinidad_All-Steel_Pan_Percussion_Orchestra
Accessed on April 27, 2018.

Canadian-Caribbean Diplomatic Relationships

The Canadian and Caribbean relationships have long been established primarily due to integration with the British Crown through the British Commonwealth. While this is most evident in the larger, English-speaking Caribbean Islands — Jamaica, Barbados, and Trinidad and Tobago, it is noticeable in other Islands within the British Commonwealth. Secondly, with Canada's unique bilingual culture of English and French, there is a natural alliance with French-speaking islands within the Caribbean, predominantly Haiti, and to a lesser extent Martinique. Full diplomatic relationship with Canada has succeeded the declaration of independence of each respective Caribbean Island, and hence those Islands that gained their Independence from Great Britain in the 1960s and 1970s have had consulate offices established in Canada shortly thereafter.

Barbados

Barbados has had a much longer relationship with Canada than any other Caribbean Island. The bilateral relationship between Canada and Barbados goes back to the early 1900s.

> "Barbados–Canada relations refer to the bilateral relations between Canada and Barbados. In 1907, the Government of Canada opened a Trade Commissioner Service to the Caribbean region located in Bridgetown, Barbados. Following Barbadian independence from the United Kingdom in November 1966, the Canadian High Commission was established in Bridgetown, Barbados on 27 September 1973. There is a High Commission of Barbados in Ottawa and a Barbadian Consulate in Toronto. The relationship between both nations today partly falls under the larger gambit of Canada–Caribbean relations. "As of 2014 it is estimated that as much as 8% of Canadian foreign investments [are] in Barbados.""[76]

---

76 *Wikipedia.* Barbados-Canada Relations.
https://en.wikipedia.org/wiki/Barbados%E2%80%93Canada_relations Accessed on April l27, 20l8.

Bahamas

"Canada established diplomatic relations with the Bahamas in 1973 after they achieved independence. The Bahamas is represented in Canada by the High Commission of the Bahamas in Ottawa. Canada is represented in the Bahamas by the High Commission of Canada in Jamaica. Canadians in the Bahamas can access consular services at the Canadian Honorary Consulate located in Nassau." [77]

Dominica

Formal diplomatic relationship between Canada and Dominica was established in 1979. Canada is accredited to Dominica from its high commission in Bridgetown, Barbados. Dominica is accredited to Canada from its embassy in Washington, D.C, United States. [78]

The Dominican Republic

Canadian diplomatic relationship with the Dominican Republic dates back to 1954. Canada has an embassy in Santo Domingo. And Dominican Republic has an embassy in Ottawa. [79]

Grenada

Canada – Grenada relations are bilateral relations between Canada and Grenada. Canada recognized Grenada and formally established diplomatic relations on 7 February 1974, as the same day as Grenada got independence from the United Kingdom of Great Britain and Northern Ireland. Both countries are members of the Commonwealth of Nations, and they share the same head of state and monarch as Commonwealth realms. Canada is accredited to Grenada from its high commission in Bridgetown, Barbados. There is no resident Canadian government office in Grenada. You can obtain consular assistance from the High Commission of Canada to Barbados, in Bridgetown. [80]

---

77 Government of Canada. Canada-Bahamas Relations. https://www.international.gc.ca/country-pays/bahamas/relations.aspx?lang=eng Accessed on February 11, 2023.

78 Government of Canada. Canada-Dominica Relations. https://www.international.gc.ca/country-pays/dominica-dominique/relations.aspx?lang=eng Accessed on February 11, 2023.

79 *Wikipedia*. Canada-Dominican Republic Relations History. https://en.wikipedia.org/wiki/Canada%E2%80%93Dominican_Republic_relations#History

80 Government of Canada. Grenada. https://travel.gc.ca/assistance/embassies-consulates/grenada Accessed on March 14, 2023.

Tulloch

Guyana

The Canadian diplomatic presence in Guyana started with the opening of the Commission of Canada in Georgetown, in March 1964. In May 1966, Guyana gained independence and full diplomatic relations were established.

In Guyana, Canada is represented by the High Commission of Canada to Guyana and Suriname in Georgetown. Since 2003, the High Commissioner is also Canada's Plenipotentiary Representative to the Caribbean Community (CARICOM), which is headquartered in the greater Georgetown area. Guyana is represented in Canada by the High Commission of Guyana in Ottawa. Guyana also has a Consulate in Toronto. Canada and Guyana have strong ties through the Commonwealth of Nations.

The strong bilateral relations between Canada and Guyana result from political ties through the Commonwealth, commercial links, development assistance and immigration. Bilateral treaties between Canada and Guyana include an Avoidance of Double Taxation Agreement (1987) and an Air Services Agreement (2005). Canada and Guyana share extensive people-to-people ties: the Guyanese Diaspora in Canada is estimated to be around 200,000. Guyana benefits from bilateral funding through the Canada Fund for Local Initiatives; and Canada's Caribbean Regional Development program, which supports Caribbean collaboration and integration efforts. [81]

Haiti

Canada–Haiti relations are relations between Canada and Haiti. During the unsettled period from 1957 to 1990, Canada received many Haitian refugees, who now form a significant minority in Quebec. Canada and Haiti only officially established diplomatic relations in 1954 when Edward Ritchie Bellemare was appointed Chargé d'Affaires of the Canadian Embassy in Haiti. [82]

Canadian International Development Agency. Caribbean Regional Program Evaluation. https://www.oecd.org/derec/canada/Caribbean-Regional-Program-Evaluation-April-2014.pdf Accessed on March 14, 2023.
82 *Wikipedia*. Haiti Relations. https://en.wikipedia.org/wiki/Canada%E2%80%93Haiti_relations Accessed on March 14, 2023.

Jamaica

Jamaica on the other hand was one of the earliest Caribbean islands to set up diplomatic relations with Canada with a High Commission in Ottawa in 1962, followed by a Consulate-General in Toronto. Since March 4, 1963, Canada has a High Commission in Kingston.[83]

Saint Kitts and Nevis

Canada established diplomatic relationship with Saint Kitts and Nevis in September 1983. Canada is accredited to Saint Kitts and Nevis from its high commission in Bridgetown, Barbados. There is no Canadian government office in Saint Kitts and Nevis. You can obtain consular assistance from the High Commission of Canada in Bridgetown, Barbados. [84]

St. Lucia

Diplomatic relationships between Canada and St Lucia were formalized in 1979. Canada is accredited to Saint Lucia from its High Commission in Bridgetown, Barbados. Updated text: Consulate General of Saint Lucia is located in Toronto. This office "provide invaluable information to Saint Lucians in Canada, potential visitors to Saint Lucia and prospective investors". [85]

St Vincent and the Grenadines

The formalization of Diplomatic relationships between Canada and St Vincent and the Grenadines occurred in 1979. Canada is accredited to Saint Vincent and the Grenadines from its High Commission in Bridgetown, Barbados. There is no Canadian government office in Saint Vincent and the Grenadines. You can obtain consular assistance from the High Commission of Canada to Barbados, in Bridgetown. [86]

---

83 Government of Canada. Canada and Jamaica. https://www.international.gc.ca/country-pays/jamaica-jamaique/index.aspx?lang=eng Accessed on March 14, 2023.
84 Government of Canada. Travel. Saint Kitts and Nevis https://travel.gc.ca/assistance/embassies-consulates/saint-kitts-and-nevis Accessed on March 25, 2023.
85 St. Lucia Consulate. https://stluciaconsulate.ca
86 Government of Canada. Saint Vincent and the Grenadines. https://travel.gc.ca/assistance/embassies-consulates/saint-vincent-the-grenadines Accessed on March 14, 2023.

Trinidad and Tobago

Canada's relations with Trinidad and Tobago are close and long-standing. A full-time Trade Commissioner was first appointed to Port of Spain in 1938. Official diplomatic relations were established on August 31, 1962, when Trinidad and Tobago became an independent country. In Trinidad and Tobago, Canada is represented by the High Commission of Canada in Port of Spain, which opened in 1962. The first Canadian High Commissioner was accredited in 1963.[87]

The Jamaican High Commission

Jamaica was the first of the Caribbean Islands to establish a High Commission in Canada.[88] This office was located at 55 Range Road in the Sandy Hill Area of Ottawa.

The Jamaican High Commission to Canada was established in 1962 as Jamaica secured the nation's independence from Great Britain. H.E. Earl Maynier, along with several diplomatic personnel including Norma McNamee, was dispatched to Ottawa to foster stronger ties with Canada and provide a channel for the growing number of Jamaican immigrants who were arriving in Canada.

Earle Maynier was a Jamaican diplomat who served as Jamaica's High Commissioner to Canada from 1962 to 1965. Having graduated from the London School of Economics in 1944, he later attended the University of Toronto. He played a part in the Trade Liberalization proposals that were made by the West Indies. Maynier died in September 1972.

Maynier was the chief economic advisor to two Jamaican leaders, Norman Washington Manley, who served as Premier before Independence and Alexander Bustamante who succeeded him to become the first Prime Minister. Maynier was married to Elsie Solomon Hylton. They had two daughters, Helen, and Shirley. His second wife was Dr. Hyacinth Lightbourne, who was among the first three female Jamaican doctors in the nation. She was a graduate of the University of London Medical School. His third wife was Ivy Lawrence, a graduate of McGill University who received her law degree from the University of Toronto.

---

87 Government of Canada. International. Trinidad-Tobago. https://www.international.gc.ca/country-pays/trinidad_tobago-trinite_tobago/relations.aspx?lang=eng Accessed on February 11, 2023.
88 The Jamaican High Commission. http://www.jhcottawa.ca/index.html Accessed on March14, 2023.

The following High Commissioners succeeded Maynier: [89]

1965 - 1970	H.E. Vincent H. McFarlane
1970 - 1972	H.E. Vivian Courtney Smith
1972 - 1975	H.E. Wills Ogilvie Isaacs
1976 - 1978	H.E. Kenneth G. Anthony Hill
1978 - 1987	H.E. Leslie Wilson

Mrs. Norma McNamee settled into her pivotal role as the main point of contact and liaison between new immigrants from Jamaica and diplomatic services that was offered by the High Commissioner's Office. Her role enabled her to become familiar with many new immigrants, and she was well known by most.[90]

The McNamee Family
Seated: John, Norma; Standing L-R: Pauline, Johnny, Sandra, Johnna, Ann.

Six weeks after her arrival, the members of Mrs. McNamee's family landed in Ottawa. She and her husband John, and their children — Ann, Johanna (late), Johnny, Sandra and Pauline — settled in Manor Park.

John secured employment with the Firestone Tire Company and the children settled into the school system. Ann, the eldest, who was nine years old when they arrived in Ottawa, recalled the McNamee's as being the only Black family in Manor Park at the time. She was enrolled at the Manor Park Public School and started in a split grade 4/5 program. Since she had started learning piano at the Alpha Preparatory School in Kingston Jamaica, she was able to continue her piano training after settling into her new Ottawa home.[91]

---

89 Jamaican High Commission. Previous Jamaican High Commissioners.
http://www.jhcottawa.ca/previous-jamaican-high-commissioners.html Accessed on March 14, 2023.
90 Information was provided during Interview with daughter Ann McNamee.
91 Ibid.

Caribbean Immigrant Groups

Domestic Workers

Domestic workers were at the leading edge of Caribbean Immigrants to the Nation's Capital. The following timeline of the "Live-in Caregiver Program" provides a historic background to how this group of Caribbean immigrants became, what could easily be the defining start of formalized Caribbean immigration to Canada. In fact, this summary shows Canada's efforts to provide domestic services assistants to families who had the capability to afford such services.[92]

Canada has been bringing in live-in caregivers for over a hundred years. Many Canadians have grandparents and great-grandparents that came to Canada through the program.

In the beginning, caregivers from Britain and Nordic countries were automatically given permanent residency. It was only when Canada started bringing in caregivers from the Caribbean and the Philippines that caregivers and Canadian families joined together to fight for and win the right to automatically apply for permanent residency.

Live-in Caregiver Program Timeline

1900: European domestics

Women from England, Ireland and Finland come to Canada as 'nannies', 'nursemaids' and 'governesses.' Their work is valued, desired and in demand. They are immediately and automatically given permanent residency in Canada.

1945: Post-war demand for domestic workers

The care gap after World War II increases demand for caregivers. The government aggressively recruits women from Jamaica and Barbados to serve as domestic workers. Unlike their Western European counterparts, however, these women were considered 'reserve' and not given permanent residency.

---

92 Inclusive Canada. LCP Timeline https://facebook.com/inclusivecanada Accessed on July 21, 2019

1955: Caribbean Domestics Scheme

Dissatisfaction with Canada's exclusionary policies towards Caribbean caregivers leads to the creation of the Caribbean Domestic Scheme. A limited number of caregivers under the program are given the ability to apply for permanent residency after one year working in domestic service. However, the women are also subjected to frequent pregnancy tests and are paid less than their European counterparts.

1966: Pearson's White Paper on Immigration

Under Prime Minister Lester B. Pearson the federal government introduces a points-system for immigration, attempting to end racial discrimination and the preference for Europeans in immigration policy.

1973: Care work becomes "disposable."

The Temporary Employment Authorization Scheme changes the rules for permanent residency, deeming care work 'low skill' and treating live-in caregivers as disposable workers. This new scheme makes it harder for live-in caregivers to qualify under the new rules. Because of the government's unwillingness to recognize care work as a permanent ongoing need, the system fails to address Canada's care-giving needs.

1976: The Seven Jamaican Mothers

Canada's high demand for caregivers leads to immigration officials advising women to not declare their children when entering Canada. Outrage ensues when seven Jamaican mothers are deported simply for following this advice, doing what they were told.

As a result, Canadian families, and caregivers joined together to fight for caregivers' right to apply for permanent residency. Protests spread from Vancouver to Ottawa and Montréal. Black community members, migrant care workers, activists, faith communities and Canadian families fight for recognition that care work is a permanent need in Canada and those caregivers should have the right to be reunited with their children.[93]

---

93 Inclusive Canada. LCP Timeline

First group of Domestic Services Providers arriving from Jamaica in August 1955.
https://www.capitalheritage.ca/virtual-exhibits/ottawas-caribbean-domestic-pioneers/

Caribbean Domestic Workers

West Indian Domestic Scheme (1955–1967)

The women who came to Canada, and specifically those who arrived in Ottawa, are in effect the pioneers of the Caribbean in the post-war era.

The West Indian Domestic Scheme was a targeted immigration program through which approximately 3,000 women from the Caribbean came to Canada to work as domestic servants. While still very restrictive, it increased Black immigration to Canada in the post-Second World War era, when discriminatory immigration policies limited the entry of non-white immigrants. The Scheme combined an immigration program with Canadian diplomacy as part of Canada's evolving economic relationships with Caribbean nations. It also contributed to the growth of Caribbean culture in Canada, especially within the Toronto and Montréal communities.

The Department of Citizenship and Immigration launched the Scheme in 1955 to help meet the demand for domestic labour. In its first year, there was a quota of 100, but the system was so successful that annual quotas increased through the 1960s. To be eligible, women had to be single, between 18 and 35 years of age, have at least an 8th grade education, and pass a medical examination conducted by Canadian immigration officials. Through this process, they were subjected to a level of 'moral' scrutiny that was not only unique compared to other immigration programs, but it also significantly influenced the way they were perceived in Canada as well as their lived experience in the program.[94]

When Canada initiated the West Indian Domestic Scheme, it effectively removed the racial barrier to immigration and opened its door to the people who are profiled in this publication. One of the prime selection criteria was that the candidate remained in domestic employment for a minimum period of one year.

Thereafter, she was eligible to apply for Landed Immigrant Status. And once a Landed Immigrant, they were allowed to sponsor other family members to immigrate to Canada. The West Indian Domestic Scheme initially set an annual quota of 100 women, and by 1965 some 2600 women had immigrated to Canada under this program.

Many of those who were selected to come to Canada, as part of the scheme were paid less than they anticipated while also being required to work longer hours. After a year of domestic work, the women were granted Landed Immigrant Status and permitted to seek educational and employment opportunities in other fields while also being able to sponsor family members' permanent residency in Canada, which the government tried to limit by only accepting single women. After five years in the country, regardless of if they continued to work in the domestic field, they were eligible for Canadian citizenship.

Once accepted into the program, women had the opportunity to select their preferred destination, with most choosing Toronto or Montréal. Between 1955 and 1961, 580 of the 1600 women who came to Canada as part of the scheme selected Montréal. There were efforts made to spread the women across the country, to rural and western Canada, but most preferred the social and economic opportunities presented by large urban centres.

Many of the women confronted racial discrimination and hostility on arrival in Canada. Few had worked as domestics before migrating and many had no plans to continue working in the domestic field after a year. This included women like the Honourable Jean Augustine, who migrated to Canada in 1960 from Grenada. Following her year working as a

94 Government of Canada. Parks Canada. West Indian Domestic Scheme (1955–1967). https://www.canada.ca/en/parks-canada/news/2020/07/west-indian-domestic-scheme-19551967.html Accessed on February 12, 2023.

domestic, she enrolled at the University of Toronto where she earned a Bachelor of Arts and Master of Education before becoming a principal and becoming involved in community activism. In 1993, she was the first Black Canadian woman elected to the House of Commons and was appointed to a Cabinet post in 2002.

Despite its success in attracting West Indian women to Canada and a seemingly unlimited demand for domestic labour, the Department of Citizenship and Immigration was reluctant to increase the number of women admitted each year. In 1967 it was announced that, with Canada moving towards a points system for immigration, the West Indian Domestic Scheme would be discontinued in January 1968.[95]

Domestic Pioneers

May Fagan

May Fagan, a 32-year-old Jamaican lady, was among the very first group of immigrants to arrive in Canada under the West Indies Domestic Scheme in August 1955, on an Air Canada flight carrying the first contingent of Jamaican women who landed in Montreal, Quebec. May explained that "they advertised for people to go to Canada as pioneers... They wanted 75 but they only got 72, [so] I came to Canada as a pioneer, to represent Jamaica."

This initial group of seventy-two Jamaican women boarded a flight at the Palisadoes (Norman Manley) Airport in Kingston Jamaica and landed in Montreal, Canada. The new immigrant ladies were not certain about their ultimate Canadian destination; however, they knew that they would be assigned to live and work with a Canadian family over the ensuing two years, in a yet to be determined Canadian city.

The Caribbean domestic caregivers encountered a few surprises once they were on the job. Many of them discovered that were being paid less than they anticipated while being required to work longer hours. After a year of domestic work, they were offered the opportunity to apply for Landed Immigrant Status and permitted to seek educational and employment opportunities in other fields. After successfully admitted as Landed Immigrants, they were then able to sponsor

---

95 Government of Canada. Parks Canada. West Indian Domestic Scheme (1955–1967).

family members for permanent residency in Canada. After five years residency in Canada, they were eligible to apply for Canadian citizenship.

May Fagan and a very close friend Florence Sinclair were among the passengers who disembarked in Montreal. They were later given a choice of three Cities: Toronto, Montreal, or Ottawa. Some of this initial group elected to remain in Montreal, and several new arrivals went to Toronto. May and her new friend, the late Florence Robinson (nee Sinclair), decided that they would go to Ottawa. May reasoned that, since Ottawa was Canada's capital city, and since she did not know much about the other cities, this choice would be a safe bet. Upon her arrival in Ottawa, May was assigned to work with the Casner family; Dr. Casner, his wife and two young children. The care of their two young children Linda and Stephen was placed exclusively in May's hands, and May's wage was set at $15 per week. By 1964 she was able to purchase a house on Tweedsmuir Avenue. May completed the full terms of her initial agreement and following her tenure with the Casner family, she secured her landed Immigrant status and then headed to Brooklyn New York. New York City has always been a dream for many of the Caribbean and so the opportunity to see this world-famous city and get a first-hand experience would not be allowed to pass. She married in 1961, and then went to New York to do short-term employment. During this period, she attended the School of Beauty Culture, where she earned a beautician certification.

But May kept moving back and forth between Canada and the US in order to maintain her immigration status within Canada while attempting to gain whatever economic benefits she could gain from her tenure in the USA. She returned to Ottawa in 1975 after the death of her husband.

MINISTRY OF LABOUR

P.O. BOX 481

JAMAICA, B.W.I.

No. C 4966/S4

24th November, 1955.

The Deputy Minister of Citizenship and Immigration,
Ottawa,
Canada.

Dear Sir,

SELECTION OF FEMALE HOUSEHOLD HELPS
FOR EMPLOYMENT IN CANADA

      I refer to correspondence on the abovementioned subject and in particular to your letter of the 15th August, 1955 in which you outlined the selection criteria and the procedure to be followed in the processing and despatch of the women selected under this scheme.

2.   I enclose for your information copy of my letters of even date addressed to Dr. M. D. Reid, Chief, Division of Quarantine, Department of National Health and Welfare, and the Director, Special Services Branch, Department of Labour, Ottawa.

3.   You will observe from these enclosures that, with the exception of completion of the Form of Undertaking which awaits final advice concerning acceptance of our selectees, all necessary arrangements have been made this end in anticipation of your Immigration Headquarters advice covering clearance to permit the final selectees to proceed by Pan American World Airways Charter Flight scheduled to arrive at Dorval Airport, Montreal at 1:00 p.m. on Friday, 2nd December, 1955.

4.   I am directed by the Minister to say that in view of the difficulty experienced in procuring a charter flight on a convenient date at reasonable cost, we now have to rely entirely on the flight which has been arranged as indicated in the preceding paragraph. I am also to say that this Ministry would be most grateful for your continued co-operation so as to ensure, as far as possible, that the full complement of 75 selectees will be flown on the 2nd December, 1955.

5.   As I have been in communication with the Canadian Government Trade Commissioner here and the British West Indies Trade Commissioner in Montreal on other matters in connection with this scheme, I propose to send them a copy of this letter by way of courtesy information on latest developments.

Thanking you in anticipation,

Yours faithfully,

Permanent Secretary
to the Ministry of Labour.

Selection letter for Domestic Services delivered to May Fagan (November 24, 1955).

Florence (Sinclair) Robinson moved to Ottawa in the late 1950s; her husband followed later, and they raised their family here. As one of the earliest immigrants to Ottawa from the West Indies, Florence completed her mandatory domestic assignment and at the end of the two-year period she married her fiancée who emigrated from the UK to reunite with her in Ottawa. Being one of the first Domestic Services immigrants from the Caribbean to establish a residence in Ottawa, the Robinson's home became a welcoming space for newer members of the community settling in the Greater Capital Region.

Milton and Florence Robinson. CHC|CPC (capitalheritage.ca)

Winnifred Stewart was one of the professionals who took advantage of the Domestic Scheme to immigrate to Canada. She was born in St. Ann's Bay, Jamaica, grew up in Spalding, Clarendon, and attended Knox College in Clarendon, Jamaica. She successfully completed the Senior Cambridge Exam. "The Senior Cambridge examinations were General Certificates of Education examinations held in Pakistan,

Bill and Winnifred Stewart

Malaysia, Singapore, India, and Jamaica."[96] This was the final high school examination to certify successful completion of the high school curriculum as established by the British. The Senior Cambridge Exam was subsequently replaced by the General Certificate of Education as the high school initial graduation standard.

Following high school graduation, Winnifred began working with the Government of Jamaica in the Ministry of Labour, which managed programs dealing with Jamaican Farm Workers. These were seasonal workers who travelled primarily to the US and Canada to work on agricultural farms during the farming season, and then returned to Jamaica during the winter months. The introduction

---

96 *Wikipedia*. Senior Cambridge. https://wiki2.org/en/Senior_Cambridge Accessed on June 26, 2019.

of the Domestic Scheme brought that program into the same department as the farm workers. Once Winnifred became aware of the nature of the Domestic Workers Program, she recognized that this program was the vehicle to further her personal ambitions aimed at improving her standard of life. She enrolled in the Domestic Workers Program, and in 1961, she was one of the 100 Jamaican women who landed in Montreal. She was among the group who were assigned to families in Ottawa.

After settling into her role with the Ottawa family, Winnifred learned that the domestic workers would meet as a group at the Ottawa YM-YWCA on their days off. She joined this group meeting and met her husband Bill Stewart at one of these get-together events. Winnifred was among a group of Domestic Workers who normally got together at the YMCA on Thursday afternoons — their normal day off. The Domestic workers were allowed time-off on Sunday and Thursday afternoons, during their seven-day round-the-clock working hours, if required. It was during one of these get-togethers that Bill showed up at the YMCA. Apparently, word had gotten around to the sparse population of Caribbean young men in Ottawa, that the YMCA was the meeting place for Caribbean Domestic Workers. It was during one of these afternoons that Winnifred and Bill met, and the couple was married shortly thereafter on December 21, 1963. By this time, Winnifred, no longer bound by the Domestic Scheme, had an office job as a secretary with a private company using the skills that she had learned at Knox. Later, she was hired by the Federal Government where she successfully worked until her retirement.

The domestic services providers from the Caribbean proved their worth under some very difficult working conditions. There were many other Domestic Services immigrants who came to Ottawa during the intervening years between the mid-1950s until the program was terminated in 1978. Some of the other notable Domestic Services pioneers who made the City of Ottawa their home include Daisy Gordon, Doris Campbell, and Phyllis Pinnock.

Daisy May Gordon
CHC|CPC (capitalheritage.ca)

Daisy May Gordon was born in Jamaica in 1925. She attended a domestic science school as a young woman, and later moved to Kingston where she worked with diplomats as a domestic worker. Daisy had learned about the Domestic Scheme from her mother who encouraged her to apply. In her interview, she recounted her work experience as a domestic worker for diplomats in Canada, and the changes she adjusted to while settling into her new life in Canada.

Doris Campbell was born October 9, 1923. She was among the first wave of young ladies who migrated to Canada in the early 1950s under the West Indian Domestic Scheme. In subsequent years she sponsored other family members to Canada.

Doris Campbell
CHC|CPC (capitalheritage.ca)

Phyllis Pinnock who migrated to Canada in December 1955 was among the pioneering group of domestic workers who arrived in Ottawa shortly after the program began.

Each one of these women, along with many of the others who came to Canada under the Domestic Scheme, has made lasting and positive impacts on the City of Ottawa largely because they were responsible for bringing up two generations of Canadian children. Some of their stories have been archived on YouTube video recordings and also referenced at the Capital Heritage site.[97]

Phyllis Pinnock
CHC|CPC (capitalheritage.ca)

Family Reunification

Shortly after successfully executing the terms of their original agreement to provide domestic services to Canadian families, almost all of the women were able to become Landed Immigrants. While some continued as domestic workers with either the same or other families, the vast majority branched out to chart their own course forward. Some enrolled in courses at adult training centers to upgrade their academic standings. Others enrolled in college courses to upgrade their skills, or in university programs to obtain degrees. And while studying, primarily

---

97 Capital Heritage. Ottawa's Caribbean Domestic Pioneers, Doris Campbell's Story. https://www.capitalheritage.ca/virtual-exhibits/ottawas-caribbean-domestic-pioneers/doris-campbells-story/ Accessed on June 27, 2019.

in part-time arrangements, most of the ex-domestic group held down part-time or full-time jobs. When they later became Canadian residents, they had two additional objectives once the qualification period was met: to sponsor their family members, and to become full-fledged Canadian citizens.

The family re-unification was immediate. The Landed Immigrant Status allowed the ex-domestic worker to sponsor family members so long as they were able to support those they sponsored until the family member became self-sufficient. Beginning in the latter part of the 1950s, new members of Caribbean residents in Ottawa began to arrive under the auspices of their family members. Some of these new immigrants were students, others were professionals, and many older family members who would be of retirement age within the near future.

Lucille Campbell (nee Small) came to Ottawa in 1957 under the Domestic Workers Program, two years after the first group of Caribbean domestics arrived in Ottawa. Lucille hailed from the parish of St. Ann, Jamaica. She was assigned to work with an Ottawa family for five years during which she became a Landed Immigrant and subsequently obtained Canadian citizenship. Lucille then began re-uniting her family. First, she sponsored her brother, Cleveland (Vannie) Small, to join her in Ottawa. Cleveland was a competent carpenter and made the transition quite easily. Shortly after Cleveland completed his transition Lucille moved to Brooklyn, New York, and arranged for her elder sister **Lynette Walker** to join her in New York.

Lynette Walker

Lynnette had completed two years at Kingston Technical School and then began working for a University of the West Indies professor in Kingston, Jamaica. She then headed off to the USA leaving her family behind with the objective of sending for them once she was settled. Unhappy with living in New York, she arranged with her brother Cleveland, now a Landed Immigrant, to sponsor her to come to Canada.

Lynette Walker arrived in Ottawa in 1967; Cleveland's wife helped Lynette find work as a domestic worker with a family living on Range Road with whom she worked for four years, before obtaining Canadian Citizenship.

Lynette then began family reunification. She promptly sponsored her four sons — Donald, Noel, Robert, and Michael, who were attending school in Kingston to join her. Her eldest child Evelyn, who had migrated to the UK earlier, would also join her family in Ottawa. Lynette then secured new employment in food services with the Island Lodge Nursing Home operated by the City of Ottawa. She worked at Island Lodge for over three decades and retired after 34 Years.

Cynthia Ashley arrived in Ottawa in November 1958. Cynthia had been the chief accountant at a shoe manufacturing establishment in Kingston Jamaica. Like many of the other professional women who immigrated to Canada under the Domestic Scheme, Cynthia felt that this opportunity would allow her to advance her education and improve her own standard of living. She recognized that she would be able to better position herself to assist her family once she had obtained a Landed Immigrant Status, which would allow her to sponsor family members and enable their entry into Canada.

Cynthia Ashley

While continuing to work at her full-time profession, she enrolled in a Domestic Training program and gained the graduate certification as a pre-requisite to qualify as a domestic services provider. Once qualified as a Domestic Services Provider her application to migrate to Canada was accepted. Cynthia worked in this capacity for about nine months before deciding that she had had enough. Her initial employer was a family in the Rockcliffe area. Similar to several Domestic Services Providers from the Caribbean, this initial assignment did not work out well. In fact, her tenure with two subsequent families was relatively short-lived. Determined to return to her professional role, she secured a release from her domestic contract and was immediately hired by Metropolitan Life Insurance as a secretary. She fell back on her professional training to obtain employment in the Federal Government, and later began reunifying her family. Cynthia's career continued to rise within the Federal Government. She progressed through several Government departments until she landed in the department of Industry, Trade and Commerce (ITC), remaining there for over 30 years; progressing to the level of Commerce Officer, she held this position until she retired.

Naylor-Rose Ashley

Naylor-Rose Ashley, Cynthia's youngest sister and the first member of the family to arrive in Ottawa under her sponsorship, arrived in Ottawa on July 22, 1967. Naylor-Rose, motivated by the desire to improve her life, had expressed an interest in migrating to Canada. Knowing that she was being re-united with her elder sister eased the immediate transition from the Jamaican environment to Canada. Sadly. she had to return to Jamaica to attend her mother's funeral three months after her arrival. On returning to Ottawa, she found work with the City of Ottawa as a nursing assistant at the Island Lodge Nursing Home. She worked for a few years before moving to New York City in a quest to fulfill her childhood dream of living in the United States. However, she soon realized that living in New York was not what she had envisioned; before the end of her first year in the US she returned to Canada and enrolled in an accounting course at Algonquin College. She secured employment at Bell Canada where she worked for several years, and in 1976 she transitioned into the field of social work with the Children's Aid Society. During this period, she set her sights on a Real Estate profession; successfully completing the qualification requirements, she became a licensed real estate agent.

Naylor spent her remaining working years in real estate sales. While working in real estate she became active in volunteering and community building initiatives. She was instrumental in the establishment of the Chair in Black Studies at Dalhousie University.

"Established in 1991, the James Robinson Johnston Chair in Black Canadian Studies at Dalhousie University, Halifax, Nova Scotia, is a significant senior academic post in Canada. Based in Halifax to honour the unique historical presence of African Nova Scotians, the position connects local Black communities with a national and international perspective. The goal of the chair is to develop Black studies in Canada, to produce significant scholarship, and to create bridges between academia and the wider African descended communities."[98]

98 Dalhousie University. History of the Chair.
https://www.dal.ca/faculty/jrj-chair/about/HistoryoftheChair.html Accessed on June 27, 2019.

Under the sponsorship of Senator Donald H. Oliver, "the first African-Canadian to have a seat in the Senate,"[99] and Senator Consiglio Di Nino, she was a key member of the committee that developed the funding mechanisms that would establish and facilitate this Chair. Other volunteer efforts included a major fund-raising initiative sponsored by Bell Canada and hosted by CJOH to assist Jamaica with relief following hurricane Gilbert, and CUSO fund raising initiatives. Naylor was one of the founding members of Black History Ottawa. Black History Month Committee was inaugurated in 1986 and later renamed Black History Ottawa. Since then, Black History Ottawa has been coordinating and presenting activities celebrating Black History Month in the Nation's Capital.[100]

---

99 *The Canadian Encyclopedia.* Donald H. Oliver.
https://www.thecanadianencyclopedia.ca/en/article/donald-h-oliver Accessed on March 14, 2023.
100 Black History Month. https://www.blackhistoryottawa.org/about_us Accessed on March 14, 2023

The Johnson Chair in Black Studies
A night at the races

Approximately 100 people turned out to the Rideau Carleton Raceway on Friday, July 23 to support the James Robinson Johnson Chair in Black Studies. The event was staged by the Ottawa Committee, chair by Naylor Ashley, with a mandate of raising some $200,000 of a $2.5 million endowment fund. Approximately $1.3 million have been raised to date.

The James Robinson Chair in Black Studies has been established with its base at Dalhousie University in Halifax, and with a national scope, where visiting lecturers will make presentations at other universities across Canada. This is a significant Canadian initiative. While US universities have established some 118 Chairs in Black Studies, this is the first of its kind in Canada.

This fund raising event was sponsored by Interlanguages, Daniel Medical Laboratories, Carling Motors and Bio-Test Laboratories. The event netted over $5000 and provided fun, good food and entertainment for those who participated, over 80% had not been to the races.

Donations can be made to the Dalhousie University Development Office, Halifax, Nova Scotia, B3H 3J5. Cheques should be made payable to the "James Robinson Johnson Chair". A receipt for the full amount of the contribution will be issued.

Members of the Johnson Committe (in picture): Horace Alexis, Naylor Ashley, Keith Charles, Merle Howard, Sam Kwofie, Carl Nicholson, Richard Menard, Dave Tulloch, Fred Wein. Seven other committee members are absent.

The Johnson Chair in Black Studies: a night at the races.
Source: *The Spectrum,* August 1993

Caribbean Students

Students from the then British Commonwealth countries and specifically from the Caribbean were some of the earlier Black immigrants to Canada. It is worthwhile noting that not all Caribbean students who came to Canada to study were Black, but to a great extent, the population of Caribbean student immigrants, especially those who were afforded scholarships, reflected the racial demographics of their home country, and hence a large proportion were Black. Some of the Caribbean students who arrived during the 1950s, prior to the inception of the Canadian International Development Agency (CIDA), were sponsored through academic grants or scholarships and the vast majority who arrived during this early period were university graduates who sought to pursue post-graduate studies at Canadian institutions. Despite their initial objective to complete their course of study and return to their native land, many chose to remain in Canada. Some of these students, who went on to exemplary careers and made significant contributions to Canada, are profiled in this publication.

In order to facilitate its development priority, the Canadian International Development Agency (CIDA), offered academic scholarships to selected students from developing countries.

> "The Canadian International Development Agency (CIDA) is the federal government agency responsible for administering most of Canada's official co-operation program with developing countries and countries in transition. Formed in 1968, CIDA now has a presence in over 100 countries and manages a budget of approximately $2.1 billion a year. CIDA's mandate is to support sustainable development in developing countries in order to reduce poverty and to contribute to a more secure, equitable and prosperous world. To achieve this purpose, CIDA concentrates its efforts on the following priorities: basic human needs, full participation of women, infrastructure for the poor, human rights, democratic development, governance, private-sector development, and the environment. Approximately 25% of CIDA's resources are devoted to basic human needs."[101]

---

101 *The Canadian Encyclopedia.* Canadian International Development Agency.
https://www.thecanadianencyclopedia.ca/en/article/canadian-international-development-agency
Accessed on July 21, 2019.

Beginning in 1969, students under CIDA sponsorship started to trickle into Canada. The terms under which they were granted CIDA scholarships stipulated that they should return to their home country immediately following graduation. They would have to return home earlier if they failed to meet the academic standards during any semester. Most of these Ottawa bound students were successful in completing their course of study. But a few returned to their home country prematurely. Some returned by choice and others because of academic failures. Many of the CIDA graduates faced a dilemma following graduation. While some were eager to return home, others saw potential benefits in remaining in Canada. However, they were bound by the terms of the CIDA agreement. So many graduates returned but others sought ways to remain in Canada. For those who graduated in the spring of 1973 and remained in Canada up until September of that year, the answer came in the form of the 1973 immigration amnesty program:

> *OTTAWA, September 6—Canada has opened an intensive two-month search for foreigners who are in the country illegally not to get them out but to welcome them in. The purpose of the drive which is being widely publicized here in two dozen languages besides English and French is to give illegal immigrants a last chance to regularize their status — or as one newspaper advertisement puts it, "to make our country your country."*

> *Indirectly, the campaign also reflects Canada's gradual move toward heterogeneity and away from a society in which nearly everybody could trace his ancestry to either Britain of France.*

> *Between now and October 15 the standards by which resident permits are granted — such things as education and possession of needed skills—are hence all but ignored for people who have already been living here since at least last fall.*

> *Instead, illegal immigrants who present themselves before the cut-off date will be allowed to stay and to move into the legal process that leads to citizenship, if they have jobs or job prospects, if they have close family ties here, or if they can show by some other means that they can "become established in Canada".*

> *"What we're really saying is, look, if you're here in Canada, and you're generally getting along O.K., we're going to let you stay, and we're not going to ask how you got here," explained J. E. McKenna, who is running the program.[102]*

---

102 Canada Is Offering Amnesty to Illegal Immigrants Citizenship. New York Times. https://www.nytimes.com/1973/09/09/archives/canada-is-offering-amnesty-to-illegal-immigrants-citizenship.html Accessed on February 13, 2023.

A number of graduate CIDA students took advantage of this program and were granted Landed Immigrant Status. While some of those who had returned to their home countries remained there, others returned to Canada as Landed Immigrants under the immigration point system program. The fact they had studied in Canada was also an advantage to those who applied for re-entry under the points system. Because the natural tendency is towards the familiar, many of those returning came back to the locale of familiarity; most of the students who studied in Ottawa returned to Ottawa, and a number of these people are profiled here.

There might have been a handful of Caribbean students who made Ottawa their study destination in the early 1950s, however the first documented wave of Caribbean students arrived during the mid-to-late 1950s. A number of these early arrivals are profiled herein. Several students who initially attended universities primarily in Hamilton, Toronto, Kingston, and Montreal made Ottawa their city of residence soon after they earned their respective degrees or diplomas. During this period, a very small number of student nurses arrived in Ottawa, and at that time nurses were trained in a hospital setting. Just about all of these earliest student arrivals have, in some manner, made their own positive contributions to the evolution of Ottawa's Caribbean community, which in many cases benefited the broader Ottawa community. Indeed in several notable instances, Canadian society overall has benefited tremendously from the contributions made by some of the Caribbean students, who had packed their bags to continue their academic development in Canada.

Once the student gates were pried open by this pioneering group, the student population grew annually with the start of each school year. Many early student immigrants arrived in Canada by way of student visas. Many of these students were provided scholarships under the auspices of CIDA. In general, the CIDA students pursued post-secondary studies in colleges and universities. So many of these Ottawa-bound CIDA students were to be found on the campuses of Algonquin College, Carleton, or Ottawa Universities.

There was also another much younger student cohort growing. They were primarily the children of domestic workers who had completed their initial tenure, had been granted Landed Immigrant Status, and were now sponsoring other members of their families. And although one of the conditions was that the domestic Immigrant was to be a single woman, there was no condition precedent that they could not be mothers. And in fact, some of the ladies that qualified to become domestic immigrants were in fact married women, who suddenly "became single" to obtain a Domestic visa. Nonetheless, their offspring who had been left behind were now able to join them in Canada. The children and, in some cases, the spouses of many of these initial domestic workers were arriving in Canada to join their mother or wife. Most of these children were either of primary or high school age causing the school system to experience an influx of students from the Caribbean that would forever change the demographics on the playground of Canadian schools.

Immigrant Students' Life

Many of the earliest students from the Caribbean who attended educational institutions in Ottawa were either pursuing undergraduate degrees or college diplomas. A smaller number were graduate students primarily from the University of the West Indies who came to Ottawa to continue post-graduate studies. Carleton University was the beneficiary of the largest contingent of Caribbean students starting in the late 1950s and through the ensuing few decades. Carleton was an easier transition for those students who arrived from English Caribbean islands, simply because most of the Caribbean students were from English-speaking islands; unlike the University of Ottawa there was no mandatory requirement to study French in certain disciplines. Nonetheless a substantial number of Caribbean students from English-speaking islands attended the largely francophone University of Ottawa. Those Caribbean students who came to Ottawa to obtain College diplomas went to Algonquin College. The Algonquin College Lees Avenue campus which focused on Science and Technology experienced an annual increase in the number of Caribbean students starting in the late 1960s throughout the 1970s. Medical Laboratory Technology, Electronics Engineering Technology and Civil Engineering Technology were the predominant disciplines sought by Caribbean students.

There were a handful of students who self-financed their education but most of the Caribbean students in Ottawa were under the auspice of the CIDA scholarship initiative. CIDA fully funded the student's academic fees including books, and provided each student with a monthly living allowance to cover rent and other living costs. Non-CIDA students would have to fund all related expenses to accomplish their academic objectives. Regardless of the conditions that governed the student's expenses, practically every student had to operate within a very tight budget. Many students found themselves creative ways to earn a few extra dollars to augment their monthly expenses. And to balance the ledger, they looked for cost-saving approaches to minimize their spending.

The two most popular revenue sources were driving taxis and working as security guards, both advantageous for the male student. The taxi driver could select a schedule that would have minimal impact on mandatory study time, and the security guard could study while on the job, usually during the night shift. Female students on the other hand were very

L-R: Barry Davis, Errol Latty, Dave Tulloch, Richard Davis, Michael Ashman

constrained vis-à-vis additional revenue opportunities. And while many Canadian female students were able to augment their income by working as waitresses, there were very few female Caribbean students who took this route.

The monthly rental expense was by far the largest component of the student's living expenses. Finding a landlord who would rent their space proved challenging. It was easy to identify a place that was advertised for rent. The 'For Rent' sign was usually posted at a window facing the road. By simply walking around any neighbourhood, one could see many places with these signs. Nevertheless, many Caribbean students, including the author, who walked up to a front door to inquire about the rental, would be told that the apartment had just been rented, or something along those lines. If you circled back, sometimes days later, the 'For Rent' sign would still be there. In some cases, even though the place was up for rent as the sign indicated, the prospective landlord would be very explicit in letting one know "for you it ain't!"

With these rental barriers, many Caribbean students recognized that it was much easier to approach this matter by forming small groups to share accommodation and enable them to rent complete units. This would increase their ability to get accommodation while simultaneously reducing their rental expenses. This shared accommodation arrangement became standard and was very popular, not only among Caribbean students. In some cases, students from the Caribbean

Student Residence ("Frat House")
198 Gladstone Avenue

teamed up with students from other countries and sometimes with Canadian students under the shared accommodation model.

While most of the Caribbean students' communal living arrangements were done by renting apartments in a 'high-rise' building, a group of students from Jamaica rented a house at 198 Gladstone Avenue, at the corner of Gladstone and Elgin. This student residence became well-known within the Caribbean student community and within the relatively small Ottawa-Caribbean community in the early 1970s. Initially, there were four Jamaicans, three of whom were students and a med school student from Guyana. Errol Latty, a Chemical Engineering student at Algonquin who had migrated to Ottawa in the late 1960s, had encouraged Michael Ashman and Richard Davis, two of his childhood friends who had recently migrated to study in New York, to study in Ottawa instead. Errol also recruited Barry Davis (no relation to Richard) another of his Jamaican friends, and a recent associate Victor Holder who was studying medicine at the University of Ottawa, to rent the house on Gladstone Avenue. This became the reference location for many new incoming students from the Caribbean. And although there were no established Fraternities to which these students belonged; the house was akin to a Fraternity House. The student from Guyana, the late Dr. Victor Holden, left within the first year and another Jamaican student, Dave Tulloch, took his place. This arrangement was maintained until everyone had graduated from college, some three years later.

One of the first realities of this accommodation was that their roommates could be from any of the other islands. This living arrangement brought students from different Caribbean islands together for the first time in their lives, in a very close-knit communal living experience. This was a microcosm of the Caribbean immigrant experience in Ottawa. People from the various Caribbean Islands were constantly in social contact with each other through their involvement in sports or other entertainment. As a result, a number of these contacts resulted in partnerships and ultimately marriages that produced families with parents from different Caribbean Islands. Caribbean students were also able to learn much more about their neighbouring Caribbean Islands than would have otherwise been the case. But the key rationale and the major upside to this student living arrangement was the ability to manage limited financial resources more efficiently.

The Caribbean Professionals

By the mid-1960s the three categories of immigrants from the Caribbean that had already been established were the Domestic Services immigrants, their re-unified family members, and the student immigrants. Before the initiation of the Domestic Scheme, international students who had the economic means or those who were able to secure scholarships were gaining admittance to Canadian institutions of higher learning. Then in 1967 the Professional Class of immigrants was incorporated into Canada's immigration policy.

This new immigration category targeted individuals with higher education and professional skills:

> "professional class or skilled worker class and the application are assessed based on a point system. An individual should make an application under this class if he/she wishes to come to Canada based on his/her qualification, work experience and knowledge of English or French language."[103]

And, in October 1967:

> "The points system was incorporated into the Immigration Regulations. The last element of racial discrimination was eliminated. The sponsored family class was reduced. Visitors were given the right to apply for immigrant status while in Canada."[104]

In addition,

> "In 1967, a points system was introduced to determine immigrant eligibility with preference given to educated French and English speakers of working age. A little more than a decade later, the Immigration Act of 1976 (which was rewritten entirely rather than modified from an older version) officially made Canada a destination for migrants from all

---

103 Canada Immigration Visa. https://www.canadaimmigrationvisa.com/ Accessed on June 27, 2019.
104 Canadian Council for Refugees. A hundred years of immigration to Canada 1900 - 1999 (Part 2) http://ccrweb.ca/en/hundred-years-immigration-canada-part-2 Accessed on February 15, 2018.

countries. The new Act was constructed around three pillars of admission. These were: independent applicants assessed on the basis of points awarded for employment skills, education, and language abilities rather than national or 'racial' origin; sponsorship by close family members; and refugee status.

The 1976 Act, which emphasized family reunification and humanitarian concerns over economic interests, was replaced in 2001 with the Immigration and Refugee Protection Act, a policy that stresses education, language, and adaptability. Those applicants with trade certificates and second degrees are awarded more points, and experience points are skewed to favor younger workers.

The 2001 Act has begun to influence migration flows to Canada and has generated public debate about the capacity of the Canadian economy to absorb many highly skilled migrants. Highly educated immigrants typically gain entry through the economic class, which now makes up more than 60 percent of all admitted immigrants.

Since the introduction of the points system in 1967, Canada has sought to target its immigration benefits toward potential immigrants with characteristics that coincide with Canada's evolving needs and interests. With the introduction of the Immigration and Refugee Act in 2001, new classes and procedures were created in order to further Canada's goal of building human capital."[105]

---

105 Migration Information Source. Canada's Immigration Policy: A Focus on Human Capital. https://www.migrationpolicy.org/article/canadas-immigration-policy-focus-human-capital Accessed on February 15, 2018.

Caribbean Community Associations

An inevitable outcome from the growth of the Caribbean immigrant population in Ottawa and other Canadian centres was the need to connect with others from one's home country. While the people from the Caribbean had many things in common, there are some obvious and certain subtle cultural differences between the people of different Caribbean Islands. Ottawa was not unique in this regard. The sharing and closer integration of Caribbean cultures than that which existed in the Caribbean emerged in cities like Ottawa, by virtue of the on-going close contacts between Caribbean immigrants from the different islands. As the number of immigrants from each individual island continued to increase, specific island groups saw the need to establish individualized island clusters where the sharing of their own cultures could become more meaningful. The result was an emergence of Island-specific community associations.

Barbados (Ottawa) Association Inc.

The Barbadian immigrants in Ottawa were the first Caribbean community to establish an Association. The Barbados (Ottawa) Association was formed on November 30th, 1966, the day Barbados attained its Independence from Britain. About 75 people comprised Ottawa's Barbadian community at that time. A group of six Barbadians started the Association with a mission "to showcase Barbados in all its beauty, foster friendships and connect our communities locally in the National Capital Region and abroad."[106] The Association also intended to mobilize and assist new Barbadians who were adapting to life in Canada and to share the Barbadian heritage with the wider community.[107]

The Association elected David Barrow as its first President, Neville St. Hill - Vice President, Ena Maharaj - Secretary, Committee Members: Eric Mason, Winston Pitt, Rudolph Brathwaite, and Victor Clement.

The Association's activities were predominantly social and recreational in its initial stage. But as the organization grew, it evolved to meet the different needs of its members. The Association then focused more on the educational and cultural needs of its members. It staged discussions, forums and lectures on

---

106 Afrobiz.ca. Black Community Faith Centres. https://ontario.afrobiz.ca/Ottawa/Black-Community-Faith-Centres Accessed on January 19, 2023.
107 Barbados (Ottawa) Association. https://www.barbadosottawaassoc.com and https://www.facebook.com/barbadosottawa/ Accessed on February 15, 2018.

various topics of interest. It initiated an annual Church Service, and hosted the Barbados Independence Dinner and Dance, which became the highlight of each year. In succeeding years, the organization blended social and recreational activities along with educational and cultural interests.

The Barbados Association in Ottawa continued to monitor the immigration patterns and changes in demographics in order to adjust its programming to meet the evolving needs, while simultaneously, maintaining a meaningful relationship with the homeland, Barbados.

Over the years the Association continued to donate to charities both in Canada and in Barbados, to such organizations as: the Canadian Cancer Society, Canadian National Institute for the Blind, Camp Sunflower, the Public Library, the Queen Elizabeth Hospital and the Ministry of Social Transformation, Mavericks Soccer Club, and Sickle Cell Parents Support Group.[108]

The history of the Barbados (Ottawa) Association executive leadership is: Mr. David Barrow (1966-1968), Mr. Winston Pitt (1968-1970), Mr. Hartley Richards (1971-1972), Mr. Gregory Richards (1973-1974, 1976), Mrs. Joyce Clement (1975, First Female President), Mr. Neville St. Hill (Dec.) (1977), Mr. Rudolph Brathwaite (1978), Mr. Berkley Harris (Dec.), Mrs. Myrle Mayers (1979). [109]

Jamaican Ottawa Community Association

The Jamaican-Canadian Association was founded right after Jamaica's Independence in 1962 by a group of Jamaicans then living in Toronto. The impetus for the creation of the association was the emergence of Jamaica from colonial status to becoming an independent nation in August, 1962. Two years later, in 1964, students at Carleton University formed the West Indian Association of Ottawa which put on programs in Ottawa and worked with student associations in Montreal to create the Conference on West Indian Affairs in Montreal in 1965, 1966 and 1967. The next year it morphed into the Black Writers Conference. But in 1967 the Carleton-based West Indian Association of Ottawa decided to be more than just a campus organization and sought to embrace the domestic workers and other Blacks in the city. It became the Jamaica Canadian Association (Ottawa Chapter) to include Domestic Scheme workers and other Jamaicans, but not

---

108 Canada Helps. Barbados Canada Foundation.
https://www.canadahelps.org/en/charities/barbados-canada-foundation/ Accessed on February 15, 2018.
109 Facebook. Barbados Ottawa. https://www.facebook.com/barbadosottawa/about_details Accessed on March 25, 2023.

before establishing at Carleton University a small scholarship for Caribbean students in need. In the meantime, another organization started operating under the name of the Jamaica Ottawa Community Association. It eventually took off under the leadership of Clyde Shaw in 1976 and continues to this day.

The formation of the Jamaican-Ottawa Association as described by Gil Scott, its first president, was triggered by a

> "call to action in support of one of our compatriots who had an encounter with the legal system. One member of our Jamaican community had been charged with a crime and the community organized a meeting to see how it could support this member. The call to action was issued by Clyde Shaw. I attended this meeting. And the majority of those who attended became the core and founding members of the Jamaican Ottawa Canadian Association (JOCA). I was elected President of the Association at the first formal meeting that was called to elect officers. This would turn out to be a pivotal determinant of my career in the Federal Government."[110]

The Jamaican (Ottawa) Community Association Inc. (JOCA) is a registered not for profit organization whose mission is to engage residents in community stewardship; to impact decisions that affect the community; to raise awareness; to foster a sense of spirit and pride; and to encourage participation in community issues, solutions, projects and events.

> "The Jamaican (Ottawa) Community Association is the heart of the community offering diverse and relevant activities for all. It is a place where neighbors meet, learn and volunteer. The Association provides physical, intellectual, social and cultural services and programs that contribute to individual and community health and development."[111]

The Trinidad and Tobago Association of Ottawa

> "The Trinidad and Tobago Association of Ottawa is a community-based, non-profit organization, operating in the National Capital Region. Established in 1983, the Association regularly sponsors cultural and social programmes and projects intended to benefit the Trinidad and Tobago community, as well as the wider community in the National Capital Region.   (continued)

---

110 Interview with Gilbert Scott.
111 The Jamaican (Ottawa) Community Association Inc. Who We Are. https://jocainc.com/who-we-are/ Accessed on January 19, 2023.

(continued) The Association maintains relationships with organizations, Caribbean and otherwise, in the community, Trinidad and Tobago Associations across Canada, and, through the High Commission in Ottawa, with the Government and people of Trinidad and Tobago, as well as community service organizations or other institutions in the twin island state of Trinidad and Tobago."[112]

Other Caribbean Cultural Institutions

In the ensuing years most of the other Caribbean Islands having a representative group of immigrants in Ottawa established their own community associations with similar objectives as those established earlier. And these community structures have continued to thrive with the support of their members through time.

Harambee

Florence Redman

Florence Redman is a quiet, modest woman who enjoys her job. She is Executive Director of the Ottawa chapter of Harambee Centres Canada.

Harambee, from a Swahili word meaning 'let us all pull together,' was founded in 1985. Harambee Centres Canada is a nationwide organization which integrates Anglophone and Francophone Black and Caribbean people into Canadian society. Chapters exist in Toronto, Montreal, Ottawa, Halifax, Winnipeg, Edmonton and Vancouver. A national board of directors is comprised of the heads of the various chapters as well as a select group of individuals also associated with Harambee.

The reality of Harambee came as a result of questions raised by a 1984 conference entitled 'Crossing Bridges and Standing Together'. The Ottawa Barbados Association, a local Caribbean culture and socialization group, was the seedbed for Mrs. Redman.

Harambee is made up of individuals; this conscious decision was made to focus on individual efforts that allowed everyone to focus on what Harambee needed and what they could offer, rather than having an attitude that reflected an organizational culture perspective.

---

112 The Trinidad and Tobago Association of Ottawa. https://ttao.ca/about.html Accessed on February 15, 2018.

The National Capital Region chapter of Harambee focuses on education. This concentration has directly lead to the now popular Saturday morning education program, the 'Stay in School' initiative, and summer employment and training programs now available for youngsters. Black children who are not doing well in school are now often brought to Harambee for some positive image building, through task assignment, cooperative work projects, socialization with other black children. Here they are given genuine affection, that builds on the relationships that the kids share with their parents, but adds the necessary real world employment skills and outlook necessary for success. The Saturday morning program is mainly academic, which provides the necessary scholastic training in a comfortable, supportive environment. Many of the children who begin these programs have already been written off by teachers and the system for many reasons, including prejudice and cultural misunderstanding. Often native-born black Canadian kids need the assistance, seemingly having less self-esteem and no real focus, compared to recent immigrants who are permeated with education-as-greatest-goal mentality.

The Ottawa chapter has over one hundred volunteers, serving over 1500 people within the local black community. Volunteers help with training, confidence building, and become friends with the children. Mrs. Redman fondly recounted the story of her early years.

As a girl, in St. Philip's parish, Barbados, she walked miles to and from school daily. She said, "they could just as easily feed me as punish me", referring to neighbours along the way. This sense of responsibility and family commitment extends to her present life. Her husband, on the police relations committee in 1992, and daughters, local volunteers, are also involved with Harambee. Speaking about her experience at Harambee, she called it, "a real family affair".[113]

Florence and Morris Redman along with **Mairuth Sarsfield and Carrie Best** were founding members; their stories are found in the Profiles.

Caribbean Entertainment

The passion for indigenous Caribbean entertainment, sports and the arts are woven into the culture of the peoples from the Caribbean. While various types of Caribbean sports activities are universal, many of the arts and entertainment have

---

113 University of Pennsylvania – African Studies Center
https://www.africa.upenn.edu/Newsletters/IFP_1_2.html Accessed on March 14, 2023.

been uniquely Caribbean and would not normally be found in any area where the people from the Caribbean would not be found as well.

The sports activities of the Caribbean Islands are mostly adopted from the British. Cricket, soccer (football) and netball are standard British sports that are integral aspects of Caribbean culture. The people of the West Indies are passionate about cricket, soccer and to a lesser extent netball. It stands to reason that those Caribbean immigrants who were involved in these sports would extend their passion to whatever locale they found themselves residing.

These three team sports became another aspect of the cultural glue that facilitated the merger of the immigrants from different Caribbean Islands. The desire to express their passion in the areas of sports, arts, and entertainment, broke down any barriers that may have been perceived between Caribbean immigrants from the different Islands of the West Indies. Once in Ottawa, the integration of peoples from the Caribbean in sports teams, choral groups, and the performing Arts became the norm. In these areas and in other aspects of the new Ottawa experience, Caribbean Immigrants viewed themselves as a composite group, while simultaneously maintaining their individual Island's identity.

The result of this coming together of Caribbean Immigrants was the mixing of islanders in sports teams, dance groups, performing arts and in most other aspects of Caribbean-Ottawa life where groupings made sense to pursue our social activities. And in most cases, 'making sense' meant that the numbers were just not sufficient for individual islanders to form a viable group in any of these areas.

The Flamingoes Steel / Strings Band

Musical entertainment is endemic to Caribbean culture, specifically two authentic genres have been endowed by the Caribbean Islands of Trinidad & Tobago and Jamaica respectively. Trinidad and Tobago created the Steel Pan and the associated Calypso music in its various forms from used oil drums. And from the island of Jamaica, the morphing of Mento, to Ska, to Rock-Steady and the ultimate Reggae in various forms have become enduring genres of music worldwide.

Allan McIvor

Noel McIvor

Ian McIvor

Ottawa happens to be one of the earliest Canadian cities to benefit from Trinidad's steelpan music. Records indicate that the Steel Pan was first introduced in New York in 1949 by a Trinidadian named Rudy King who introduced the "pan" to America.[114]

This indigenous Caribbean music from the steel drums was introduced to Ottawa long before it became known anywhere else in North America. In 1962, a few years before the first recorded appearance of a steel band in North America, three Trinidadian brothers had assembled a small steel band ensemble, and this was the resident band at the Coral Reef Club in Ottawa.[115] At that time the Coral Reef was located at the corner of Sparks and Kent streets in downtown Ottawa.

During the 1960s, the Coral Reef was the only place that one could experience Caribbean entertainment in Ottawa. It was frequented by people from the Caribbean with a yen for the back-home vibes. More significantly, the Coral Reef was also frequented by curious Canadians as well as those who had visited the Caribbean Islands and had delighted in sampling its unique form of pan music.

An integral part of Coral Reef's entertainment package was its resident band The Flamingoes. This was not a touring group. It was a local steel band formed by recent Trinidadian immigrants. The core members of the Flamingoes Band were three brothers from Trinidad who had migrated to Canada beginning in the mid-late 1950s. **Donald McIvor** was the first of six McIvor brothers to arrive in

---

114 Pan on the Net. Examining the Roots of Steel Band Activity in New York. https://www.panonthenet.com/news/2010/mar/NY-forum-3-19-10.htm Accessed on March 14, 2023.
115 Interview with Alan McIvor.

Canada. Within a few years, his brothers **Bruce, Stewart, Noel, Ian, and Alan** also came to Canada and initially settled in the Ottawa area.

The Flamingoes band was formed specifically to provide Caribbean music, in keeping with the theme for the Coral Reef club. Bruce McIvor initially teamed up with his brother Ian and along with a few other musicians from the Caribbean to form a five-piece steel band combo, and in 1959 they formed the first steel band to perform in Ottawa. This is also the earliest record of any steel band to have performed in Canada. Caribbean music in its authenticity had become an integral part of Ottawa's Caribbean culture and with a much broader appeal to the wider Ottawa Community. And as time progressed, there was a natural diffusion to infect many other non-Caribbean residents of Canada's capital city. During the 1960s two other McIvor brothers joined the group; Noel played tenor pan and Alan played string instruments.

The Coral Reef Night Club became a success. And it remained at the Sparks Street location until the late 1960s when it moved to a new location — Nicholas Street at Besserer. But in the intervening years, the Flamingoes band was forced to transition from primarily a steel band to a hybrid ensemble; the group found it difficult not only to get the steel band equipment, but also to get them tuned. They morphed into a strings ensemble retaining the tenor pan and xylophone as the centerpieces of the band. And by the time the club had relocated to the Nicholas location, Noel who played these two instruments had assumed leadership of the Flamingoes.

Marty McIvor, wife of band leader **Noel McIvor** provided some of the historical content on the Flamingoes Steel band. Marty met Noel who later became her husband at the Coral Reef club. In the early 1960s, Marty was working within the Unemployment Insurance Department when they created the 'Women's Bureau', a sub-unit designed to manage the inflow processing of domestic workers from the Caribbean. She transferred into this unit and became involved in facilitating the immigration process related to the West Indian Domestic Scheme. "Getting the people through all the paperwork, the immigration needs and everything and placing them." And because of this work, she became familiar with Caribbean issues. Having heard from her friends that there was a Caribbean night club in Ottawa, she went with them to get first-hand Caribbean cultural experience at the Coral Reef. Her visit turned out to be a life-changing experience. She became a regular patron at the Coral Reef, recalling that the patrons were a mixture of predominantly Canadian and Caribbean people.

Noel and Marty got married in early 1964; she soon discovered that her Trinidadian husband had an intense yearning for Caribbean food, none of which could be found in Ottawa. The closest substitutes were to be found at 'Top Banana' a fruit and vegetable store on William Street in the Byward Market. But authentic Caribbean foods were virtually non-existent. By coincidence Marty's high school classmate and close friend was the wife of Moe Saslove who owned Top Banana. This friendship enabled Marty to influence the importation of some Caribbean foods that turned out to be the genesis of Caribbean produce in Ottawa.

The Coral Reef ran into some political headwind while at their Sparks Street location. Noise complaints reached the Mayor's office. As a result, Mayor Charlotte Whitton had the club closed down. The operation re-located to Besserer and Nicholas Street (currently the Rideau Centre). This change saw a transformation of the Flamingoes Steel Band. Predominantly a steel band, the ensemble began to transition away from the full steel band instruments towards a larger component of string instruments. At the end of this transition phase, the band only retained the tenor pan that was played by Noel, who also played the vibes.

The Flamingoes later moved out of the Coral Reef club and began to freelance around the Ottawa area up until 1970; the Flamingoes Steel Band was the only Caribbean entertainment band in Ottawa. The band grew a substantive number of clients in the Golf Club communities and in other venues where they needed live Caribbean entertainment. It continued to transform over the ensuing decades, and presently the next generation of McIvor family members continues to provide contemporary entertainment to audiences around the National Capital area.

Sound of Freedom Reggae Band

During the early 1970s the Flamingoes continued to entertain Ottawa patrons primarily with Calypso music interspersed with several Caribbean and international favourites such as 'Yellow Bird'. But by 1972, Reggae music began to take North America by storm. The Ottawa Caribbean community had been growing rapidly. Many of

Sound of Freedom Reggae Band (1972): Lennox Charles (d), David Carty, Lionel (Bingie) Barker, Fred Ming, Dave Tulloch, Randy Greenaway

the early Caribbean pioneers had now been well established as Canadian citizens and permanent residents in the Nation's capital city. And under the auspices of some of the community associations Caribbean bands from larger cities and in some cases, directly from the Caribbean, began to make appearances at venues in Ottawa. The Ottawa Civic Center (now TD Place) was one of the most prominent venues for touring bands. With this new trend of touring Caribbean bands, came the expanded genres of Caribbean music with Soca, Calypso and Reggae at the forefront.

It was in this environment that the Sound of Freedom reggae band emerged as the first reggae-focused band in Ottawa. The band, comprising mainly recent Caribbean immigrants, emerged at a time where Reggae began to expand its boundaries outside the Caribbean community. Reggae groups from Kingston, Jamaica, such as 'Byron Lee & The Dragonaires' who played in Montreal at Expo67, and 'The Fabulous Five (Fab5)' were now making Ottawa a routing stop while touring Canada. Many music lovers in the city, especially those who had been exposed to Reggae music through their visit to the Caribbean began to absorb and enjoy this new genre of Caribbean music.

Performing Arts - The Third World Players

Along with the growth of the Caribbean immigrant community in Ottawa, the cultural expression of the Caribbean people in the Arts began to evolve. The earliest expression came to Ottawa with the establishment of a theatre group 'The Third World Players'. This Caribbean performance group was spawned from the members of the Bel-Air Cricket Club. **C. Lloyd Stanford** was one of the founding members of the Third World Players theatre group in Ottawa. Stanford was one of the early Caribbean immigrants to Ottawa, arriving in 1959 to attend Carleton College, now Carleton University. Stanford, who was an avid cricketer, explained that the idea came out of discussions among friends from the different islands at cricket gatherings. It soon became evident that they shared similar interests in the performing arts. They decided to structure a Caribbean-focused theatre group that would bring Carib-centric plays to the Ottawa-Caribbean immigrant community, and with a broader objective of promoting Caribbean artistry to the wider Canadian community within the Ottawa-Carleton Region (now the City of Ottawa). C. Lloyd Stanford provides 'A Tribute to the Third World Players' (see Appendix D).[116]

---

116 Flo's Seniors. C. Lloyd Stanford. A Tribute to the Third World Players. https://floseniors.com/event/1285/ Accessed on February 15, 2023.

Carib Dancers

Bernice Tait-Frank was one of the early immigrants from Trinidad & Tobago who decided to settle in Ottawa. Arriving on September 27, 1967, she was under the sponsorship of her sister **Jocelyn**, who had arrived in Ottawa three years earlier. Bernice, a dancer in Trinidad, had received professional dance training from leading Trinidadian dancer, Beryl McBurnie whose influence in dance had a positive impact on creative dancing in Trinidad.

Bernice Tait-Frank

"Beryl Eugenia McBurnie (2 November 1913 – 3 March 2000) established the Little Carib Theatre, and promoted the culture and arts of Trinidad and Tobago as her life's work... McBurnie dedicated her life to dance, becoming one of the greatest influences on modern Trinidadian pop culture. "[117]

Bernice was also active in athletics and other sports, and she represented Trinidad and Tobago in international netball competitions. "Coming to Canada was an experience for me. It was cold and I had to get adjusted to the change in climate." Bernice joined her sister in Ottawa, and shortly after settling in she came to realize that there were very few Caribbean nationals living in Ottawa. However, she did find the Caribbean Cultural Association, the Hurricanes Sports and Cultural group. This relatively small Caribbean association frequently met at 36 Elgin Street. At these gatherings, new arrivals from predominantly the Caribbean Islands would have the opportunity to meet existing expatriates.

At the time of Bernice's arrival, her sister Jocelyn, a Landed Immigrant, was employed at Bowmar Canada, an electronics manufacturing firm. Bowmar was one of the leading technology companies at the onset of the digital age.

"Portable devices got a major boost from an LED technology developed by Bowmar Canada. Their small, red numeric LED displays enabled the

---

117 Wikipedia, Beryl McBurnie. https://en.wikipedia.org/wiki/Beryl_McBurnie Accessed on August 21, 2018.

first hand-held digital calculator, and the company went on to produce some of the world's first digital watches with the same technology."[118]

Bernice lived with her sister for the first three years after her arrival, working at various jobs over short periods of time. After she married, Bernice began to chart her own course that would create a series of Caribbean Cultural entities focusing primarily on dance.

In 1970 she joined together with several other Trinidadian friends — one of whom was the late Nancy Awang, a professionally trained dancer — and worked with Rod Scott, an American Trained choreographer, to establish a dance group initially called the Rod Scott Dancers. They became the Carib Dancers and the first Caribbean dance troupe in Ottawa, appearing regularly at cultural and social events around the Ottawa area for several years. By the mid-1970s many of the initial Rod Scott dancers had started their own respective families and the interest waned. Bernice turned her focus to the young children of Caribbean parents and established a young Caribbean-centric dance troupe called 'The Little Carib Dancers'.

The Little Carib Dancers became popular performers during the Canada Day celebrations at Major's Hill Park in downtown Ottawa, and expanded their territory to perform in neighboring towns. The group continued for approximately fifteen years when the performers made their transition from adolescence to adulthood.

Bernice subsequently turned her attention to another of her Caribbean cultural passions, Caribbean cuisine. She successfully transferred this aspect of Caribbean culture to the many people who signed up for her classes on 'Caribbean Cuisine' at the Rideau High School during mid-2000. And true to her love of dance, she continued to introduce Caribbean dance styles to audiences around the City of Ottawa.

Caribbean Voices

Several members of the Link-up team decided that they should create a singing group beginning with team members who had musical talent. All team members were invited to audition, and the singers chosen for the choir called themselves the 'Caribbean Voices'. After a period of rehearsal, the group made its debut appearance at the Holiday Inn as part of the entertainment lineup at an event held

---

118 Ottawa Magazine. "Society" by Emily Kennedy, Posted April 5, 2017.
https://ottawamagazine.com Accessed on August 21, 2018.

by the Jamaica Ottawa Canadian Association. This performance at the annual Jam Day festival was the first of many as the Caribbean Voices continued to perform at a variety of events in the ensuing years. They sang at weddings, funerals and regular entertainment venues.

Caribbean Voices:
Ruben Brown, Victor Laing, Maureen Ghosh, Miriam Edwards, Lorna Townsend, Sandra Latty, Paulette Barker, Sylvia Taffe-Hemmings
Source: *The Spectrum,* November 15, 1989

Over time the choir gained in popularity and found itself in demand to perform as backup singers to visiting, high-profile performers. Caribbean Voices performed at the Civic Centre (TD Place) with the rock band Foreigner on August 24, 1985, at Landsdowne Park; Michael Boulton - Civic Centre on August 27, 1992; Celine Dion at the Corel Centre on May 31, 1996 and at the Canadian Tire Centre, and with other renowned performing artists, such as Rita McNeill and New Kids on the Block[119]. As Caribbean Voices evolved, the group began writing and performing plays, expanding their repertoire of entertainment offerings to many enthusiastic audiences. Even today Caribbean Voices continues to perform at many cultural events in and around Ottawa.

The Barbados Singers

Another Caribbean singing group, The Barbados Singers, emerged from predominantly Barbadian nationals in Ottawa, expanding the breadth of Caribbean cultural entertainment to Ottawa audiences.

---

119 Interview with Sylvia Taffe-Hemmings - of the Caribbean voices. Also see Concert Archives Ottawa. https://www.concertarchives.org/locations/ottawa-on?page=289#concert-table Accessed on March 3, 2023.

Sports

Upon arrival, West Indian immigrants with a passion for Cricket found that the game had long been established in Ottawa. The Ottawa Cricket Club had a long history, established even before the Canadian Confederation in 1867.

> "Ottawa Cricket Club (OCC) one of the oldest established cricket clubs in the world was founded in 1849. The Ottawa Cricket Club plays on the grounds of the Governor-General of Canada at Rideau Hall in Ottawa."[120]

Many decades later the New Edinburgh Cricket Club came into being.

> "The club was founded in 1928, in Ottawa, Canada. Since its inception, NECC has used the cricket pavilion at the Governor General's official residence at Rideau Hall as its home. NECC initially consisted of members who resided in the New Edinburgh district of Ottawa, an area within walking distance of the cricket grounds at Rideau Hall."[121]

By the early 1960s the Ottawa Caribbean immigrant population started to increase. The passionate Cricketers saw the need to build a core West Indian Cricket team in Ottawa, not unlike the established tradition within the British Commonwealth. This gave birth to the Coral Reef Cricket Club which later became the Bel-Air Cricket Club. Some members of this new West Indian Cricket team, such as **Lloyd Stanford**, had previously played in the New Edinburgh Club. However, the Coral Reef team ran into a racist obstacle when it attempted to join the already established Ottawa Valley Cricket Council. However, like many other aspects of the Caribbean peoples experience in Ottawa, this obstacle was soon overcome. The History of the Bel-Air Cricket Club as documented by Ewart Walters is attached in Appendix E.

Soccer

The game of soccer was also well established in Ottawa by the time the Caribbean immigrant inflow began in the mid-1950s.

> "The Ontario Soccer Association, founded in 1901, is one of the oldest and largest sport organizations in Canada. The OSA currently has more than 500,000 registered participants and provides development

---

120 Ottawa Cricket Club. https://ottawacc.wordpress.com/about/ Accessed on September 2, 2018.
121 New Edinburgh Cricket Club Ottawa History. New Edinburgh Cricket Club history - 80 years and growing strong! https://www.burghscricket.com/history/default.aspx Accessed on September 2, 2018.

opportunities for players, coaches, referees, and administrators. The OSA has its headquarters at The Ontario Soccer Centre in Vaughan. The OSA has 21-member District Associations [Districts]. Each of these Districts has many Clubs as member organizations and there are approximately 900 Clubs province-wide."[122]

The OSA's most coveted award is the Ontario Cup that is the envy all registered clubs within the league.

"Beginning in 1901, with the exception of 14 years during the war, the Ontario Cup has been Ontario's most prestigious award. The largest competition of its kind in Canada, the Ontario Cup is every Club's shared passion. No other sport boasts greater geographical representation in Ontario at more age levels and in both genders."[123]

By late 1960s the Caribbean immigrant soccer enthusiasts had become a critical mass. They were primed to build a team that would compete with the established teams in Ottawa. The Ottawa and District Soccer League (ODSL) was then a member of the Eastern Ontario District Soccer League. ODSL membership was comprised of teams/clubs that were primarily ethnic in nature. The Falcons Soccer Club which began in 1946 appears to be one of the oldest clubs in Ottawa. The St. Anthony Club, founded in 1952, was basically Italian. Lusitania, a Portuguese Club was founded in 1963. The Ottawa Royals, established in 1966 included predominately United Kingdom, English and Scottish soccer players. The Maple Leaf Almrausch Club were predominantly German immigrants. The Lynwood Centennials started in 1967. Mid-1960 ushered in the Hellenic Soccer Club of Greek immigrants and the South Ottawa Internationals, a mixture of nationalities as the name depicts. The Glengarry Soccer League (or GSL as it is commonly known) was established in 1924 making it one of the longest running leagues in North America. And by 1970 these teams were the leading players of the EODSL.[124]

Owen (Bill) Stewart, an immigrant from Jamaica, felt that the soccer players from the Caribbean, many of whom were playing for fun in open fields and parks, could become organized as a West Indies Soccer team and become a member of the official league. Bill himself was an avid soccer aficionado, though not a great soccer

122 *Wikipedia*. Ontario Soccer Association. https://en.wikipedia.org/wiki/Ontario_Soccer_Association Accessed on June 18, 2020.
123 Ibid.
124 Glengarry Soccer League. https://glengarrysoccerleague.ca/about-us/ Accessed on December 3, 2023.

The Hurricanes Soccer Team 1971
Front: Patrick Hall, Dave Tulloch
(2nd Row) Trevor Edwards, Garrinchi, Dave
Fredericks, Andre Lashley, Jimmy Young,
(3rd Row) Roy Gobin, Henry Lewis, Blaze,
(Back Row) Trevor Grant, Desmond Lungrin,
Clyde Bailey, Pat Mohammed, Keith Woleston.

player by his own admission. As the Ottawa-Caribbean community increased in numbers, he recognized the need to form a soccer team where players from the Caribbean would feel culturally at home. This prompted Bill to establish the Hurricanes Soccer Club as the first Caribbean Soccer Team in Ottawa. The Hurricanes team, with players predominantly from Trinidad, Barbados, Jamaica, and St. Lucia, competed in the Ottawa District Soccer League (ODSL). The ODSL had four tiers of competitive teams: Divisions 1, 2, 3 and the Recreational Division at the entry level. The top two teams at the end of each season were promoted to the upper divisions — three, two and one, respectively. Simultaneously, the bottom two teams were demoted in the reverse order.

In 1972 several Jamaican players from the Hurricanes team began to play soccer with other new Jamaican-immigrant friends at Strathcona Park on Range Road in Sandy Hill. These were predominantly students who attended Algonquin College or the University of Ottawa, both of which are located nearby. Since it was natural for students to find accommodation near the campus they attended, many of these soccer players lived in the same area. Those who were on the Hurricanes team continued to play with the Hurricanes during the season, but often would join other Jamaican compatriots at Strathcona Park for fun pick-up games.

In the summer of 1973, a number of these students had graduated, primarily those from Algonquin College, Lees Avenue Campus. Others who were still in college had become core players in the newly formed Algonquin College soccer team. Since many of the remaining college group attended the Woodroffe Avenue Campus, the pick-up games moved from Sandy Hill to a park at the corner of Meadowlands Drive and Inverness. The number of players at soccer park outings increased to the point where a full core soccer team became viable. It was about this time that **Lionel Barker**, a student in the Algonquin College accounting program, and who had played major league soccer with several division-one teams — Railway, YMCA, Cavaliers and Santos, and had represented Jamaica on its Under-19 and National teams, proposed that the group form their own team and join the EODSL.

Officials at the EODSL would have none of this. They flatly denied the request from the newly formed Rockers United Soccer Club. One official stated that the proposed entrants should merge themselves with the then fledgling Hurricanes Team. But the Rockers Group was persistent. They continued to pound on the EODSL doors demanding entry. The EODSL ultimately relented, and the team began its debut in the Recreational league.

Rockers Soccer Club, 1976:
L-R Standing: Milton Rodney, Alic Edgar, Lionel (Bingie) Barker, Patrick Muir, Keith Woleston, Dave Knibbs, Charles Haven, Michael Dixon, Errol Nelson, Donald Dixon, Richard Davis, Desmond Brooks, Dave Tulloch; [Kneeling] Michael Ashman, John Price, Noel Dixon, Al Miller, Desmond Price. Front: Courtney Latty

Rockers United outclassed their divisional Competitors every successive year to rise to Division one and ultimately became league champions. But the journey to the top was fraught with many tough battles both on and off the field. On the field, referees took great pleasure handing out red cards to Rockers players for the slightest infringement and in some cases for no infringement at all. Each of these red cards came with a hearing, and most of these hearings resulted in a player suspension. But this was no deterrent to success and even though the Rockers could only field ten players on some of their games due to player suspensions, the team continued to win. The Rockers Club decided that something had to be done to stem the unfair disciplining measures. They commissioned two of their members, **Alic Edgar** and **Dave Tulloch** to attend league meetings in order to understand the inner workings of the ODSL. At one such ODSL meeting at the National Library on Wellington St, there was a call for volunteers to perform various tasks that were essential to league operations. One of these was to schedule 'Cup' games and assign referees to each game scheduled. Cup games were special non-league competition. There were two separate knock-out competitions – an Ontario Cup and an Ottawa Cup. Dave Tulloch volunteered to assign referees.

The volunteers were given full responsibility, authority and discretionary powers to perform their assigned tasks: scheduling and referee assignment, and selecting which referee would call specific games. Referees were paid a stipend $35 per game, and considering that in 1970 the minimum wage in Ontario was $1.50 per hour, a referee would make approximately $23 an hour for refereeing a game. Once the referees realized that the person enabling them to make this kind of money was in fact one of the Rockers Club members, they drastically diminished handing out frivolous red cards to Rockers players. The Rockers went on to win the Ottawa Cup and the Ontario cup for several seasons. The Rockers Soccer Club, a fixture in Ottawa, continues to operate some 40-plus years later.

Netball

Front: Avril Tulloch, Allison Charles, Sylvia Taffe, Back: Loretta Pitt, Sandra Latty, Elaine Jones, Adassa Davis, Ann Trout are the **Link-Up Netball Team.**

As subjects of the British Commonwealth, the Caribbean Islands had adopted predominantly British Sports activities. Netball is one of those sports that can be considered traditionally British.

"Netball traces its roots to basketball. Basketball was invented in 1891 by James Naismith, a Canadian physical education instructor working in the United States, who was trying to develop an indoor sport for his students at the YMCA Training School (now Springfield College) in Springfield, Massachusetts. ... Basketball was first introduced to England in 1892 through the YMCA at Birkenhead in Merseyside, although the sport did not gain significant popularity in that country for another two decades. Basketball was taught at other institutions in England, either by visiting

American instructors or by English people returning from visits to North America." [125]

"In 1893, Martina Bergman-Österberg informally introduced one version of basketball to her female physical training students at the Hampstead Physical Training College in London, after having seen the game being played in the United States. The rules of this game were modified at Madame Österberg's college (which moved to Dartford, Kent in 1895) over several years. Substantial revisions were made during a visit in 1897 from another American teacher, Miss Porter, who introduced rules from women's basketball in the United States; the game moved outdoors onto grass courts, the playing court was divided into three zones, and the baskets were replaced with rings that had nets. By this time, the new sport had acquired a new name: 'net ball'. The first codified rules of netball were published (between) 1900 (and) 1901 by the Ling Association (later the Physical Education Association), with 250 copies of the rules published. From England, the game of netball was spread to all corners of the British Empire. "Netball" was also being played in schools in Jamaica (and other Caribbean Islands). Netball spread throughout much of the British Empire during the first half of the 20th century."[126]

The Ottawa Link-up Netball club was organized by **Babagene Barrett**, a Jamaican national Netball player, along with **Tony Branka** and **David Barrow**, two Barbadian immigrants to Ottawa. The club was a merger between two fledging netball teams of Jamaican and Barbadian players. Following the merger, the Link-up Club joined the Ontario Netball League and played in several annual tournaments across the province and also in the province of Quebec.

---

125 *Wikipedia.* History of Netball. https://en.wikipedia.org/wiki/History_of_netball Accessed on June 22, 2020.
126 *Wikipedia.* History of Netball in the British Empire.
https://en.wikipedia.org/wiki/History_of_netball#%22Net_ball%22_in_the_British_Empire
Accessed on June 22, 2020.

PROFILES

How you confront obstacles determines how your story ends.
— TD Jakes, b.1957-

Immigrants from the Caribbean who made the City of Ottawa their home embarked on the life journey that they envisaged as the primary reason for coming to Canada. They came to Canada "to improve" their lives. Approximately sixty individuals were interviewed for this publication. The main objective of the interview was to obtain a condensed version of each person's life story, starting with the circumstances relating to their decision to immigrate to Canada and how their stories evolved following that decision. These individuals arrived in Canada either as domestic workers, students, professionals, or family members of those who preceded them. As the Ottawa-Caribbean community grew, the Caribbean immigrants became Canadian citizens, who over time immersed themselves into just about every segment of the Canadian socio-economic system.

Caribbean immigrants excelled, leaving a lasting impact on Canadian society. Following are the primary areas in which respondents built their own careers along with the community structures that contributed to making Ottawa a vibrant city:

Business & Commerce
Public Sector
Academia
Religion
Health Care
Media, Public Service and Community
Law & Justice
Science & Technology
Transportation Services
Beauty & Aesthetics
Other Notables

Business & Commerce

Dry Cleaning

Mr. **Herbert (Pops) Brown** was the earliest Caribbean immigrant on record to have arrived in Ottawa. Brown had migrated to Canada in 1937 with the intent of relocating his family once he was settled. He secured employment as a steward for the Canadian National Steamship line.

Herbert (Pops) Brown - Brown's Cleaners

> "Canadian National Steamships began as part of the Canadian National Railway, which was established in 1919. During this year the Canadian parliament passed an act to incorporate the Canadian National Railway Company Limited, and a few years later the Canadian National Railway was fully in operation. In addition to a railway service, it operated a telegraph company, hotels, and the steamship line. Canadian National Steamships operated routes to the ports of Halifax, Boston, the West Indies, Alaska, and Australia." [127]

On September 10, 1939, Canada declared war on Germany. At that time Brown's cruise ship was docked in the Port of Montreal, located on the St. Lawrence River in Québec, Canada. Three days later Brown, who had served with the British Army in Jamaica, promptly enlisted in the Canadian Army. During his tenure, he became a gunner, then an instructor

Sgt. Herbert Brown (second from left, front row) seen in a photo alongside members of the military during WWII. Copy of Albert Bedward's photo, by Laura Pedersen / Postmedia, The Ottawa Citizen (February 19, 2017).

---

127 Royal Museums Greenwich. House flag, Canadian National Steamships. https://collections.rmg.co.uk/collections/objects/188.html Accessed on June 22, 2020.

and later was promoted to Sergeant. At the end of the war, he returned to Montreal to learn the dry-cleaning business. Branching out on his own, he opened his first dry cleaning operations in Montreal. But as the business evolved, Brown became dissatisfied with its progress, and decided to settle in the Hull/Gatineau area, where he re-started his dry-cleaning venture.

Estelle Brown

Herbert Brown's daughter, **Nessa Bedward-Sherwood** (nee Brown), related the family story. Once Brown was firmly settled in Hull, he began the process to re-unify his family. "My father sent for us. My mother (Estelle), my brother (Herbert) and my sister (Velma) came up in 1953."

When the family arrived in Canada, their father Herbert was working at a Golf Club near Hull, but in 1957 Brown opened his first dry-cleaning business venture. Brown's Cleaners and Tailors, was opened on Murray Street downtown Ottawa, the first Black owned business in Ottawa. Brown's Cleaners incorporated a tailoring service that was operated by Estelle, his wife. Estelle was an accomplished seamstress and the business soon moved to a location on Bank Street. Brown's Dry Cleaners expanded and flourished over the ensuing decades. The business, with about eighteen locations in Ottawa, was finally sold.

Real Estate

Carleton Braithwaite

Carlton Braithwaite graduated from the University of the West Indies in 1962. Shortly after receiving his honors undergraduate degree in Economics, Carlton was awarded a Teaching Fellowship to pursue post-graduate studies at McMaster University in Hamilton Canada. McMaster was selected from at least two other offers since Joyce, his fiancée, was already in Canada pursuing her undergraduate studies in Manitoba. Braithwaite enrolled to start a Master's Program in Economics in the fall of 1962.

Carlton found the transition from Jamaican to Canadian society to be smooth and pain free. Sponsored by a Fellowship, his accommodation was pre-arranged in the student's residence on campus. These living arrangements made it relatively easy for him to forge friendships and to integrate with the Canadian students; his engaging personality facilitated amicable associations with many of his fellow students within a very short period after taking up residence. Many of his new associates were from the United Kingdom but there were a few students from the Caribbean with whom he forged natural friendships. Ernest James and Gurnus James, a talented cricketer, came to mind as he recounted his McMaster experience. Carlton was particularly drawn to Bob Headley, a brilliant Canadian with a physical disability, who performed so exceptionally despite his physical drawbacks.

In September 1962 Carlton began his first post-graduate semester at McMaster in Econometrics; "the branch of economics concerned with the use of mathematical methods (especially statistics) in describing economic systems"[128]. His focus was on the development and application of econometric models that were more appropriate for the Canadian Manufacturing environment, as opposed to the current models which were biased towards the manufacturing sectors within the United States. The Canadian Manufacturing sector needed a 'Made-in-Canada' approach to fit the domestic environment. Carleton tackled this problem in concert with his academic studies and with his innovative mind. His work caught the attention of leading academics in that field, and he was encouraged to rapidly pursue Doctoral Studies with this work at its core.

Soon after commencing his academic studies, Carlton was selected to join the McMaster University track team as a 100 and 200-meters sprinter and as a member of McMaster University 4x100 Sprint Relay team.

In the spring of 1963 after the first academic year at McMaster, Carlton transferred to Queens University in Kingston Ontario to complete his Master's program and to begin Doctoral Studies in Econometrics. While at Queens he met several other Caribbean students; (Late) Dr. Keith Chang (MD) from Jamaica, who was then studying medicine and later practiced family medicine in Ottawa, and Dr. Dennis Awang (BSc, 1960; PhD, 1967) from Trinidad. As he was approaching the end of his Doctoral studies, Carlton was offered an assignment at Statistics Canada as a research intern. This provided him with the opportunity to

---

128 Northwestern University. Economics.
https://economics.northwestern.edu/undergraduate/why-economics/ Accessed on March 22, 2023.

apply his econometrics models in analysing a number of real-world economic issues. Within a few years he became Chief of the Analysis division at Statistics Canada. He was then offered a new position at the Economic Council of Canada, and during his tenure Dr. Braithwaite authored or co-authored a number of published works including his book "The Impact of Investment Incentives on Canada's Economic Growth".[129]

After fourteen years at the Economic Council of Canada, Dr. Braithwaite branched out in new ventures, investing in real estate. He built up a very successful real estate portfolio, amassing some C$17M of net worth from his business ventures. During this period, he also ventured into a number of auxiliary activities with a focus on community development. He formed a group of entrepreneurs to establish 'The Commonwealth Club', a social-focussed organization to facilitate the enhancement of the lives of primarily Caribbean peoples in Ottawa. The Commonwealth Club, having a full-service facility on Frank Street, downtown Ottawa, provided dining and meeting rooms, and a small conference centre; it became a magnet for up-and-coming business and politically oriented Caribbean immigrants. The Black Business and Professional Association presented Dr. Braithwaite with the Harry Jerome Business Award in 1990:

> "'Harry' Winston Jerome OC (September 30, 1940 – December 7, 1982) was a Canadian track and field sprinter and physical education teacher. He won a bronze medal at the 1964 Olympics in Tokyo and set a total of seven world records over the course of his career."[130]

Dr. Braithwaite explained his philosophy of life in his acceptance speech (see Appendix F: Harry Jerome Business Award acceptance speech).

Caribbean Food Services

First Caribbean Grocery in Ottawa

Dr. **Eric Samuels** during the late 1960s recognized that new Jamaican immigrants needed information on how to navigate through the Canadian system and how best to integrate into their new community. He decided to focus on ways to assist the emerging Jamaican-Ottawa community to meet their most basic needs for

---

129 Carlton Brathwaite. The Impact of Investment Incentives on Canada's Economic Growth. (Ottawa: Economic Council of Canada, 1983). Canadian Govt. Pub. Centre.
130 *Wikipedia*. Harry Jerome. https://en.wikipedia.org/wiki/Harry_Jerome Accessed on February 15, 2018.

food products that were part of their home cultures.[131] At that time, the only grocery store that carried any semblance of Caribbean foods was 'Top Banana', a fruit and vegetable outlet on William Street between Rideau and George Streets. The selection of Caribbean foods at Top Banana was sparse. However, despite the lack of selection, Top Banana and the lower-town market area had become the central location for Caribbean immigrants to shop for their food products. Fish could be purchased at 'Lapointe Fish Market' and there was a variety of meat shops in close proximity. The Caribbean immigrant had no difficulty with the availability of meats. In fact, Caribbean consumers could load up with some of their favorites — like oxtail, just by asking the butcher. Oxtail was simply a discarded meat product because the public had no interest in it. When people from the Caribbean requested oxtail, the meat shop owners would simply give it to them free of charge. The irony is that oxtail is now the most expensive beef item.

Dr. Samuels teamed up with two of his cohorts, Mr. Henry Cadogan and Mr. Rawle Scott to establish the first Caribbean grocery store in Ottawa. The SCS Tropical Enterprises (Samuels, Cadogan & Scott) was initially located on Bank Street, later moving to William Street in the Market Area where it served the Caribbean consumer for several years. Subsequently, the SCS partnership was disbanded, and Dr. Samuels started Otaheiti, his own retail establishment on Bank Street near Argyle, which remained there for several decades. In the interim, the Caribbean community had expanded significantly opening up opportunities with other Caribbean grocers. Negril Foods was one of the next stores to follow this trend. The food store was opened on Somerset Street by the Brown family (relatives of 'Pops' Brown).

Dr. Samuels later expanded his food services by entering the farming industry. He and his family relocated from their Bellamy Street residence to a farm in Osgoode to grow some of the products that he sold. At the time, he was also searching for a location to build a cricket ground for the Bel-Air Team. His real estate agent showed him a farmhouse and associated property, and he saw the potential for producing some of the same Caribbean type vegetable products that he sold at Otaheiti. Dr. Samuels' son **Colin** continues to operate the farm with several acres of farm produce that he distributes to local restaurants, hotels and retailers, and sells himself at the Farmers' Market.

---

131 Information based on Interview with Nye Samuels, wife of Dr. Eric Samuels (late).

Spicey Lukes - Restaurant

Elisha "Luke" Campbell

Elisha 'Luke' Campbell grew up on a farm in *"Somerton-Lime Tree Gardens* (Parish of Saint Ann), a town in Jamaica about 46 mi (or 74 km) north-west of Kingston, the country's capital city."[132] In 1963 he began his career as an apprentice chef at the Runaway Bay Golf and Country Club. After a few years he was promoted to sous-chef; an opportunity soon arose where he could engage in further culinary studies to specialize in international dishes. He chose Canada partly because he had two sisters who were already living in Ottawa, and a brother living in Toronto.

"Luke Campbell arrived in Canada from Jamaica in 1966. Schooled by international chefs, he was quite able to turn out duck a l'orange at time when most Canadian restaurants were still dishing out meat loaf."[133]

Upon arrival he began job hunting and prepared for classes. Within a week he landed a job at the Del Mar restaurant located at Rideau and Sussex Streets. He showed up, eager to start as a chef. But to his chagrin, he was shuttled down to the basement to do food prep. His debut at the Del Mar restaurant lasted for one week. As fate would have it, the main chef fell ill on the Friday and the owner had little choice other than to allow him to do the cooking that day. One of his first customers was so thrilled with his meal that he called for the chef, gave him a five-dollar tip, slipping him his business card for the Beacon Arms Hotel. Luke accepted a new job at the start of his second week in Canada as Chef at the Beacon Arms Hotel (now Capitol Hill Hotel) at 88 Albert Street.

Luke enrolled at Algonquin College to pursue his Culinary Arts program while holding down a full-time job at the Beacon Arms; he completed the program after three years. As a certified International Chef, he continued working there for another two years. In the meantime, he had part-time positions at two

---

112 Trip Mondo. Lime Tree Garden in Parish of Saint Ann
https://www.tripmondo.com/jamaica/parish-of-saint-ann/lime-tree-gardens Accessed on August 2, 2019

133 "Spicy Luke" (Documentary) CBC Radio Sunday Edition 10:47 . https://www.cbc.ca/radio and Accessed on August 2, 2019 and https://www.alignable.com/ottawa-on/.

other Ottawa hotels. But his long-term plan was to open his own restaurant. The owner of the Beacon Arms assisted him by facilitating the financing of his start-up. He secured a location at Prince of Wales Drive near Meadowlands Drive. He began operating the existing 'Canadian Chef' restaurant in 1973 and subsequently re-branded it 'Spicy Lukes'.

Luke continued to deliver Jamaican patties and other Caribbean dishes at this location until 1988. The patties — a big hit, became a wholesale business unit with many

Campbell with Prime Minister Brian Mulroney

other food outlets as customers. An active member in the Canadian Federation of Chefs, Luke launched a catering business; he continued to operate both his restaurant and catering business for 36 years, earning several prestigious awards during his career.

Luke immersed himself in the Jamaican Ottawa community through the association. But his most lasting contribution to the immigrants from his home island of Jamaica was the opportunities that he provided through his restaurant business. The Spicy Luke Restaurant became the source of employment for many new immigrants, primarily from Jamaica. Countless students found part-time employment at Spicy Luke while pursuing their studies, and Luke provided the first job to many new adult immigrants as an entry point until they were able to land other jobs more suitable to their skill-set. Over time, his community involvement extended beyond the Caribbean immigrant population, including volunteering at the Ottawa Mission:

> "I retired from the hospitality industry 20 years ago but am still active as a member of the Canadian Culinary Federation Ottawa Branch. I also volunteer at the Ottawa Mission for special events and conduct some classes for their food service training program. The Ottawa Mission in Ottawa has a great program for anyone who would like to do something else – a change of profession. Please check the Ottawa Mission's web site,

it is not just a place to get a hot meal each day, but offers other programs and great opportunities."[134]

"Elisha Luke Campbell is resplendent in his spotless white uniform and chef's hat, moving from barbecue to stove, laughing, orchestrating dinner for a hundred people without blinking an eye. When you've managed food for 700, this is just fun. There are still regular postings bemoaning the loss of his famous Jamaican patties. And there are trophies – huge trophies - two, three feet high; the most recent awarded by the Canadian Federation of Chefs."[135]

Banking

Carolyn Mott
Branch Manager Scotia Bank

Carolyn (Carol) Mott was a Manager at Scotia Bank. Carol arrived in Ottawa on August 8, 1971. Her elder sister **Carmen Curtis** had been in Ottawa for several years and was able to sponsor her and her mother. Carolyn started her career at the Bank of Jamaica, but she intended to pursue post-secondary studies once she arrived in Ottawa. After her arrival, one of her initial observations after venturing out was the lack of Black people.

Deciding that she would need work to finance her education, Carolyn went job hunting during the first week following her arrival in Ottawa. Armed with letters of recommendations from previous employers, she polished her resume for the job search. Carolyn was hired by the first bank she inquired, and began a banking job as a teller a week later. Unfortunately she found the work environment uncomfortable, and within a few weeks she used the same job-hunting strategy to change banks. This second banking job turned out to be the start of a 30+ year career in Canadian banking.

Even though her previous banking experience had prepared her for a much more advanced role Carolyn started as a teller, remaining in this position for some three years. A new manager, Graeme Hutton, was transferred from an international posting in Kingston Jamaica to manage her bank. Recognizing that Carolyn was in a much lower position than her talent and capabilities, he solidly

---

134 "Spicy Luke" CBC Documentary
135 Ibid.

supported her application to transfer to another branch for a supervisor position. She received her first promotion to supervise the teller staff at Scotiabank on Elgin Street. She filled this role at different branches and during this period she attended several training programs to equip herself for advancement. Carolyn was later promoted to Branch manager and was transferred to manage three successive branches in Ottawa. She was then promoted to a regional office position where she was responsible for training managers at various branches across the province of Ontario. Carolyn continued in this role until her retirement after working some 33 years with Scotiabank.

Like many of the Caribbean immigrants, Carolyn immersed herself in community endeavours. She volunteered with the Ottawa Jazz Festival, and she was Treasurer for the Ottawa Chapter of the Black Business and Professional Association. Carolyn also volunteered her time at the Ottawa Food Bank, and continued as an active member and volunteer on various church committees.

Ottawa International Airport

Bill Stewart's job as a Porter at the Ottawa International Airport during the latter part of the 1960s and early 1970s, gave him the opportunity to meet a fairly large number of Caribbean immigrants as they arrived on Canadian soil. Based on his wife Winnifred Stewart's account, Bill was the only boy in a family of seven children. One of his sisters, Ellie, lived in Montreal. She had arrived in Montreal a number of years earlier, and after she obtained her Landed Immigrant Status, she subsequently sponsored her brother Bill. Initially joining his sister in Montreal, Bill then decided to move to Ottawa where he was hired as a Porter at the Ottawa International Airport. This was during the late 1950s when Ottawa's Black community, and more specifically the Caribbean sub-set, was miniscule in numbers. Most of the Blacks who lived in Ottawa knew each other, notwithstanding country of origin; if you were from the Caribbean, it was near certain that you knew just about every other person who was of Caribbean origin. Bill's job as a Porter at the point of immigrant entry allowed him to become the initial point of contact for many of the Jamaican immigrants who came to Ottawa. He provided guidance to a substantial number. Some saw him as a safe bet to support their initial arrival; others arrived knowing that their sponsoring relatives had requested Bill's assistance in facilitating their reception. This increase of new Caribbean contacts placed Bill in the center of the emerging Caribbean community within Ottawa. As the Caribbean community grew, Bill saw the opportunity to facilitate cohesiveness between immigrants from the different Islands.

One of his initial initiatives was to structure a soccer team like what the cricketers from the Caribbean Islands had done earlier in Ottawa. Although Bill was himself not the greatest soccer player, he was able to reach out to young soccer enthusiasts who had recently immigrated predominantly from Trinidad & Tobago, Barbados, Jamaica, St Lucia, and any other Islands, including a few players from African countries, to form the first Black soccer team in Ottawa. And in the summer of 1969, the Hurricanes Soccer team made its debut in the emerging Ottawa and District Soccer League (ODSL). Over the next several years, the Hurricanes advanced to become a second division participant. Bill was the team manager and player when the need arose. And as the team became more established, he quietly withdrew without fanfare, and turned his attention to other community building efforts.

By 1973 Bill recognized another opportunity to expand the entertainment choices for Caribbean music in Ottawa. At that time, the well-established Flamingoes band was primarily focused on entertaining Canadian audiences. A reggae band had also emerged with the focus on primarily Caribbean audiences. Recognizing that there was a cultural gap with Calypso and Soca music, Bill assembled a group of musicians from the eastern Caribbean to form the Dynamic Pressure Band to fill this gap. Once again Bill remained well in the background to the extent that many of his associates had no idea that he was in fact the force behind the Dynamic Pressure Band. This gave the Ottawa-Caribbean community a complete suite of musical entertainment choices to which they had been accustomed prior to immigrating to Ottawa.

After working for several years at the Ottawa Airport, Bill secured a short-term assignment within the Federal Government, followed by a permanent position at the Canada Mortgage and Housing Corporation, where he continued working until he retired.

Public Sector

Federal Government

Lloyd Stanford arrived in Ottawa in September 1959 to pursue graduate studies at Carleton University.[136] His first degree was in languages from the University College of the West Indies (UCWI) with honors in French, Spanish as a second language, and a minor in Spanish. Graduating from UCWI he took a job with the Jamaica Civil Service and was placed on the management track. He also had a passion for theatre and had been a member of the UCWI Theatre Group. He had performed in a number of plays while pursuing his undergraduate studies

C. Lloyd Stanford, Honorary Doctor of Laws

and he continued his stage activities with the UCWI Theatre Group while working. He had the opportunity to perform in the first play that was staged by the Jamaica Broadcasting Corporation (JBC) after they came on air.

The JBC was the brainchild of the Rt. Hon. Norman Washington Manley who became Jamaica's first Premier and who led the Island into its independence from Great Britain. However, Manley wanted to model the JBC after the Canadian Broadcasting Corporation. It was in this regard that a group of Canadians including Carleton University President Davidson Dunton came to Jamaica to assist. As a member of the cast that was performing the JBCs first on-air play, Lloyd was in contact with the visiting Canadian implementation team. During one of his conversations with the Canadians Lloyd talked about his career aspirations in the public sector. The Canadians encouraged him to come to Canada and pursue his public service training at Carleton University. They also showed him the Carleton University calendar with the course outline. He submitted his application, and was pleasantly surprised by the swift acceptance along with an offer for a scholarship.

"Founded in 1942 as Carleton College, the institution originally operated as a private, non-denominational evening college to serve returning World

---

136 Interview with Lloyd Stanford.

War II veterans. Carleton was chartered as a university by the provincial government in 1952 through the Carleton University Act…"[137]

In 1959 it was managed by its fourth president, Arnold Davidson Dunton, who served the university from 1958-1972. When Lloyd arrived in Ottawa, the Carleton campus was located on First Avenue in the Glebe, and was relocated to its current location shortly after Lloyd became a student. Lloyd's objective in registering at Carleton was to obtain a Diploma in Public Administration and then return to Jamaica. With this accreditation, he anticipated that his career would advance smoothly upwards within the ranks of the Jamaican Civil Service.

On arrival, Lloyd was greeted by a welcoming committee arranged by the Carleton University Student Liaison Office. His accommodation had also been pre-arranged, initially with a family who lived on First Avenue in the Glebe, affording him easy and convenient access to the campus. Completing his Diploma in Public Administration (DPA) he followed up with a Master's in Public Administration (MPA) at Carleton before going to pursue Doctoral studies at Queens University in Kingston, Ontario.

Mr. Stanford spent one year in the Province of Saskatchewan and continued to work in the Canadian Government for several decades, serving in several government departments including the Privy Council. After retiring in 1991, he held Governor–in-Council appointments with the Governments of Canada and Ontario. He has been a consultant on employment and governance issues since 1992.

He taught at Carleton and, briefly, at the University of Ottawa. His community work has included serving on the Board of Governors and the Senate of Carleton from 1993 to 1999, as president of the theatre group Third World Players, and as the Ottawa contact for the Alumni Association of the UWI.

He has received numerous awards, notably the C.A.T. Productions' Capital Award "for outstanding service to Canadian community" in 1991[138], the Prime Minister of Jamaica's Gold Medal for service to Jamaica, the Queen's Golden Jubilee Medal in 2003 and the Queen's Diamond Jubilee Medal in 2012.

---

137 *Wikipedia*. Carleton University. https://en.wikipedia.org/wiki/Carleton_University Accessed on February 25, 2018.
138 Carleton University. Newsroom Archives. Canute Lloyd Stanford Receives Honorary Doctorate from Carleton University. https://newsroom.carleton.ca/archives/2017/06/15/canute-lloyd-stanford-receives-honorary-doctorate-from-carleton-university/ Accessed on February 25, 2018.

"Lloyd Stanford is a professional public administrator who has dedicated his life in service to the governments and citizens of his native and adopted countries," said Joy Mighty, Carleton's associate vice-president (Teaching and Learning).[139] On June 15, 2017, C. Lloyd Stanford was awarded the degree of Doctor of Laws, *honoris causa*, by Carleton University.

Health Canada and Community Service

The profile of the late **Dr. Eric Samuels** was provided by his wife **Nye Samuels**. This is a broader profile of the Samuels family as they made the transition from Jamaica, their home country to Canada, and the unfolding events through the ensuing years. Eric met Nye at St. George's College Extension School in Kingston Jamaica while she was studying sciences there.

Eric graduated from the Jamaica School of Agriculture, worked for a short while to accumulate sufficient funds to finance his continuing education, and then was accepted at McGill University in Montreal, where he completed an undergraduate

Dr. Eric Samuels
(1926 -2003)

degree in Bio-Chemistry. He then completed his Master's Degree in Bio-Chemistry. While at McGill he became active in student affairs and became the first Black student council president at that institution.

After earning his Master's Degree at McGill, Eric was accepted at the University of Saskatoon to complete a PhD program in Bio-Chemistry. It was during the first year of his PhD program that he returned to Jamaica to marry his fiancée. The couple married in September 1959 and Eric returned to continue his studies, but his wife was unable to join him until a year later.

At that time Nye was working in the Ministry of Health as a pharmacist. Her mother was a primary school teacher, and Nye had obtained her primary education under her mother's tutorship. On graduating from high school, she took a short course in Commercial studies. Then a friend informed her of a Pharmacy training program at the Kingston Public Hospital; Nye enrolled in the program

---

139 Carleton University. Newsroom Archives. Canute Lloyd Stanford Accessed on February 25, 2018.

and became a pharmacist, working in the profession for about nine years until her departure for Canada to join her husband in October 1960.

She landed at the Saskatoon Airport and was greeted by a not-too-friendly immigration officer who put her through an intense investigative process. She then encountered a housing situation where the landlord thought it necessary to get permission from the neighbours to rent the apartment to the Samuels. Nye was surprised to find several other Blacks in Saskatoon, most of whom were university students.

Once settled, she received a work permit for a six-month period and then found a job with the accounts office in a private company. The work permit was not renewed at the end of the six months; she was told that the position could apparently now be filled by other qualified Canadians. Nye remained unemployed until the spring of 1963 when the couple moved to Ottawa. At this time Eric had graduated with a PhD in Biochemistry and held a position in the Radiation Protection Division of Health Canada in Ottawa.

After their first night in Ottawa which was spent at a motel, the couple had an upsetting experience when they went to pay the next morning. Checking out, they discovered that the room rate quoted at check-in had increased overnight. The attendant suggested that the rate increase was due to Nye's condition – and pointed to her. The couple was nevertheless able to rent an apartment at 649 Wilson Street in Vanier that very same day. Dr. Samuels had to obtain an official verification from the Jamaican Government that he was not indebted to them before he could start in his new job. To expedite this process, he reluctantly went back to Jamaica to obtain this official document, returning several days later with the verification that was required.

His wife was expecting their first child. Fortunately, the Samuels had a friend who lived in Ottawa who was able to give advice on how to establish themselves in their new city. They furnished their apartment after visiting the Colonial Furniture store.

Two days after settling into the new apartment. Nye decided to meet her next-door neighbour. Knocking on the door, the neighbour opened and they greeted each other. Nye invited her over for cup of tea. The woman responded that she was just moving out to a new address and was surprised that, after living at this apartment for two years, this was the first time she had had any interaction with any of her neighbors. Nye concluded that this must be a very unfriendly city. Nevertheless, the Samuels family remained in this apartment for the initial two-year lease period. When they asked to extend their lease, the Landlord would not accommodate them, claiming that they were disturbing the residents in the apartment below them. Nye found out later that the resident in the apartment below had been routinely reporting to the landlord that they were making noise even when they were away from their apartment.

With their first child approaching three years of age, the Samuels family moved to 1411 Bellamy Street, and apart from a few minor incidents with racial subtexts, living at the Bellamy Street location worked out fine. This neighbourhood was very different as most residents came from other parts of Canada and were much more accommodating towards each other.

Dr. Samuels, fully settled into his new job with Health Canada, began to reach out to others in Ottawa's small Black community, most of whom were Caribbean immigrants. His passion for cricket led to the establishment of the Bel-Air Cricket Club as a home for cricketers from the West Indies. They ran into difficulties — the norm at that period, when the team tried to join the local cricket league. The Bel-Air Club, predominantly Black players, was denied entry to play in the league based on their colour. However, since the Cricket ground was located on the Governor-General's estate, Eric felt that they had the same rights as any other Canadian to play at that facility. Leading a deputation, they met with the Governor-General and presented their case. It was determined that the League could continue to use the Governor General's cricket field only if they allowed Bel-Air in the league. "No Blacks, no Cricket" as documented by Ewart Walters in his account of the history of the Bel-Air Cricket Club.

Eric went further, building inter-racial bridges with visits by the club to communities in Kingston, Brockville, Montreal, Cornell, and Hartford. These visits and the entire deportment of the club were conducted at the highest levels of camaraderie and sportsmanship, giving club members, their wives and friends, a sense of worth and belonging in their new country. In the process, he enjoyed the game himself, served for many years on the executive of the league, and for some time held the post of Vice-President, declining to accept nomination as president.

As time went by the club grew into two teams. While some members simply wanted to be associated with the club, everybody who wanted to play could play. The inclusive nature of the club weakened its strength when it started using "A" team players on the "B" team since fewer members had a chance to play. This greatly affected the integrity of the club.

Dr. Samuels became a key point of reference for many of the other Caribbean community organizations. He was awarded the Order of Distinction by the Government of Jamaica for his community efforts in Ottawa. In addition, he earned him a place in the Cricket Hall of Fame for his intense efforts in the building of the Ottawa-Caribbean Cricket organization.

Dr. Samuels passed away on September 13, 2003. During this interview, his wife, 92 year-old Nye Samuels remained her normal self — very sharp, with an excellent memory of these historic events; she was actively organizing an extensive library containing hundreds of books in the top floor of her farm house in Osgoode.

National Defence

Dr. Stephen Blizzard
October 17, 1928 -June 9, 2020

Stephen Blizzard was born in Trinidad. After completing high school, he worked briefly for the Government of Trinidad and Tobago before being granted a scholarship to study veterinary medicine in Edinburgh, Scotland. Initially he wanted to study in Canada, but since all available spaces in his chosen field of study were filled by war veterans, he elected to go to the United Kingdom (UK). The terms of the scholarship mandated that upon successful completion of his studies, he would return to Trinidad and work with the Government for a period of five years.

Dr. Blizzard was also interested in becoming a pilot. He had been introduced to flight training in Trinidad while he was in high school. At that time he had joined the 'Air Scouts of Trinidad' and had received flight training from Royal Navy flight instructors who went to Trinidad for that purpose. He continued flying while he was at the University in Edinburgh as a member of the University Air Squadron.

He completed his course of study, and as planned, returned to Trinidad to take on the role as a Government Veterinary Officer. After completing his mandated five years with the Government, and while dis-satisfied with his situation in the government, he also recognized that there were no opportunities in the private sector. Having heard favorable reports of the Canadian experience from his peers who were then studying at the University of Toronto, Dr. Blizzard decided to leave Trinidad for Canada, discounting a return to the UK or migration to the US.

"I didn't want to live in the United States. I didn't want to live somewhere else in the Caribbean. And I certainly didn't want to live in the UK because post-war UK was something else."

The Blizzard family would arrive in Canada in 1958. Before heading to Canada, Dr. Blizzard, his wife Merle, a registered nurse, and their thirteen-month-old son Roberto sailed off to the UK to visit friends. They then flew from London to New York, and boarded a train from New York to Toronto. Dr. Blizzard reconnected with one of his earlier associates, Frank Milne, who had attended the same institution in Glasgow and was now a professor at the University of Guelph. This contact enabled him to work as a faculty assistant at the Ontario College of Veterinary Medicine at the University of Guelph. Merle had already secured employment at the Toronto General Hospital, and shortly after receiving her Canadian certification, she moved to the Doctor's Hospital in Toronto. Dr. Blizzard worked at the University of Guelph for about one year before applying to Medical School; he was accepted at the University of Western Ontario. During his studies, he enrolled in the Canadian Military initiative — the 'Forty-five Months Subsidization Plan'. This was targeted to medical students across Canada who had signed up to be a member of a Defense Reserve Unit. At that time Canadian universities had a University Reserve Training Program (URTP) as part of the Army, Navy or Air force. This plan was a part of the URTP program, a voluntary Cadet Training program in which both tuition and a stipend were paid with the agreement to provide three years of service in return upon graduation. During the summer periods the Cadets would be dispersed throughout the country serving and learning at military bases across Canada. Meanwhile Nurse Blizzard worked at the Guelph Hospital for three years while the family resided in Guelph.

During his second summer stint, Dr. Blizzard was posted in Ottawa at the Army, Navy, Air Force Hospital, later renamed the National Defense Medical Centre (NDMC), where he worked under the direction of Colonel Bailey Powell, the Chief of Surgery. Colonel Powell indicated that he wanted Dr. Blizzard back at the NDMC working with him after he completed his post-graduate internship.

In 1963, Dr. Blizzard graduated from the medical program at the University of Western Ontario, fulfilling his initial career goal to become a doctor, as well as being nominated president of his graduating class. He returned to the NDMC to work with Colonel Bailey, and at the end of the first year Dr. Blizzard was posted to the medical facility at the Rockcliffe Military Base while still retaining emergency room duties at the NDMC. Dr. Blizzard said that when he arrived in Ottawa there were very few Blacks living in the city: "At that time there were very few of us." However, his experience with regards to racial interactions within the Canadian Forces was pleasant. He could not recall encountering any racial incidents worth noting.

Nurse Blizzard had been trained as a midwife in Trinidad, a practice not recognized in Canada at that time. However, when the Blizzards moved to Ottawa, she was able to practice nursing at a number of hospitals on an on-call basis. She had stints of work at the Ottawa General, the Civic Hospital and the Grace Hospital. Her midwife skills were recognized by the Grace Hospital, which had a highly reputed maternity ward, but not at the other hospitals where she worked. Interestingly, there were several Caribbean nurses who had midwifery training in the UK before immigrating to Canada; they were able to use their skills in midwifery without restrictions.

The Blizzard family objective was to ultimately return to Trinidad in order to serve the people in their home country. Notwithstanding that he was among the six officers who were selected for permanent commissioning and were offered a permanent job within the Canadian Forces, he elected to return to Trinidad to take up a job offer in his home country. However, after Mrs. Blizzard and their children moved back, with Dr. Blizzard remaining in Canada to settle remaining family business, he was informed that the job offer in Trinidad was frozen. The separation placed a tremendous strain on the family, especially with their children starting school in Trinidad. Dr. Blizzard decided to remain in Canada and visit with his family in Trinidad as frequently as possible.

The Canadian Forces posted him to Moose Jaw where there was a fighter pilot training operation. With his previous pilot experience he enrolled in the fighter pilot training program and became the first and only Black doctor to have earned his wings in the Canadian Forces: "I am the only Black doctor in this country who has carried out his full job as a doctor on a base and simultaneously got his wings."

He completed his Moose Jaw assignment, and in 1969 he was promoted to Commanding Officer and posted to the Institute of Aviation Medicine in Toronto. An administrative position, it was not his forte. He applied for leave on compassionate grounds and returned to Trinidad to initiate a medical practice.

His return did not work out well. Mrs. Blizzard had established the office and procedures, but social and political considerations made this experience an unpleasant memory. After six years the Blizzard family returned to Canada. Dr. Blizzard immediately rejoined the Armed Forces, and the family was reunified in Canada. By this time the eldest had completed high school and enrolled in university. Things went very well for the Blizzard family throughout the remainder of his career.

Dr. Stephen Blizzard passed away on Monday June 15, 2020, at the age of 91; leaving Merle, his wife of 65 years, his children Roberto, Gloria, and Carlos (Fabienne), and his grandchildren Desirée, Kevin, Bianca, Zev, Tyra and Danté.[140]

How does a young man from the outskirts of Port-of-Spain ascend to become one of the most respected servicemen, and most decorated West Indians in the Canadian Air force? By determination, focus and self-confidence, Dr. Stephen Blizzard straddled two professions and became a celebrated trailblazer in the little-known field where they both merge – aviation medicine.

Public Service Commission

The Government of Canada publishes the names and images of those who served as Public Service Commissioners since 1908. One of those images stands out conspicuously. **Gilbert (Gil) Scott**, who served from 1988 to 1994, is the lone Black face in this group.[141]

Gilbert Scott 1988-1994
Public Service Commissioner of Canada,

Gilbert Scott attended Kingston Technical School in Jamaica. Established in 1896, Kingston Technical High was the first technical school in Jamaica, and as such, introduced curricula that represented alternative educational directions to the traditional academic programs of study in the high schools.[142] He graduated in 1959 and had a brief internship with the Jamaica Public Service Company (JPS), the sole distributor of electricity in Jamaica. He then moved into the field of meteorology, working at the Jamaican Meteorological Services in Kingston Jamaica. After eight years Gil found that the shift-work inherent to this profession had become onerous, motivating him to

140 T+T Icons in Science & Technology Volume 3. http://icons.niherst.gov.tt/icon/stephen-blizzard-tt3/ Accessed on February 2, 2018.
141 Government of Canada. Public Service Commission of Canada. https://www.canada.ca/en/public-service-commission February 20, 2018.
142 Kingston Technical High School. http://kingstontechnicalhighschool.edu.jm/about-us/ Accessed on 3/14/23

explore other avenues to avoid this type of work environment. His primary objective was to retrain in computer software development overseas and then return to Jamaica upon graduation. He applied for entry to Canada under the professional class (Points System), and in 1968 migrated to Canada. Shortly after his arrival, Gil was hired by the Canadian Meteorological Services in Toronto. After six months, he was promoted and transferred to Ottawa, and seven years later he entered the Federal government as a Program Manager. Gil tells the story of his professional career in his own words in *Meteoric Rise to Public Service Commissioner.* See Appendix G.

In response to the economic downturn in the early 1990s, the Federal Government went through a period of re-organization aimed at meeting a downsized budget. The target was a reduction of 30% within three years. Gil was appointed to Regional Director for Ontario to execute the re-organization plan. He immediately recognized that Ontario with the largest budget, which was a compliment of 1100 staff and a budget of $1.2B Canadian dollars, would be most difficult to reduce to the 30% target within the three-year timeframe. Nonetheless, he set out to accomplish this and was successful in meeting the targets within the given timeframe. He served as the Regional Executive Director, Ontario Region, in the newly created Department of Canadian Heritage from 1994 to retirement in 1997.

One of the casualties in this downsizing effort was Gil himself. At the completion of the assignment, his own job had been made redundant. He had two options; take a demotion after one year, or return to Ottawa to seek other opportunities within the Federal Government. Gil chose a third option. He retired from the Federal government and returned to his native Jamaica where he now resides.

During his tenure with the Federal Government, Gil was appointed to be the Administrative Head of the Canadian Delegation to the Second World Festival of Black and African Cultures (FESTAC '77) in Lagos, Nigeria – 1977. He was also a Member of a Six-Person Canadian Delegation to South Africa to assist the African National Congress (ANC) to prepare for governance in advance of the first ever national democratic election in 1994. And subsequent to his retirement, he was invited to be the Executive Director of the Canadian Delegation to the Second World Conference Against Racism in Durban, South Africa – 2001.

Agriculture Canada

In March 1956 **Desmond (Des) Doran** boarded an airplane at the Palisadoes (Norman Manley International) Airport in Kingston Jamaica. He had a Canadian student visa to pursue an undergraduate degree at the Ontario Agricultural College (O.A.C) in Guelph Ontario. He also had a visitor's visa to the United States. Desmond's initial destination was New York City; he spent some time visiting with his elder brother who then drove him to Guelph Ontario where he would begin his course of study.

Desmond (Des) Doran
Agricultural Economist
January 3, 1936 -May 18, 2020

Although Des was looking for the opportunity to further his education it was by chance that he learned about the Ontario Agricultural College from one of his school mates at Jamaica College. Des recalls that time:

> "During my two years of full-time employment, I saved for study abroad. A high school classmate told me of the Ontario Agricultural College, the O.A.C., now part of the University of Guelph, in Guelph, Ontario. I came to Canada in September 1956, and enrolled at the O.A.C., which I attended from 1956 to 1961."

Des was impressed by the highway system and the spectacular Niagara Falls as he and his brother drove across New York State and entered Canada. They arrived at their OAC destination close to midnight. He met with his roommate, a Trinidadian student, and settled into his college life.

In order to finance his education, Des intended to enroll in the Canadian Regular Officer Training Corps (R.O.T.C.) which allowed students to gain military training, and guaranteed paid summer employment:

> "The thing that you must remember is that I'm a product of the 2nd World War. I grew up in those years when Spitfire pilots were the envy of every little boy and young man. That's what you wanted to be. Spitfire was the outstanding part of the military service. So that was my plan when I was planning to come to Canada. The University calendar showed that you could join the Canadian forces, what they call the R.O.T.C. at the time, which is an officer training corp. My plan was to join the Air Force and be a fighter pilot and to pay my way through university. … Unfortunately, the year that I came was the year that they stopped allowing non-Canadians

from joining the university Air Force training course. You could still join the army or the navy and the beauty with that was you got a full-dress uniform and you got a small salary. So for the formal events at the university there was nothing sharper than to be in full military dress to attend a formal dance, this meant that you didn't have to rent a tuxedo."

The fact that Des was no longer able to gain entry into the R.O.T.C. program meant that he had to look for alternate ways to earn money. "I worked every summer and paid my entire university training." He found interesting work:

"I was active at university and so one of the clubs that I joined immediately was a fish and wildlife club. I was student assistant to the district biologist in Kirkland Lake northern Ontario. I spent my entire summer traveling around the bush being dropped into a remote lake by Air Beaver airplane which is a float plane, and three of us would spend the entire week in our canoes there studying the fish in the lake. The biologist would inspect them to see what species of fish were there and what they were eating.

The second summer I worked with a construction company. And I did a small stint with Canada Packers in Toronto pouring meat and making Spam. And then I had a beautiful job with my department of agricultural economics at the University. I was doing a survey [of] all large-scale hog production. With an assistant I visited all of the hog producers in Ontario who produce 800 or more hogs each year. That research later became the subject for my master's thesis."

In 1960 Des graduated from the Ontario Agricultural College with a BSc in Agriculture, and in 1961 he completed his MS in Agriculture with a major in Agricultural Economics. He then attended McGill University in Montreal and pursued PhD studies in Economics, majoring in Economic Development. He then began to teach and conduct agricultural research. He taught at Bishop's University in Lennoxville, Quebec, and was a Professor of Agricultural Economics at the Nova Scotia Agricultural College in Truro. He also worked as a Research Associate at the Department of Agricultural Economics at the University of British Columbia in Vancouver.

"The major focus of my work was world food and agriculture issues, and Canada's participation and contribution to resolving issues such as food scarcity in developing countries, use of food as aid to economic development in Third World Countries and was on Canadian Delegations to the Food and Agriculture Organization (FAO), Rome, and the Inter-American Organization for Cooperation on Agriculture of the OAS."

His career focus afforded him a number of special assignments related to international agricultural development. These included project assignments in Irrigation Development in Malawi, Africa, with visits to Kenya, Mozambique, Ivory Coast and Ghana. Des was also a consultant on a number of Caribbean Development Projects in Haiti, Grenada, St. Lucia, and Barbados, as well as giving input to other Caribbean projects.

Des was an active community leader in Ottawa. He was the Chair of the Canadian Race Relations Foundation, a member of the Ottawa Police Services Board and a member of the Regional Ethnocultural Advisory Committee of Correctional Services Canada. He was a very active participant in the Jamaican Ottawa Community Association. And in recognition of his contribution to the building of the Jamaican community in Ottawa, Des was awarded the 'Prime Minister's Medal of Appreciation' by the Jamaican Prime Minister, for his many years of service to Jamaica and to the Jamaican community in Ottawa.

Immigrant Services

Carl Nicholson was born in Port Maria, originally 'Puerto Santa Maria', the capital town of the northern Jamaican parish of Saint Mary.

Carl Nicholson

> "Puerto Santa Maria, it was the second town established by Spanish settlers in Jamaica after Christopher Columbus brought his conquistadores in the 15th Century. Port Maria has a population of some 7,500 people." [143]

I interviewed Carl on May 17, 2018, in his office at 219 Argyle Avenue. He was the Executive Director at The Catholic Immigration Centre, Ottawa, although the Centre changed its name to Catholic Centre for Immigrants. Carl had graduated from Kingston's Calabar High School in 1961. He found work in the Courts Office, and applied to study Law at Gray's Inn in London to further his career in Legal Services.

> "The Honourable Society of Gray's Inn, commonly known as Gray's Inn, is one of the four Inns of Court [professional associations for barristers

---

143 *Wikipedia*. Port Maria. https://en.wikipedia.org/wiki/Port_Maria Accessed on March 22, 2023.

and judges] in London. To be called to the bar and practice as a barrister in England and Wales, an individual must belong to one of these Inns."[144]

Around the same time he was offered a scholarship by the Canadian Government to study *Sociology and Economics* at Carleton University in Ottawa. At that time Canada provided assistance to developing nations under its External Aid program, the predecessor to CIDA. Carl packed his bags, heading off to Canada. Before his plane landed in Toronto, he 'adopted' a mother to ease his transition into the Canadian society.

> "I was sitting on the plane and there were two women sitting behind me. One of these ladies was Isis Officer, she was a nurse, and her friend was also a nurse. We struck up a conversation and as it turned out they were both coming to Ottawa as well, returning from their vacation."

Upon learning that he was headed for Ottawa, Isis Officer gave Carl a standing invitation to Sunday dinners at her home. As Carl puts it, this was one of those instances where planning and opportunity intersected since Carl had no family in Ottawa. He knew two of his former schoolmates, Ewart Walters and Claude Robinson, both of whom were studying Journalism at Carleton University. Carl spent his first night in Ottawa at the Lord Elgin Hotel under the auspices of the Canadian Government and then secured accommodation at a boarding house on Cambridge Street.

Carl initiated his studies in Sociology and Economics at Carleton in the Fall Semester of 1966. But in 1968 he developed an interest in the emerging discipline of computer systems and veered off to do a six-month program in Systems Analysis with an institution downtown. This was essentially a programming course. He benefited by gaining part-time employment at a technology company, as well as at the Carleton University computer center. Resuming his fulltime studies at Carleton, he completed his program in 1971. Carl had moved from the boarding house at the end of his first year and established a new living arrangement with a group of Jamaican students. He had also fully immersed himself into the Canadian culture and was rapidly building an extensive network of Canadian friends and associates. Carl later moved into a Co-op living arrangement on James Street with a number of his new Canadian friends.

During his university years, Carl worked a number of odd jobs in order to sustain himself financially. Like a lot of students from the Caribbean, he drove a taxicab, and he worked at the LaPointe Fish Market downtown. And while his

---

144 *Wikipedia.* Gray's Inn. https://en.wikipedia.org/wiki/Gray%27s_Inn Accessed on May 16, 2018.

taxicab experience provided the opportunity to learn the city, the LaPointe Fish Market job provided him with a steady supply of fish at zero cost.

Upon graduating from Carleton University, Carl decided to remain in Canada and applied for his landed status. Still sharing the James Street Co-op with Canadians, he was also still driving a taxicab. During 1972 a couple of his roommates approached Carl with a business proposition. The proposal would be to evaluate the effectiveness of Federal Government programs across Canada. His potential business associates thought that with Carl's technical computer skills, along with his training in Sociology and Economics, he would be a perfect fit for the project they were planning. The new business secured an initial contract to evaluate a project relating to 'Opportunities for Youth'; other contracts would follow. Each required field travel across Canada, all paid by the Canadian Government. And on his first Trans-Canada trip to Vancouver, Carl reflected on how far he had advanced in such a relatively short time, marveling at how well his life had turned out so far. He went to other Canadian cities including Winnipeg where he met up with two of his sisters who had recently migrated.

After a few years in this consulting role, the Canadian Government recognized the added value from this initiative and decided to establish evaluation units in other Government departments where appropriate. The Secretary of State initiated this program and initially hired Carl's organization to begin the effort. The work that Carl's group had been doing would now be folded into the Department of Secretary of State. The Federal Government encouraged the participants in Carl's consulting team to apply for internal jobs with the newly instituted Program Evaluation teams associated with various Government Departments. Carl was offered a job with the group at Statistics Canada: "The StatsCan evaluation unit was new. I was being initiated to assess the value of the work being carried out internally at Statistics Canada." Carl would essentially be performing the same task that he was doing before, but now he would be working with StatsCan as an employee of the Canadian Government. Motivated, he applied for and was granted Canadian Citizenship.

Carl's first project at Statistics Canada would provide him with an expansive view of how many of the Government Departments operated. His initial project, the Federal Statistics Activities Secretariat (FSAS) project, was to examine the data that was collected by other Government Departments in order to determine where the elements of the collected data had statistical value and how it could be used. This further allowed him to participate in policy discussions relating to issues such as individual privacy, access to information, human rights, information-sharing between government departments, and other policies relating to what the Government could or could not do with the data that it collected from its citizens.

In 1976 Carl then went to work as a Field Staff Officer with Canadian University Service Overseas (CUSO) and was immediately posted to Ghana. His job was to select and place Canadian Resources in areas where those skills were needed. Carl also worked with the local communities to identify what each community needed to facilitate their development. He would then work with international suppliers and the local groups to carry out relevant projects to fulfill the needs that the Ghanaian communities had expressed. Constructing Health Clinics, erecting Electrical Grids and digging wells were examples of some of the projects implemented under this program. After five years Carl recognized that the posting of human resources by CUSO to aid the development of targeted countries, while a principal mandate, was just an important first step. But the real impact in facilitating country development was in implementing projects that solved native problems. He returned to Canada to promote this vision to the CUSO management team and was placed in charge of the West Africa area to execute this vision. He then began fund-raising to finance international development before ending his tenure at CUSO in 1989.

Carl transferred these skills initially to a fund-raising and management consulting firm, FLA-Fran Loe and Associates, and then branched out, forming his own company, Carl Nicholson & Associates, to do essentially the same work until 1993 when he came to the Catholic Immigration Centre.

In December of 1993 Carl took on the position as Director of the Catholic Immigration Centre, now the Catholic Centre for Immigrants (CCI) - Ottawa, which is a non-profit organization whose mandate is to assist immigrants and refugees in Ottawa, or those selected by Immigration, Refugees and Citizenship Canada (IRCC) to migrate to Canada.[145] Carl inherited an organization with about $1M in assets and a debt load of some $6 M (CD). Among a host of other challenges, one of his most pressing tasks was to restore the organization to financial health, which he did. As of May 2018, the non-profit organization had amassed some $12 M (CD) in assets and was also debt free. The Catholic Immigration Centre is primarily funded by the various levels of Government: Federal funds account for about 60%, Provincial and Local governments provide another 30%, and the remaining 10% is raised from private sources. These

---

145 Catholic Centre for Immigrants – Ottawa. http://cciottawa.ca/ Accessed on May 6, 2018.

funding sources enable the Catholic Immigration Centre to operate with an annual budget of approximately $10M (CD).

Carl views his job as having two primary missions. The first is to welcome and facilitate the assimilation of new immigrants into Canadian society, and the second is to enable the harmonious co-existence between immigrant and Canadian citizens. He can accomplish these by influencing policy decisions at various government levels. In addition to his role as the Director of the CCI, Carl was instrumental in transforming the Somali Center for Family Services that started out to assist a specific Somali group to become a viable organization that assists the Somali community at large. Also a member of the Ottawa Police Services Board, he promoted an agenda to improve the relationships between the police services and the predominantly Black immigrant community. He views Canada as a better place for its inhabitants, and his operation as a small part of Canada's role in that regard. His only regret is that he did not return to Jamaica to apply his acumen in further developing his native land. As a testimony to his contribution, Carl was awarded the 'Order of Ottawa' and an Honorary Degree from Algonquin College. Overall, the boy from Port Maria is humbled by the myriad accomplishments he has achieved in his adopted country.

Provincial Government

Morris Redman arrived in Canada in May 1968, firstly to re-connect with his fiancée who was already in Canada, and secondly to continue his education. Florence had arrived in Canada some nine months earlier to work with the Sun Life Insurance Company in Montreal. Morris, arriving in early May, found it very cold. In fact, the weather turned so cold that it snowed shortly after his arrival; disappointed, he immediately considered returning home, but his family convinced him to remain. Fortunately, he had an aunt who had been living in Montreal. He married his fiancé Florence shortly after settling in. The Redman family was later prompted to move to Toronto when the Front de libération du Québec (FLQ) became active in Montreal.

Morris Redman

"The FLQ was a militant independence movement that used terrorism to try and achieve an independent and socialist Quebec. FLQ members — or felquistes — were responsible for more than 200 bombings and dozens of robberies between 1963 and 1970 that left six people dead. Their actions culminated in the kidnapping of British Trade Commissioner James Cross and the kidnapping and subsequent murder of Quebec cabinet minister Pierre Laporte, in what became known as the October Crisis." [146]

Shortly after settling in Toronto, Morris registered at Ryerson College to study business administration and landed an accounting job with Community and Social Services in the Ontario government. The following year, **Florence** registered at Ryerson College to study accounting. In 1973 Morris earned his Certified General Accountant (CGA). He was hired by the Holiday Inn, and in 1974 was re-located to his native Barbados on a short-term assignment with the Holiday Inn. The Redman family spent approximately five years in Barbados, returning to Canada after the assignment period ended. Upon returning to Canada in 1980, Morris was offered a job with the National Capital Commission (NCC). The couple now had three children, one born in Montreal and the other two born in Barbados. Once the family had re-settled in Ottawa, Florence began working as a consultant. The couple immersed themselves in community development activities. Florence and Morris engaged other leaders within their community to address one of the pressing concerns that the immigrant communities were grappling with. The need to facilitate the educational development of their children was paramount. There was also an opportunity to assess the ability of adults with enhanced training to further develop their English speaking and writing skills.

---

146 *The Canadian Encyclopedia*. Front de libération du Québec (FLQ). https://www.thecanadianencyclopedia.ca/en/article/front-de-liberation-du-quebec Accessed on February 14, 2023.

Academia

Ottawa Catholic School Board

Yvonne Harper and her husband Rod arrived in Ottawa from the island of Trinidad in 1967. She graduated from high school with the Senior Cambridge School Certificate, the predecessor in the Caribbean and many Commonwealth countries to the General Certificate of Education (GCE). In 1955 Yvonne started her teaching career while taking courses to prepare herself for entry into Teacher's College. Eventually she enrolled, completed the Teacher's College training program, and continued her career as an elementary school teacher in Trinidad. "Teaching has been in my family, and I've always wanted to teach," she said. When Yvonne heard that Canada

Yvonne Harper

had initiated a recruitment program to source teachers from Caribbean countries, she became interested in teaching in Canada. Yvonne applied and succeeded in obtaining a teaching position in Ottawa. She also had an open invitation to contact the Ottawa Catholic School Board upon arrival.

Rod arrived in Ottawa several weeks ahead of the family in order to secure living accommodations, and within a few weeks he landed a job with the Ottawa Journal newspaper. Since he had worked as a printer at the Guardian newspaper in Trinidad, his friend Anthony Boissiere, also living in Ottawa, took him to the newspaper office. Rod was hired immediately because of the high demand for his skills. He recognized that the work environment was very friendly, and he believed that this in part contributed to the ease with which he handled the job. Anthony, who had encouraged Rod to immigrate, was instrumental in facilitating the Harper family with their transition once they arrived.

Three weeks later, on November 16, 1967, Yvonne and their two children arrived in Ottawa. The school term was already in full swing and the only teaching position available was special education or supply teaching. Yvonne elected to work as a supply teacher for the rest of that school year, and started in

December within weeks of their arrival. She then was offered a full-time teaching position at the Our Lady's Primary School downtown Ottawa.[147]

In 1971 the students from Our Lady's School and St. Brigid School on Murray Street were integrated into an amalgamated environment at St. Brigid School at 200 Springfield Road, bordering Rockcliffe Park. Yvonne explained that the move improved the lot of these students from "lower socio-economic backgrounds". Indeed, the School Board's effort to elevate the educational standards of the Lower-town children, who were primarily from lower income families, was a very successful initiative.

The new school drew students from the middle-income families in Manor Park and the surrounding neighbourhoods. And this mix of students from varied backgrounds resulted in a more challenging educational environment. During her tenure at St. Brigid, the minimum standards for teaching were elevated such that all elementary school teachers were required to have a Bachelor's Degree. To meet this new teaching requirement, Yvonne enrolled in part-time night studies at Carleton University. She continued to teach elementary students at St. Brigid until 1975, and after obtaining her Bachelor of Arts (BA) from Carleton University she was transferred to St. Luke's School at 2485 Dwight Crescent, Ottawa.

St. Luke had a student socio-economic demographic similar to St. Brigid. However, many of the students at this school were low performers. Yvonne embraced this challenge as an opportunity to raise the level of the low performers until there was little disparity in the overall academic achievement of the students. She immersed herself in seminars, garnering as much knowledge as she could to arm herself with tools to improve the academic performance of her students, and she used these skills effectively. Much to her satisfaction, her students began to demonstrate higher levels of achievement. Their improved achievement level caught the school board's attention. As a result, they offered Yvonne an administrative position as a Curriculum Consultant with the objective of having her propagate her learning techniques across the school district. After 18 years in the classroom, Yvonne began her new role as an administrator with the Catholic School Board in Ottawa.

---

147 Heritage Ottawa. "Our Lady's School, an Anglophone Catholic school, was built in 1904 on the intersection of Murray and Cumberland Streets in Lowertown West, Ottawa. The school played an integral role in education for Catholic boys and girls, supporting them spiritually and morally during the early 1900s." (2013). It was closed in the 1970s and sold by the Ottawa Catholic School Board. https://ottawaschoolheritage.wordpress.com/ Accessed on October 28, 2021

GOVERNMENT TRAINING COLLEGE
EMERGENCY COURSE - 1961
TUTORIAL GROUP TWO

Front Row: (Left to Right)
C. SPENCER (SRC),   Mr. A. PIERRE (Tutor),   R. OXLEY (SRC).

Middle Row:
G. R. JOSEPH,   B. WILTSHIRE,   R. SADEEK,   N. SAUNDERS,   M. CRUICKSHANK,   L. DEO,   R. JULIEN,
S. SURAJ,   M. MOHAMMED,   K. ALI,   J. SALICK,   B. SHAH,   G. BOOS,

Back Row:
K. MANUEL,   H. HARPER,   V. HAREWOOD,   N. HONORE,   J. CLARENCE.   C. REID,   I. WINTER-GITTENS,
J. LUCAS,   A. ALMARALES,   G. ALI.

The group of Teachers from Trinidad that was recruited to teach in Canada during the 1960s.

She began working with the Superintendent of Curriculum Development. Diving headlong into her new role, she built a revised curriculum, and conducted workshops for teachers in order that they implement the new curriculum. Concurrently, Yvonne returned to the University of Ottawa to obtain her Master's Degree, and followed with courses to become a school Principal.

After completing half the program, she was offered the position of Interim Principal at St. Luke, one of her former schools. She held this for a year and then returned to the Board to continue her role. Soon after, she was offered the Principal's position at St. Brigid, the second school where she had taught for seven years. After her five years mandated tenure, she was reassigned to Prince of Peace School at 1620 Heatherington Rd, Ottawa, and retired at the end of the year.

Despite being fully immersed in her career as an educator, Yvonne still found time to involve herself in community initiatives. She was one of the five women, including Carmen Hajdu, Claudine Awang, Yvonne Codette and Myrtha Peters who initiated the Impact Heritage program that provided the facility and activities to enable the development of predominantly young Black children. She was awarded a 150th Anniversary Confederation Medal for her work as an educator and community builder. Rod's career wound down with the closing of the Ottawa Journal, and he moved on to work with OC Transpo until he retired.

Ontario Ministry of Education

June Girvan

June Girvan is mother to three and grandmother to five. Her motto is "I can do this". Her favourite word is 'gratitude'.

Newly married, June left Jamaica for Canada in 1957. Her husband had graduated from the University of the West Indies and was accepted at the University of Toronto to pursue post-graduate studies in Chemical Engineering. The couple had been married just two weeks prior to heading off to Canada. Upon arrival in Toronto, they learned that finding a place to live was very challenging. "It was a horror story because the only places available were questionable rooming houses." The horror was alleviated by the kindness of the Rotary Club of Bowmanville, whose members would arrive in Toronto each weekend, to 'rescue' overseas students. Through them, she was introduced to Canadian culture. The couple settled into a tight attic space, and June found work with the King Edward Sheraton Hotel as assistant to the Food and Beverage purchasers and the Executive Chef, and then as local contributing editor to the Sheraton News. Her working days included navigating the St. Lawrence Market, the hotel's kitchen, and the hotel's public spaces. In these places, she gained valuable exposure to the community in Toronto, to culinary skills and knowledge about social and cultural happenings in the city. From the Beverage Purchaser, a former high school history teacher, she learned Canadian history.

Upon graduation in 1959, June's husband secured an internship with the National Research Council (NRC) in Ottawa. The couple moved from Toronto to take up residence in Ottawa. They found an apartment in a new building on Cummings Avenue near NRC, where June declared them to be "a model couple in a model apartment". One day, walking along Metcalfe Street on her way to write the Civil Service Exam to gain entry to a job in the Public Sector, June saw a sign in the window of a legal firm. In her words, "I pushed the door open, and I walked in and said, I'm looking for a job". June was offered a job as legal assistant to Peter Newcombe, a lawyer with the law firm, Gowling, MacTavish, Osbourne, and Henderson. He would become a life-long friend, mentor, protector.

Having settled in Ottawa, the couple started a family. They faced many challenges. She encountered disconcerting reactions to herself and her children's African descent. Wanting to protect her children, she was determined to gain the qualifications to access the education system from within. June began her pursuit of a first degree and of teacher training. In 1970, thanks to Madeline Tufts, the only woman principal in Ottawa, she accessed the education system, beginning as an outdoor education teacher. In 1977, thanks to the support of persons like John Jarrett, Superintendent of Schools, she began service in positions of responsibility, including Vice Principal, Acting Principal, Special Assignment Teacher for Mathematics K-6. Thanks to the insight of persons like Mike Perry, Superintendent of Education, Ontario Ministry of Education (Eastern Ontario), she was appointed to serve in the position of Education/Supervisor Officer with the Ministry.

Ten years after beginning part-time studies, June acquired a first degree, B.A. in History of Art. She has qualifications from Carleton University, Ottawa University and Queen's University.

In 1983, June won an annual school board sabbatical competition for one year's leave of study on a topic of her choice; she chose to study French in France. In 1989, distressed at the continuing inability of the system to adequately protect and promote the human rights of children of African descent, June withdrew from the system for a year's reflection. While on leave of absence, she was asked to assist with the assimilation of children from East Africa who had secured refugee status in Ottawa. In response, she returned to the Adult High School as a student, in order to interact with the young people on their own terms; learn their stories and give them a platform for their own voices to be heard. This engagement led her to East Africa, to learn from Elders and a local anthropologist, how to better serve the young refugees in Ottawa. She was pleased to be invited by the Ministry of Education and Training (Eastern Ontario) to return to service as a Supervisory Officer, with responsibilities for equity in education.

On retirement, June Girvan became intensively involved in community building with specific focus on Ottawa's children of African descent. She established the *J'NiKira Dinqinesh* Education Centre – Every Child is Sacred in honour of her children. 'J'Nikira' is a contraction of the names of her children. The aspiration, which dates back to the basinet, home and neighbourhood she worked to create for her children, is for Ottawa to be experienced as a safe, child friendly place for all children of the maple leaf; children of all human colours of the sun and having systems that respect them throughout the municipality. June hosted the annual Era 21 Networking Breakfasts in the Parliamentary Restaurant for young people of African descent and their guests to break bread with parliamentarians and senators, affirming their sense of belonging and ownership in the 'halls of power'. Since 2018, she has worked to have the UN International Decade for People of African Descent adopted throughout the municipality. For her work, she has received a number of awards. These include, the Community Champion Special Award from the Canadian Race Relations Foundation, the Martin Luther King DreamKeepers' Award for her distinguished community leadership and engagement, a Youth in Leadership Award, the Mayor of Ottawa's Community Builder Award, along with the prestigious Order of Ontario, by the Honorable Elizabeth Dowdeswell, Lieutenant Governor of Ontario and Chancellor of the Order of Ontario. June acts as President, Elder-in-Residence, of Black History Ottawa.

She initiated a Robert Sutherland scholarship at Queen's University and has provided the June Girvan Bursary at Carleton University for students with ancestry in the Middle Passage and Plantation Slavery. One citation read:

> "June Girvan has devoted her life to nurturing, protecting, affirming, and giving voice to children and young people. Since moving to Canada from Jamaica in the 1950s, Ms. Girvan has invested her talents and resources in bettering the lives of newly arrived Canadians, vulnerable children in the school system and at-risk youth. Her career included positions in teaching and curriculum development, and she also served as an Education Officer with the Ontario Ministry of Education…Mrs. Girvan also founded the J'Nikira Dinqinesh Education Centre* (JDEC) in Ottawa, where she is the

Volunteer-in-Chief. The JDEC's community work is based on honouring and celebrating the moral compass of fellow Canadians, both historic and contemporary, for their efforts in fighting against slavery and championing human rights and social justice in Canada."[148]

In 1969 **Maud Pitters** was a teacher at the Middlesex All-Age School in Jamaica. She was married to Glen Pitters, the couple having five children attending school. She and her husband sought opportunities to improve the lives of the family members. An opportunity to migrate to Canada presented itself, and Mrs. Pitters arrived in Ottawa on May 5, 1969. She left her family in Jamaica with the intention of having them join her as soon as possible. Her sister **Vernie Hall** sponsored her to visit Canada. Vernie had been a Public Health Nurse in London, England. But she had emigrated from the UK to Canada several years earlier to work as a school nurse in St.

Maud Pitters

Catharines, Ontario. She later moved to Toronto where she met her husband; the couple subsequently moved to Ottawa, shortly after which Vernie sponsored her sister Maud.

"The trip was very long," she said, but once she arrived, she found that "the people were quite welcoming." She took up residence in Britannia at 2656 Don Street, and even though she arrived in May she was welcomed with a snowfall when she looked out the window on her first morning in Ottawa. She initially secured a job at a nursing home in the Glebe and then she began working at another nursing home, 'The West End Villa'. But her passion for teaching burned deeply, and she secured a part-time tutoring position at Algonquin College to assist adult students. Her sister helped her secure the application documentation to apply for a position with the Ottawa Board of Education, and even though she thought this a long shot, she submitted her application. About one year after she arrived in Ottawa, she was offered her first real teaching position at Mutchmor Elementary School on 5th Avenue.

---

148 Black Ottawa Scene. June Girvan awarded Order of Ontario.
http://blackottawascene.com/june-girvan-awarded-order-of-ontario/ Accessed on August 14, 2018.

"Mutchmor Street Public School, was erected on December 23, 1895, is dedicated to John Mutchmor, military veteran of the War of 1812, an Upper Canada homesteader, and a farmer. Mutchmor Public School opened under the name Mutchmor Street Public School taking its name from the adjacent Mutchmor Street, which was later renamed Fifth Avenue".[149]

Once back into her teaching career, Mrs. Pitters enrolled at Carleton University to pursue an undergraduate degree in order to bolster her teaching credentials. By this time her family had been re-united in Ottawa. Her husband **Glen**, along with the younger siblings, Patrick, Joni, Blair and Glenor, had arrived in Ottawa in January 1970, several months after her arrival. The eldest, Carrol remained in Jamaica to complete her final year at St. Andrew High School. Mrs. Pitters worked during the day and attended classes at night while she also took care of her family.

Shortly after Glen arrived, he found a job with the Federal Public Service doing social work, a job similar to what he had in his native Jamaica. He remained in this position until he retired at age 65. The family's home became a welcoming place for many of the new immigrants, mainly students who were new to Ottawa. The Pitters family often invited students and other new immigrants to join them for dinner, usually on Sunday. Their hospitality helped many new immigrants make the cultural transition from their native land to the Canadian environment.

Ted Guillaume arrived in Canada in June 1976. He had left his native Haiti in the summer of 1972 to study in the USA around the time that his fiancée Mitsy also left Haiti for Montreal where she had relatives who had earlier migrated to Canada. After graduating from high School, Ted taught in Haiti. He initially began mathematics and sciences but switched over to languages – English and Spanish because of the dire need for teachers of these subjects at that time. After about five years he was awarded a scholarship to pursue an Education degree in the USA.

He enrolled at the Ottawa University in Kansas USA to pursue a three-year Bachelor of Education degree and settled into his student role there.

---

149 Canada's Historic Places. Mutchmor Public School. HistoricPlaces.ca https://www.historicplaces.ca/en/rep-reg/place-lieu.aspx?id=18490&pid=0 Accessed on October 29, 2021.

"Ottawa University-Kansas City (OU) is a private, non-profit, faith-based liberal arts college located in Ottawa, Kansas, United States. It was founded in 1865 and is affiliated with the American Baptist Churches USA. Ottawa has approximately 600 students on its main campus, with a total of about 7,000 students across all of its campuses and online." [150]

Ted Guillaume

Meanwhile Mitsy had secured a job as a bookkeeper in Montreal and settled into her adopted city; in 1975 just before the completion of Ted's undergraduate degree, they married in Montreal and the couple returned to the USA where Ted was now teaching Spanish in an Ohama, Nebraska school district. After teaching for a year, the couple returned to Canada, taking up residency in the Ottawa area. Ted secured his first teaching job at a private school in Ottawa, shortly after moved into the Ottawa Catholic School Board, and then onto the Catholic School Board. During his tenure as a teacher, Ted found it "useful and interesting to pursue a Master of Arts degree in Psycho-pedagogy at the University of Ottawa (Canada)." Later he enrolled in International Affairs, earning a second Master's degree in 1983.

Ted became very active both within the school environment and within the Ottawa community. As a language teacher, he initiated a Spanish Language Club for his students that went on for eighteen years. He was also very active within his church, holding the position of Youth Choir Director and establishing a public speaking forum to equip the young people in his Church.

Ted was an active member of the Haitian Community Association where he held the position of Treasurer. He later was involved as President with the Black Canadian Scholarship Fund for a period of four years. He carried out these extra-curricular roles while continuing his teaching career with the Catholic Board and the Public Board for several decades until he retired in 2004.

Following his retirement, he worked as a supply teacher for two years. Then turning his attention more seriously to real estate investments, he secured a few rental properties on both sides of the Ottawa River which he continues to manage.

---

150 *Wikipedia*. **Ottawa University.** https://en.wikipedia.org/wiki/Ottawa_University **Accessed on April 20, 2018.**

Religion

The Ottawa Church of God

The people of the Caribbean are very religious and church attendance in Caribbean Islands is normally high. The religious denominations in the Caribbean are like those in Canada, with traditional Catholic, Episcopal, Baptist, and other Protestant groupings, along with a growing Pentecostal movement.

As the Ottawa Caribbean population increased, there was a growing awareness that new immigrants would be much more comfortable if they had a place of worship where they were reflected in the congregation. Up until 1970, there was no predominantly Caribbean or Black Church assembly of any denomination within the City of Ottawa; the Caribbean immigrants attended places of worship that were close to the church denominations with which they were originally affiliated.

Rev Dr. Jeremiah McIntyre

As the mid-1970s approached, the larger Caribbean immigrant population in Montreal had become more mature than that of Ottawa and the first predominantly Caribbean Congregant Pentecostal Church was established there under the leadership of Pastor **Jeremiah McIntyre**. Rev. Dr. Jeremiah McIntyre was born in St James, Jamaica, on the 1st of July 1931. Dr. McIntyre was converted at age 19 and migrated to England in 1956. He pastored five churches by the age of twenty-five (1950-1956). From his arrival it was known that his passion was evangelism and church planting. By 1957 he was a licensed minister, and was ordained in 1964.

After a successful twenty years of evangelism and church planting in the UK, he immigrated to Canada in 1976 and successfully organised churches in Montreal and Ottawa (Bilingual-speaking cities). To enable him to communicate effectively with the French-speaking Canadians, Dr. McIntyre undertook the task of learning to speak French.[151]

---

151 NTCG History. Dr. Jeremiah McIntyre. https://ntcg.org.uk/about/history/dr-jeremiah-mcintyre/ Accessed on October 19, 2019.

In September of 1974, **Pastor Blake** came to Canada from his native Jamaica. He had been content to lead his congregation in the Parish of Trelawny. "I had no intention to travel." He was encouraged to visit Canada by a ministerial colleague **Pastor Moncrieffe** who had first migrated to England, lived there for several years, and then migrated to Canada. Meeting Pastor Blake while on a brief visit to Jamaica, Moncrieffe encouraged him to come to Canada. Pastor Moncrieffe initiated the formal invitation

Bishop Canute Blake

to facilitate Pastor Blake's migration and made arrangements for his interim accommodation.

Pastor Moncrieffe welcomed Pastor Blake upon his arrived in Montreal and provided him with temporary residence at his own home. Shortly after settling in, Pastor Blake recognized two problems that he thought he could do something about. First, he came to realize that Canada was not the Christian country he had envisaged, and so he thought about the many opportunities to evangelize. Then he recognized that there were many migrants from the Caribbean living in Montreal who regularly attended Church; however, they felt some level of discomfort in the church environments that were available to them. Hence Pastor Blake saw the opportunity to establish places of worship that would be more amenable to Caribbean immigrants. During the time when he was familiarizing himself with his new country, he met Ethel Adams who would later become his wife. These three factors solidified his desire to remain in Canada. Pastor Blake went back to Jamaica to close out his personal affairs and once this task completed, returned to Montreal and embarked on the mission of evangelism working with Rev. McIntyre.

Rev. Blake then became the Associate Pastor at Rev. McIntyre's Church in Montreal and while in this role, Rev. McIntyre expanded his outreach to establish the Ottawa Church of God. Rev. Blake was then given the responsibility to pastor the new Church in Ottawa where he remained as the Senior Pastor of the Ottawa Church of God for approximately 19 years. During this period, the Church experienced tremendous growth from its early beginnings, through to its Wellington Street location, and ultimately to the current location at 1820 Carling Avenue.

Health Care

Physicians

Dr. Garth Taylor

Garth Alfred Taylor, the brilliant, humble, outspoken, kind-hearted, and generous ophthalmologist and humanitarian was born in Jamaica on April 29, 1944. He died in November 2005 after emergency surgery at the Ottawa Heart Institute. He had taken his skills to more than 40 countries, where he treated thousands of patients and trained many doctors and surgeons. The ophthalmologist who lived and worked in Cornwall, Ontario, joined Orbis, the new flying eye hospital, as a volunteer who was committed to curing blindness and eye diseases in developing countries. Two years later, he became president of Orbis Canada, focusing on eliminating preventable blindness around the world. Orbis Flying Eye Hospital converted a DC-10 with a high-tech mobile surgeon suite and lecture theatre, as the world's only airborne eye hospital and training facility. At the time of his death, Dr. Taylor had completed 111 missions with Orbis, the last being to China. He trained many doctors and surgeons in cornea, cataract, and refractive procedures, including the treatment of ocular parasites.

Orbis is an international non-profit humanitarian agency[152] that grew from a vision that Houston ophthalmologist David Patton had established. The current president of Orbis Canada, the famous Ottawa retina surgeon, Dr. Brian Leonard, who interned with Dr. Taylor at Ottawa Civic Hospital, said,

> "We considered him a legend. No one knew more about global blindness. The ORBIS team is devastated by the loss of our dear friend and colleague. Dr. Taylor gave his life completely to the service of others. A humanitarian, Dr. Taylor truly embodied the spirit of ORBIS, working tirelessly so that no human being should be needlessly blind. He will be greatly missed. On behalf of the ORBIS family around the globe, we extend our deepest sympathies to Dr. Taylor's family and loved ones." [153]

---

152 Orbis Canada. www.orbis.org Accessed on August 12, 2019.
153 ibid.

According to the World Population Clock there are about 8 billion people[154] on the planet; the WHO estimates that there are 135 million with low vision: 90% of the world's blind live in developing countries, with nine million in India, six million in China, and seven million in Africa.[155] Dr. Taylor was convinced that as much as 80% of global blindness is avoidable – 60% treatable and 20% preventable. He repeatedly said, "Tell me and I will forget; show me and I may remember; involve me and I will understand."

In 1976, after becoming the first Black ophthalmologist to graduate from Queens University, he became a pioneer in cornea transplants and laser-eye surgery. Soon he became Chief of Ophthalmology at Cornwall Community Hospital and a lecturer at Queens University. After joining Orbis and volunteering in the third world, he recruited other Canadians as volunteer surgeons and staff.

He was also a co-founder of CanSEE Surgical Eye Expeditions, the Canadian arm of the eye-aid agency, and used to donate a week of his time annually with the Canadian National Institute for the Blind's Eye. For his contribution to international ophthalmology, Dr. Taylor received many awards and distinction including the Meritorious Service Cross of Canada, the Paul Harris Fellow Medal from Rotary International, the Harry Jerome Award from the Black Business and Professional Association of Toronto, the Jackie Robinson Award from the Montreal Association of Black Business Persons and Professionals, and the Lifetime Achievement Award from the Academy of Ophthalmic Education. Most notably, Dr. Taylor was named at the top of *Maclean's* magazine's Honour Role in July 2004 and was awarded the prestigious Order of Jamaica in 2005.

In Dr. Taylor's words,

"I found my nirvana 23 years ago aboard my first ORBIS flight... By treating avoidable blindness, people don't just get back their sight, they get back their self-esteem and their respect through their ability to act as society expects... Nothing is more important than what we are able to do for patients through our combined efforts as participants in the ORBIS sight-saving program."[156]

154 Worldometers. World Population Clock. https://www.worldometers.info/world-population Accessed on November 23, 2022
155 World Health Organisation. Up to 45 Million Blind People Globally---and-Growing. https://www.who.int/news/item/09-10-2003-up-to-45-million-blind-people-globally---and-growing Accessed on August 12, 2019.
156 Orbis Canada. www.orbis.org Accessed on August 12, 2019.

Before his death, he mentioned to his friends that one simple letter from a patient touched him deeply, "I write this letter to you because prior to meeting you, I could not see to write."

For his outstanding service to international ophthalmology and humanity, Dr. Taylor (1944-2005) has truly left an extraordinary legacy. But for Dr. Taylor, these accomplishments were simply part of his calling:

> "Until I have a breath to breathe, I will continue to do this because I think I was chosen for this, not for money, not for compensation, but just to make the quality of life of my fellow human being better. That's all I ask." [157]

The task of treating and preventing blindness around the world remains with humanitarians like Dr. Taylor, who relentlessly dedicated his time, skills, and kindness to the dream of bringing vision to the world.

"I came into this world with nothing, and all I'm going to leave with is my conscience."[158]

Sports Medicine

Dr. Rudolph (Rudy) Gittens
Dec. 30, 1932 – Sept. 18, 2013

Born in Trinidad and Tobago, **Rudolph (Rudy) Gittens** arrived in Saskatchewan, Canada in 1953 as a student at the age of 21. He went on to obtain pharmaceutical and medical degrees from the University of Saskatchewan. He also held a fellowship in orthopaedics at the University of Ottawa.

Dr. Rudy Gittens served as team doctor for the Ottawa Rough Riders Football team for more than 20 years before taking the same role with Canada's national soccer teams in 1984. The legendary sports medicine physician, also known in Ottawa for his work with the Ottawa 67s Hockey Club, was inducted into the Soccer Hall of Fame in 2007. Gittens was team doctor for the Canada national team that won CONCACAF[159] championships in 1985 and 2000.[160] He was also a member of

---

157 Orbis Canada. www.orbis.org
158 Dr. Taylor's godfather Garth Taylor: A heroic Fighter Against Global Blindness - By The Ambassadors Research Foundation. Orbis Canada. www.orbis.org Accessed on November 23, 2022.

the CONCACAF Hall of Fame, and worked as a volunteer leading the Canadian Soccer Association Medical Committee for more than 20 years.

"[Dr. Gittens was the] head of the Canadian Soccer Association's sports medicine committee, [and was] part of the [FIFA and Biokinetics start heading research] team to direct the clinical aspects of the work. For many years, he [had] been a strong proponent of involving more disciplines in the understanding of injury in sports."[161]

Internationally, Gittens served on sports medical committees, including committees for the Atlanta 1996 Olympic Football Tournament, the FIFA Women's World Cup USA 1999 and three successive FIFA World Cups from 1998. In 2007, he was the general medical officer for the FIFA U-20 World Cup Canada, which was held in six cities across Canada including Ottawa.[162]

Family Medicine

In 1958, **Horace Clayton Alexis** migrated to Canada from Trinidad with $200 in his pocket and one goal – to become a doctor. Dr. Alexis practised family medicine for more than 40 years, but never forgot his roots or the sacrifices he made to reach his goal. In fact, his own challenges, and the difficult times he faced in those earlier years led him to create the Black Canadian Scholarship Fund (BCSF), one of his proudest achievements. The goal of the BCSF is to help promising Black students in financial need attend university. To date, more than $200,000 in scholarships has been awarded to some 40 students.

Dr. Horace Alexis (BA, MD)
May 6, 1931 -February 7, 2019
(Black Ottawa Scene)

The premise behind the scholarship is that providing someone with the means to get an education, we create a ripple effect that has a positive impact on

159 CONCACAF refers to the Confederation of North, Central America and Caribbean Association Football . https://www.concacaf.com/ Accessed on November 24, 2022.
160 FIFA. FIFA and Biokinetics Start Heading Research.
https://www.fifa.com/development/news/y=2002/m=3/news=fifa-and-biokinetics-start-heading-research-81587.html Accessed on August 12, 2018.
161 Canada Soccer. Profiles. https://www.canadasoccer.com/profile/?id=1307 Accessed on August 12, 2019.
162 Ottawa 67's. SEPTEMBER 20, 2013 67's Mourn The Loss of Rudy Gittens http://ottawa67s.com/ Accessed on March 23, 2023.

generations to come — something Dr. Alexis has experienced firsthand within his own extended family.

The capital fund, initially endowed with a $5,000 gift from Dr. Alexis in 1996, is now worth a healthy half million dollars. The far-reaching impact of the BCSF is due in great part to Dr. Alexis himself, who struggled to ensure the survival of his scholarship, at times against great odds.

Recognized for his involvement in the community, he has put his talent and skills to work over the years to help ensure the success of many other projects and organizations, including the Victorian Order of Nurses Canada, the James R. Johnston Chair in Black Canadian Studies at Dalhousie University, the Community Foundation of Ottawa, and The Trinidad & Tobago Association of Ottawa.

The University of Ottawa is proud to recognize a community leader who knows so well the vital role education plays in building a better future.[163]

"Dr. Horace Alexis, founder and chairman of the Black Canadian Scholarship Fund, yearned to help young people reach their full potential, thanks to his experiences in Canada."[164]

When Dr. Horace Alexis set up practice in Ottawa in the early 1970s, multicultural meant English and French. There wasn't much room for a Black physician who'd grown up dirt poor in Trinidad. Prejudice was a part of daily life.

"That made him stronger," said his wife, Christiane Millet-Alexis. "Instead of being angry and bitchy, he said, 'We're going to do something.' He believed in action. He did not believe in bitterness."

Alexis, one of the first Black graduates from the University of Ottawa medical school, a tireless supporter of Ottawa's Black community and founder of the Black Canadian Scholarship Fund[165], died on February 7, 2019. He was 87.

"He led the path for the rest of us," said Rachel Décoste, a software engineer, author and motivational speaker, whose family was among Alexis' huge roster of patients.

"He gave us a model of a life lived, not just for himself, but to give back," she said. "I try to emulate it myself."

Horace Clayton Alexis was born May 6, 1931, in Trinidad. He was a brilliant student, who graduated high school at age 16 and dreamed of being a doctor like

---

163 University of Ottawa. Awards of Excellence. https://www.uottawa.ca/alumni/awards-excellence/award-community-service Accessed on August 14, 2019.

164 Suzanne Bird / Suzanne Bird - The Ottawa Sun August 24, 2019.

165 Black Canadian Scholarship Fund. http://bcsf.ca/ Accessed on August 24, 2019.

his older brother, Carlton. But the family being poor, Alexis went to work instead, spinning records as a DJ on Radio Trinidad.

He was 27 when he was finally able to immigrate to Canada where he enrolled in pre-med studies at the University of Ottawa. To make ends meet, he worked nights in the post office and weekends with a moving company.

After graduation, he ended up in Petrolia, Ontario, where he set up his first family practice. Alexis' decision to set up practice after his internship ended was met with opposition. "There was a petition to run him out of town because a Black doctor in the 1960s wasn't welcomed,"[166] said software engineer and motivational speaker Rachel Decoste who was born and raised in Ottawa. A petition circulated pressuring him to leave. He refused. Instead, he went to work bettering the community. His practice grew, he was named Chief of Staff at the local hospital and became head of a local credit union.

When he left to return to Ottawa in 1974, moving his children closer to the university, another petition was circulated, this time begging him to stay.

"It was the proudest moment of my life," he told the Ottawa Citizen in 2008.

"After people got to know him, they didn't see his colour anymore," Millet-Alexis said. "They just saw a very competent doctor."

Alexis set up his first Ottawa practice on Sunnyside Avenue before moving to Main Street. He was soon the go-to doctor for many Black families in Ottawa.

"In the '70s and '80s, there were no studies that proved that medical services were rendered differently according to race," Décoste said.

> "But local minorities knew. That's why almost every Black person in town was his patient. He provided culturally attuned care decades before it became a buzz word....You knew that unless you were the first patient of the day, you had a half-hour, or an hour wait. He had more demand than there were hours in the day."[167]

Dr. Alexis loved being a general practitioner. "We get to see everything," he said; and his caring manner and sense of humour made him popular with his patients.

---

166 Ron Fanfair. Dr. Horace Alexis has left lasting legacy. https://www.ronfanfair.com/home/2019/3/6/yfqmv0jjdd1o8kromid586rdrrdrn7 Accessed on August 24, 2018.
167 Idem.

"He had such a positive attitude, even patients with a dramatic condition he would make them laugh," Millet-Alexis said. "You could hear his laugh all the way to the elevator." Dr. Alexis closed his practice in 2004.[168]

Forensic Psychiatry

Dr. Shirley Brathwaite

Dr. Shirley Brathwaite arrived in Ottawa in the summer of 1974. Born in Barbados where she received her early education, she had first worked as a teacher before completing her medical degree at the University of the West Indies (Mona Campus) in Kingston, Jamaica. After completing her studies at Mona, she decided to specialize in psychiatry; the University of Toronto accepted her application. However, the circumstances at that time prevented her from heading off to Toronto. Returning to Barbados, she worked at what was then called 'The Mental' Hospital.

Soon after she began practicing in Barbados, she re-applied to the University of Toronto and also applied to the University of Ottawa. Ottawa responded first with a letter of acceptance. She would begin her specialization, through the University of Ottawa, first at the Ottawa General Hospital then located on Bruyere Street in the Byward Market. The General Hospital was founded in 1845. In 1947 "a clinical teaching program was set up with the University of Ottawa"; and later during the 1950s, "the General Hospital was the first to be affiliated with the University of Ottawa, School of Medicine."[169]

Dr. Brathwaite talked about her initial experience upon arrival in Ottawa.

"I had been told that Ottawa is cold six months of the year. But my first summer, it was good. I had the interesting experience of being hosted by someone that I did not know, someone that I only met when I arrived at the airport."

One of her friends had planned for a Canadian lady to receive and host her. Dr. Brathwaite was very impressed by the very warm reception that she received

---

168 The Ottawa Citizen. B Crawford. https://ottawacitizen.com/author/bcrawford10 Accessed on August 24, 2018.
169 *Wikipedia*. The Ottawa General Hospital.
https://en.wikipedia.org/wiki/Ottawa_General_Hospital Accessed on July 5, 2018.

from this lady to whom she was a complete stranger. Before the end of her first week, one of the diplomats at the Barbados High Commission had invited her to go to a cricket match at the Governor-General's cricket grounds. And immediately upon her arrival she saw two people that she knew from her neighbourhood in Barbados. Their aunt had been Dr. Brathwaite's next-door neighbor, and she knew the family very well. But she did not know that these two brothers and their sister were here in Ottawa. Suffice to say that she was very pleased when she discovered her two Barbadian counterparts on the cricket grounds. She knew of one other Barbadian, who lived in Ottawa; she contacted the woman who was a nurse at the Ottawa Civic hospital, was invited to her home for dinner, and provided with salient advice on where she might choose to live.

Her initial residence was on Wilbrod Street, and she was able to walk to the General Campus several blocks away. However, she was surprised by the prevalence of the French language within the work environment. As far as Dr. Brathwaite can recall, at that time she was the only Caribbean working at the General Hospital.

After completing her first year at the General Campus, Dr. Brathwaite went to the Royal Ottawa Hospital (ROH) on Carling Avenue to continue her specialization training. The ROH, a full Psychiatric Hospital, enabled Shirley to discover the emerging branch of Forensic Psychiatry. After resolving a number of obstacles, she became the first Forensic Psychiatry resident in Ottawa.

During the early stage of her Forensic Psychiatry practice, Dr. Brathwaite was asked to sit on the Ontario Lieutenant Governor's Review Board, later renamed the Ontario Review Board (ORB). The Ontario Review Board (the 'Board') has jurisdiction over individuals who have been found by a court to be either unfit to stand trial or not criminally responsible on account of mental disorder.

> "The Board is an independent tribunal established pursuant to the Criminal Code of Canada which stipulates that each province and territory must establish or designate a Review Board to oversee these individuals. Individuals subject to the jurisdiction of the Ontario Review Board are referred to in the Criminal Code of Canada as 'accused'."[170]

Indeed, Dr. Brathwaite was the first person of colour to sit on this review board that served a very critical role in the criminal justice system. And a person of colour appearing before the Board would have a sense that at least one of the

---

170 Ontario Review Board. http://www.orb.on.ca/scripts/en/about.asp Accessed on August 27, 2018

reviewers could be more in tune with his or her situation. The ORB process outlined below explains the nature of the work Dr. Brathwaite performed in this role.

> If a client has been found to be unfit to stand trial or not criminally responsible, the client must appear before the Ontario Review Board (ORB) and receive orders. The process is comparable to appearing before a judge. An ORB hearing consists of a panel of professionals and may include the following: psychiatrists, psychologists, lawyers, community members, and retired judges. This panel is responsible for making decisions regarding the client's current situation and status. This can include making decisions regarding the level of security that the client requires, and the client's community privileges.
>
> A client will have his or her first ORB hearing within 45 to 90 days of being admitted to the forensic mental health system. In general, the client and his or her lawyer attend one ORB hearing per year. At the hearing, the panel will receive evidence and testimonies from the clients the client's lawyers, the client's psychiatrist, other specialists, and other appropriate people, such as family members. The panel will receive a hospital report, which details the client's history and progress in the forensic mental health facility. This includes a risk assessment, which determines the client's potential threat of violence or harm to the public and/or themselves.
>
> The ORB panel would then make decisions based on a majority vote regarding the client's status for the upcoming year in the form of a disposition. Unlike a jail sentence, clients of the forensic mental health system do not have a predetermined release date. They remain in the system until they are no longer considered a public threat, which could be indefinitely. It considers the client's risk to the community, his or her progress over the past year, the prospective outcomes of the client's return to society, and additional factors that are unique to that client's case. Following the panel's decision, the client does have an opportunity to appeal the decision. If a client decides to pursue an appeal, he or she would have to develop a case with his or her lawyer to demonstrate that the panel's decision was unfair or unwarranted.[171]

Dr. Brathwaite's primary professional practice was as a Forensic Psychiatrist at the Royal Ottawa Hospital (ROH) which is affiliated with the University of Ottawa. She also held the position of Assistant Professor at the University of Ottawa. In her role at the Royal Ottawa, she provided consultation services to the

---

171 Forensic Mental Health. https://forensicot.weebly.com/ontario-review-board-orb.html Accessed on August 27, 2018.

courts, to lawyers and to the Ministry of Corrections of Ontario, the latter through assessing and treating inmates held at the local detention centre.

Dr. Brathwaite also became socially active, primarily within the Barbados-Ottawa community. She became a member of the Barbados-Ottawa Association and later served as President. She was an Executive Committee member of the National Council of Barbadian Associations in Canada. She participated actively in the Harambee organization, starting at its inception and working through to the end of its existence, and served on the Hard to Serve Children's Committee of Ottawa, and on other community boards such as the Ottawa Community Immigrant Services Organization (OCISO). She was a member of Third World Players, and is also very active in her Church, holding positions as a Synod Representative, as a Rector's Warden, and was the first Black, Indigenous and People of Colour (BIPOC) Coordinator.

Quite a number of the early Caribbean immigrants to Ottawa spoke of their encounter with racial incidents, and Dr. Brathwaite was no exception. She had her own encounters within her work environment, one where she was overlooked for an assignment for which she knew categorically that, in comparison to her counterparts, she was the closest fit. In 2011 she was honored by the University of the West Indies with the Doctor of Science (Honoris Causa) degree.

> "In 1992 Dr. Brathwaite was awarded the Commemorative Medal celebrating the 125th anniversary of Canada's confederation. In 2009, she established the Dr. Shirley Brathwaite Foundation to support African-Canadian children at risk."[172]

Her community service has also been recognized by the province of Ontario.

Ottawa Children's Hospital

Carrol Pitters arrived in Ottawa in September 1970 to reunite with her family who had migrated to Canada previously. The family migration process started shortly after her mother, Mrs. Maud Pitters, came to visit her sister who had migrated to Ottawa earlier. Carrol's aunt convinced her mother that Ottawa could provide the Pitters family with great opportunities for their five children, Carrol being the eldest.

---

172 University of the West Indies (UWI), Campus News. Regional University names twenty Honorary Graduands. https://sta.uwi.edu/news/releases/release.asp?id=818 Accessed on August 27, 2018.

Dr. Carrol Pitters, Chief of Staff, Children's Hospital of Eastern Ontario. (Black Ottawa Scene)

Mrs. Pitters remained in Ottawa and within several months her husband Glen arrived with the two youngest siblings, Glenor and Blair, leaving the three older children behind in Jamaica to complete their current year of high school.

Although Carrol had some apprehension about coming to a new country, she was also excited to reconnect with her family. Once in Ottawa, her first impression was the cold weather, and the density of the housing. When she took the bus two weeks later to start her first year at the University of Ottawa, she immediately realized that she was the lone Black person on the bus and was conscious that this was the first time in her life when she found herself in an extreme racial minority situation. "It felt really strange about being the only Black person on the bus." Once she reached the University, and trying to find her way around, she suddenly saw another Jamaican student whom she knew very well. Although she knew that Hal Pape was in Ottawa, she had no idea that they would re-connect under those circumstances.

Hal immediately connected Carrol to a network of Caribbean students who attended the University of Ottawa and other learning institutions in Ottawa. Making the transition into the University culture was relatively easy. On the academic side, Carrol had not yet fixed her gaze on pursuing a career in medicine. And even though she liked sciences she was not planning to become a doctor. However, she was encouraged by one of her mentors to apply to the University of the West Indies after it occurred to her that proceeding to get entry into the Canadian medical schools was very difficult. She was accepted at the UWI. She completed Medical School and her internship, and then returned to Ottawa after a period of six years. Her plan was to complete a Pediatric residency, which she completed at the Children's Hospital of Eastern Ontario (CHEO). Following this she studied another year in Epidemiology and Community Medicine at the University of Ottawa.

Carrol went back to Jamaica to look for work in Pediatrics with the mindset that this was where she should serve. Ultimately, this return was especially disappointing, since she had earlier turned down an offer from CHEO to pursue a job opportunity in Jamaica. Returning to Ottawa, CHEO's offer for work was still open. On July 1st 1985, Dr. Pitters began her career in earnest at the Emergency Ward. Dr. Pitters worked in the Emergency Ward at CHEO for approximately two years, and was then promoted to Associate Director of the Emergency Department. In this role, she acted as the Chief in the current Chief's absence.

> "After serving as Associate Director of the Emergency Department for four years, she was appointed Medical Director and Chief of Emergency Medicine in 1996, a position she held for ten years. She then became the Chair of the Board of the Children's Hospital Academic Medical Organization (CHAMO). In 2010 Dr. Pitters was appointed Chief of Staff. As CHEO's senior physician leader, she is responsible for organizing the activities of the medical staff and for ensuring the quality of clinical care and patient safety. In this role, she reports directly to the Board of Trustees."[173]

Dr. Pitters continued in this role until her retirement in 2018, while also assuming a number of ancillary roles; she chaired the board of the Children's Hospital Academic Medical Organization (CHAMO), and advocated for Emergency Physicians among others.

> "Dr. Carrol Pitters was honoured with the Health Sciences Award for Excellence at the 33rd Annual Black Business and Professional Association (BBPA) Harry Jerome Awards held on Saturday, April 25, 2015, at the Metro Toronto Convention Centre.
>
> The BBPA Harry Jerome Awards is recognized as the most prestigious national awards gala in the African Canadian community and a coveted symbol of achievement. That year's winners received awards in the following categories: Academics, Athletics, Media, Entertainment, Community Service, Diversity, Health Sciences, Leadership, Lifetime Achievement, Young Entrepreneurs, Professional Excellence, Public Advocacy, Youth Advocacy, Social Engagement and the President's Award."[174]

---

173 Rotary Club of Ottawa Bytown. Chief of Medical Staff at the Children's Hospital of Eastern Ontario 2018.https://portal.clubrunner.ca/1101/speakers/1b870168-bcee-49f9-be8b-0e5396f16626 Accessed on July 7.
174 Black Ottawa Scene. Dr. Carrol Pitters receives Black Business & Professional Association award for excellence. http://blackottawascene.com/dr-carrol-pitters-receives-black-business-professional-association-award-for-excellence/ Accessed on July 7, 2018.

Nurses

Caribbean immigrants in pursuit of nursing careers began to arrive in Ottawa during the mid-1950s around the same time as the Caribbean domestic workers. One of the daughters of the earliest Caribbean immigrant in Ottawa was a pioneer in the nursing profession.

Nessa Brown, RN

Nessa (Blossom) Brown, immigrated to Ottawa in 1954 to be reunified with her mother Estelle, her father Herbert (Pops) Brown and two other siblings. Nessa came to Canada with family – husband Ven Bedward and two sons, Marvin and Dane, some fifteen years after her father immigrated to Canada. Nessa's initial impression was that "Ottawa was very quiet." Ottawa was not well developed. It was a very small town. "The streetcars stopped at Holland and Carling." This point was virtually the outer city limits going west.

At that time nurses received their training at hospitals that offered nurse training programs. The Civic Hospital on Carling Avenue and the Saint-Vincent Hospital on Cambridge Street were two Ottawa hospitals that offered such programs. In 1955 when Nessa entered the nursing program at the Civic Hospital, there was no other Caribbean nurse at that facility. At around the same time another Jamaican immigrant would arrive in Ottawa to study nursing at the Saint-Vincent Hospital. These are two of the earliest Caribbean immigrants to study and practice nursing in Ottawa.

Making the transition into this quiet environment was smooth, given that she was in the midst of family. She was able to secure her first job as a trainee nurse at the Civic Hospital in 1955, the year after arrival. "It was not comfortable working there." She was required to complete a nine-month training program. But at the five-month juncture, she became pregnant with her third child. And when this became known, she was promptly terminated. "Those were the days when if you were a nurse, you were not allowed to work if you were pregnant." Once her son was born, she decided to move across the river from Hull where she had been living with her family to the Ottawa side. But she could not find a decent place to rent "because of my colour". So she and her family remained at her parent's residence in Hull.

Following the birth of her child, Nessa elected to return to the Civic Hospital, not as a nurse trainee but as a Nurse's Aide. She worked nights for $35/week and saved all her earnings. Throughout her early tenure at the Civic hospital, she could not recall encountering another Black person. Based on her interactions with co-workers, she concluded that none of them had any knowledge or experience with Black people, so she gave them a pass whenever they would make ridiculous comments. It was not until 1968 that she encountered the first Black nurse at the hospital. This nurse, (late) Isis Officer, was trained in the UK and signalled the onset of foreign-trained Black nurses in Ottawa.

Previously a bookkeeper in Jamaica, **Ven Bedard**, Nessa's husband, secured a job at Colonial Furniture where he worked until he retired. The couple soon found that they had the financial resources to purchase their first home, a bungalow on Shillington Avenue.

In 1960 **Sally St. Louis** left her native Island of Dominica to study nursing in the UK. She "had a travel bug while growing up" and concluded that she would use her nursing profession as a way to travel and work in different countries. Sally completed her nursing program in midwifery, and because her plan was to go to Kenya, Africa to practice nursing, she also completed a diploma in Tropical Medicine. But there was political conflict and a period of high uncertainty in Kenya at the time, so she travelled to Australia instead. Her plans to work in Australia also hit a roadblock; she could only be admitted to work as a visitor and not a Landed Immigrant. Hence

Sally St. Louis - RN

would not be able to work in that country. Sally then turned her attention to Canada. Her visit to the Canadian embassy proved to be much more accepting; she would be able to immigrate to Canada and also obtain a Landed Immigrant Status after her arrival.

Sally sailed on a ship bound for Quebec City. Her final destination was Hamilton Ontario where her cousin who had immigrated to Canada earlier would host her. There was such a dire need for trained nurses in Canada at the time of her arrival, that she had no problems finding a job. She was immediately hired at the Hamilton General Hospital where she began her nursing career. Sally's transition was relatively easy for her, since "the hospital environment was just like the one in England". But in the mid-1960s, the social environment in Hamilton vis-a-vis demographics was similar to that of many other Canadian cities in that there were very few blacks at that time.

She worked at the Hamilton General for approximately 18 months and then moved to the Chedoke Hospital. Towards the end of her second year at the Chedoke Hospital, Sally met another nurse who worked in northern Canada during the summertime. Captivated by the prospect of working with the Inuit community, she decided that she too would head north for her next venture. After contacting Health Canada (then Health and Welfare), she was hired to go to Northern Manitoba as a nurse. After two years she went much further north to work in Igloolik,

> "an Inuit hamlet in Foxe Basin, Qikiqtaaluk Region in Nunavut, northern Canada. Because its location on Igloolik Island is close to Melville Peninsula, it is often mistakenly thought to be on the peninsula."[175]

After working for several years in the north, Sally and a friend Marylyn Karpa decided to travel across Canada. They rented a car, loaded it up with camping gear and headed west to Vancouver. Then they set their sights to go east and drove across the country, staying at camping grounds, eventually arriving at Prince Edward Island. They headed back to Saskatchewan where the cross-Canada journey started some six months earlier, and returned to her nursing job with Health Canada. Sally spent most of her nursing career working with Inuit and Indian communities in northern Canada. She later worked and then volunteered with the Red Cross organization resulting in her being awarded the Order of the Red Cross as well as an award from the Federal Public Service for her exemplary service.

Her tenure as in-field Inuit nursing ended when the Health Canada Director for Indian affairs called her to Ottawa to fill an administrative role which she executed until she took early retirement from the Federal Government in order to continue volunteering with the Red Cross. Sally had always volunteered with the Red Cross during her work life. She was a member of the Regional Council, the governance body for the Red Cross, and was later dispatched to serve on

---

175 *Wikipedia*. Igloolik. https://en.wikipedia.org/wiki/Igloolik Accessed on August 10, 2018.

international missions in Yugoslavia and Tanzania. Her only regret was that she was unable to stay on the front lines with the Inuit communities much longer.

Lorraine Waugh was also a student nurse who immigrated early to Ottawa from the Caribbean. She left her native Jamaica during the mid-1950s to enter the nurse training program at the St. Vincent Hospital, located on Cambridge Street in Ottawa. During that time, nurses received their training within a hospital setting, and Lorraine was one of a very small group of Caribbean nurses to gain admittance to a nurse training program in Ottawa.

Once her training completed, she continued to work as a nurse at St. Vincent and a few years later, after receiving her Landed Immigrant Status, she started to sponsor a number of her family members. Her younger brother, **Herbie Waugh,** was one of her sponsored family members to arrive in Ottawa. Herbie had been a police officer in Jamaica and after taking up residence in Ottawa, he joined the Ottawa Police Force. He was the first black police officer in the Ottawa Police Service, and although his tenure was not very long, it is clear that he pried the doors open and paved the way for the succeeding black police officers that are so obvious as a part of the local police force.

A second wave of Caribbean immigrant nurses would arrive in Ottawa more than a decade later. By the early to mid-1970s, several Caribbean immigrants who had been trained as nurses in the United Kingdom immigrated to Ottawa. By this time, the nurse training programs were more formalized, and the colleges and Universities had begun to offer Degree and Diploma certifications in Nursing. The nursing profession became more open to Immigrants and many of the Caribbean immigrants took advantage of this opportunity. Those who were trained in the United Kingdom found that they had to re-certify in order to obtain a license to practice in Canada, and a number of them proceeded with the re-certification program which entailed additional university or college courses.

Elaine Skeete - RN

Shortly after completing High School in 1957, **Elaine Skeete** left her native island of Barbados to join her older brother and his family in the UK. She enrolled in the nursing program at the

Hospital in Coventry and successfully completed her RN certification in 1963. She moved to nearby Reading to take up a position as a nurse and continued in this role until 1970 when she left the UK for Canada. During her time in the UK Elaine married John Skeete a childhood friend whom she knew from grade school and the couple had two boys.

With encouragement from her cousin Joyce Williams who lived in Toronto, Elaine decided to move the family to Canada. Their initial intention was to head for Toronto, but John's sister Eulene Clark lived in Ottawa. And from their discussion with the immigration officer, they learned that there were many opportunities for nurses in Ottawa. So the family decided to move to Ottawa. They arrived on May 25, 1970, and almost immediately, Elaine was hired by the Ottawa General Hospital, located on Bruyere Street at that time.

Once on the job, she found that the Ontario College of Nurses' Policy did not recognize her RN certification from the UK. She would need to take additional courses and pass the College of Nurses Certification exam in order to work as a registered nurse in Ontario. Although she thought that this was not right, she decided to continue working as a graduate nurse, and to find a way to get the College of Nurses to come around to her point of view. Elaine enlisted her MP, Michael Cassidy and after a five-year battle, the College of Nurses agreed to allow her to take the RN Certification Exam without having to take pre-requisite courses. She passed the exam and was able to register as an RN in Ontario. Elaine continued to practice nursing at the Ottawa Hospital through the transition from the downtown campus to the new facilities on Smyth Road. She was ultimately promoted to Team Lead on the Orthopaedic ward at the General and she executed this role up until her retirement.

Mitsy Guillaume – RN

Mitsy Guillaume and her husband Ted moved to Ottawa in 1976 after having lived in Nebraska for a short period after Ted completed his degree in Education. The couple, who had met in Haiti, were married in 1971, and she immigrated to Montreal in 1972. Shortly after arriving in Ottawa, Mitsy secured a job as an office administrator for a company in Gatineau; she worked in this position for a short period. Since she had been trained as a bookkeeper in Haiti, she registered with a Manpower organization and had a number of temporary book-keeping assignments. Deciding to enrol in the Nursing program at Algonquin College, she completed her nursing program, and was hired by the Ottawa General Hospital, located at 43 Bruyère Street downtown Ottawa. The General Hospital was relocated to its current site at 501 Smyth in 1980. Mitsy practiced nursing at this facility for several decades until she retired.

Avril Tulloch had immigrated to Ottawa Canada from the UK after she completed her training at the Harrogate General Hospital in Yorkshire England. She had graduated from St. Hugh's High School in Kingston Jamaica, worked for a few years at Scotia Bank, and then went to the United Kingdom to study nursing. She graduated as a Registered Nurse in 1975, and shortly after her marriage to Dave Tulloch (Author) she immigrated to join him in Ottawa.

Avril Tulloch, RN

Within weeks after her arrival she obtained employment with the City of Ottawa, working as a graduate nurse at the Island Lodge facility. At that time Ontario required that all foreign-trained nurses obtain re-certification in Ontario before they could apply for a provincial nursing license. Avril enrolled at Algonquin College to complete the requirements mandated by the Ontario College of Nurses, and in 1976 was granted her Ontario Nursing License.

Avril secured a nursing position at the Ottawa General Hospital, and after her arrival on the job she found that there were a handful of predominantly British-trained Nurses at the General. Avril worked at the Ottawa General Hospital for just over twenty years. She started as a staff nurse, was soon promoted to Nursing Supervisor, and then Clinical Nurse Coordinator. She also completed a Bachelor of Arts in Psychology (BA. Psych.) as well as a Bachelor of Science in Nursing (BSc. N). She later resigned her position at the Ottawa General to manage the medical unit at a psychiatric hospital for the State of North Carolina in the US. During this period, she pursued post-graduate studies towards an MSc in Nursing Administration.

Media, Public Service and Community

Ewart and Merle Walters
At 4th Avenue Baptist Church
Ottawa 2008

Ewart Walters is one of those people who cannot be pigeon-holed into any one category. A graduate of Calabar High School for Boys in Kingston, Jamaica, he was one of the earlier Caribbean students to have been awarded a scholarship by the Canadian government to study in Ottawa.

"Calabar High School is an all-male secondary school in Kingston, Jamaica. It was established by the Jamaica Baptist Union in 1912 for the children of Baptist ministers. It was named after the Kalabari Kingdom later anglicized by the British to Calabar, in present-day Nigeria. It has produced at least five Rhodes Scholars, and is respected for its outstanding performance in track and field."[176]

Ewart arrived in Ottawa in September 1964 to begin his studies in Journalism at Carleton University. Canada's External Aid Office enabled students from the Caribbean and other countries to advance their education as part of its mandate to assist developing countries.

"In 1968, CIDA (the Canadian International Development Agency) succeeded the External Aid Office, the agency through which Canada had directed official aid to poorer 'developing' countries since 1950."[177]

At boarding school, the making of the man was evident through scouting, literature, drama, cricket, swimming, football, singing, and the Student Christian Movement. Leaving school he worked in teaching and the civil service for a few years before entering journalism as a reporter on the weekly newspaper Public Opinion, where he learned just about everything about news and newspaper production. The paper closed after the first year, and he was hired by the much larger Daily Gleaner. There he was presented with a cross-section of life that can

---

176 *Wikipedia.* Calabar High School. https://en.wikipedia.org/wiki/Calabar_High_School Accessed on November 25, 2022

177 Publications Canada: Political and Social Affairs Division. Aid to Developing Countries. http://www.publications.gc.ca/Collection-R/LoPBdP/CIR/7916-e.htm#abrieftxt Accessed on November 25, 2022.

only be experienced by covering stories in Parliament, the courts, the education system, the church, and in the various and widely differing parts of the country where people and mores vary. This was supported by a home grounding from parents who were primary schoolteachers and deacons in the Baptist Church.

While at the Gleaner, Ewart saw an advertisement for a journalism scholarship to 'a Canadian university'. His 'key points' (close friends) had already emigrated for studies at Howard University in the USA but he had set his mind on Canada and embraced this opportunity immediately, applying for the scholarship and obtaining it. Ewart, en route to Ottawa and Carleton University with Claude Robinson, his schoolmate and colleague, arrived in Toronto on an early September evening in 1964 — the temperature a deceivingly balmy 55 degrees Fahrenheit. After a short connecting flight, they were picked up at the Ottawa Airport by two members of the University's Students Council and taken to a home on Euclid Avenue near the university.

With a few years of practical journalism experience behind him, Ewart embarked on the formal study of this discipline at Carleton University. He immediately recognized that Ottawa was 'culturally bereft' and set out on a mission to rectify this cultural chasm. He began to expose the Ottawa community to the external world, beginning with international music. "I had to let Ottawa know that there was a world, a bright pulsating world beyond the Rideau Canal," he wrote in his autobiography To Follow Right – A Journalist's Journey. Drawing on his journalistic acumen he soon persuaded radio stations CKOY and CKPM to do programs on Jamaican music. He also arranged with the CBC to broadcast students' Christmas greetings to their families back home in the West Indies during his first year at Carleton University. That summer he returned to Jamaica to marry, and brought his wife Merle back with him two weeks after the wedding. That year he became the first Black editor at the university student newspaper, The Carleton, and was selected by his professor to lead his class in a challenging adventure to Carleton Place where they set up a newsroom, sent out reporters, and created a newspaper in one day. On completion of his degree Ewart returned to Jamaica to honour the terms of his scholarship and pick up his career with the island's premier newspaper, The Gleaner. Ten years later he came back to Ottawa, once again returning to Carleton University to get his Master's Degree in Journalism. By this time, he had made a career transition into the Jamaican Diplomatic Service, and his day job was Information Counsellor with the Jamaican High Commission in Ottawa.

Four years later during a period of political turmoil in Jamaica, he was posted as Jamaica's Consul in the New York Consulate-General with responsibilities for the Jamaican mission to the United Nations there. But with the eventual change of government, he ended his tenure and returned to Ottawa as a Landed Immigrant with his family, making Ottawa their permanent residence. Once the family had planted themselves firmly at their new Ottawa residence, Ewart began to make an impact, not only on the Ottawa community, but on the Canadian community at large.

The Ottawa Civic Hospital gladly welcomed Merle back into her old job in medical technology. However, Ewart's expectation that his two Canadian degrees would grant him ready access to the job market was soon extinguished. There was no media house in Ottawa that wanted to employ a Black man with a Master of Journalism degree, even though he was Canadian. Beyond that he sent out 124 job applications, received four interviews, but no job offer. In June 1982, resigned he turned back to something he had done as a student, driving with the Red Line Taxi company. His fortune changed at the end of that month when he accepted a term employment offer at CIDA; once permanent, he worked there for several years.

In the meantime, he recognized that Blacks in Ottawa did not have a platform to voice their concerns. Unlike the situation of the Jews, the Italians, and people of other races and ethnicities, there was no Black institution, no Black church, no Black newspaper, no Black-named streets, no Black language — nothing to bind the Black communities together. The dominant news media ignored the city's new Black cohort except when there was crime, sports, or entertainment. "We were, in a word, invisible," he says. And so, leaning on his journalism experience and his sharpened sense of justice, Ewart and his wife Merle launched 'The Spectrum', a monthly community newspaper with the mission to "Making Minorities Visible". And with the burgeoning Black community in Ottawa, The Spectrum provided the exact media vehicle that the 'Visible Minorities' community needed at that specific time (see sample articles in Appendix H). It became a widely circulated publication in the Ottawa region and was read by residents indiscriminately giving a face to the previously 'invisible'. Indeed Ewart recognized that

> "The Spectrum became the instrument that bound the Black communities together for the first time. Ottawa being a national and international capital, was home to many who had traveled from countries served by the Canadian International Agency (CIDA). It became a widely circulated publication that attracted the attention of Prime Minister Stephen Harper who once sent one of his staff to check it out. If it was a mission of intimidation it failed; the little newspaper continued speaking truth to power."

It also served to present the Black community to white Ottawans, particularly those who through the Department of External Affairs or CIDA had made contacts with the outside world. The Spectrum serviced the city through three decades, then passed the baton to online media publications such as http://blackottawascene.com. Ewart is also the author of several books.

But there seemed to be no end to Ewart's energies. He appeared on stage at the Ottawa Little Theatre and with Third World Players where he was a member and director; he co-founded Black History Ottawa and produced the BlackMusicfest series of concerts that brought to the stage luminaries such as gospel singer Cathy Grant and jazz singer Kellylee Evans. He was a co-founder of Harambee and the National Council of Jamaicans and Supportive Organizations in Canada; he was captain and president of the Bel-Air Cricket Club; he was a Director of Ottawa Carleton Immigrant Services Organization; a member of the Carleton University President's Committee; he assisted Junior Smith launch his Reggae in the Fields radio program with seven sessions on reggae history in 1976; and he continues to be a member of the choir at the Fourth Avenue Baptist Church which he joined in 1964, and was deacon, trustee, moderator, and chair of the Music Committee there. He was also a Director of the Ontario Cricket Association, a member of the Justice of the Peace Advisory Committee of Ontario, Chair of the Ottawa-Jamaica 50th Anniversary Celebrations, and is Co-ordinator of Black Agenda Noir which seeks to restore the Black agenda to national life in Canada.

Additionally, Ewart also had a very interesting and productive career as a Federal Public Servant starting with CIDA in 1982, worked on two national multiculturalism conferences with the Department of Secretary of State, and ended with Health Canada in 2010. At CIDA he worked in communications with the Americas and Africa Branch (during the Ethiopian Famine), as well as with the Office of the President as Chief of English correspondence along with Access to Information. This gave him the opportunity to volunteer with the Agency's Visible Minority Committee and chair monthly meetings with the President in efforts to improve the condition and promotion possibilities for Black and Visible Minority people who were being left behind. This led in 2000 to the coming together of several departments to launch the National Council of Visible Minorities in the Federal Public Service in which he was Director for the National Capital Region, meeting with Deputy Ministers and attending conferences in Toronto, Halifax, Montreal, and Winnipeg.

Ultimately, Ewart became the community champion against unjust causes. When warranted, he would defend the integrity and good name of Jamaica and Jamaicans in articles in the Ottawa Citizen, the Toronto Star and the Globe and Mail. People would come to his home seeking help for their son (usually) who was in trouble at school, and they never went away disappointed. He was a prime organizer for the first protest movement against the attempt to cover up the killing of Vincent Gardner, a poor Black man, by the Nepean Police. He conferred with City Counsellors and was invited to membership of an Ottawa Police advisory panel to effect changes in policing of Blacks. He lobbied the Police Service Board to enact better strategies for the community. Ewart was a central figure in the Jamaican Ottawa Community Association for decades and continued to work tirelessly to improve the lives of Caribbean-Ottawa immigrants here in Ottawa as well as all other Visible Minorities in the National Capital Area. And for this work, he was awarded the Jamaican Order of Distinction, Commander Class (CD) in 2010.

> "The Order of Distinction is a national order in the Jamaican honours system. It is the sixth in order of precedence of the Orders of Societies of Honour, …The Order of Distinction is conferred upon citizens of Jamaica who have rendered outstanding and important services to Jamaica, or to distinguished citizens of a country other than Jamaica."[178]

He was also awarded the Martin Luther King DreamKeepers Award, and the Order of Ottawa for his service to the community. An author, Ewart has written and published a number of books, including the aforementioned autobiography, To Follow Right... a Journalist's Journey, and We Come From Jamaica – The National Movement: 1937-1962 which describes the people and the impetus that carried Jamaica from colonialism to Independence.

Fay Jarrett graduated in the early 1960s from Clarendon College, a high school in Chapelton, Jamaica, and attended the University of the West Indies at Mona, Jamaica. In the summer of 1963 during her second year at university, Fay made her initial trip to Canada, a summer vacation to visit a close friend. Her girlfriend had studied to be a lab technician in New York, and then had moved to Toronto where she was able to get employment. After spending the summer, which was for her 'an exciting experience', Fay returned to complete her Bachelor's Degree.

---

178 *Wikipedia.* Order of Distinction. https://en.wikipedia.org/wiki/Order_of_Distinction Accessed on November 25, 2022.

She returned to Toronto the very next summer. This time she was bridesmaid at her friend's wedding. And as fate would have it, Fay met her husband-to-be, a gentleman of German ancestry, during this visit.

Shortly after her marriage, Fay was offered employment with the University of Toronto as a Librarian in the Medical School Library. Her husband, who was a teacher, later secured a teaching position in Ottawa and the couple, with their first child, left Toronto to take up residence in the Nation's capital. They initially lived on Grady Crescent in the west end of Ottawa. After settling in, Fay decided to suspend her professional aspirations in order to focus on raising her child.

Fay Jarrett – Community TV

Fay explained that while this was the right decision, the ensuing period turned out to be very stressful. A new life in a new city, and at home alone with a child all day left her feeling completely isolated. During the few years that she lived in Toronto she had seen and met a handful of Black people:

> "Toronto was a small town back then. You didn't see a lot of Black people. And when you saw one across the street you'd immediately approach and greet each other."

The situation in Ottawa was much more acute. During the mid-1960s the Black population in Canada's capital was even smaller, so any sighting of another Black person was extremely rare. Fay and her family found themselves living in an all-white neighbourhood. She quickly determined it was not too amenable to their being there. She immediately recognized that her neighbours were not too friendly or accommodating; indeed a number of her neighbours explicitly voiced their opinion that Fay did not belong in their neighbourhood.

Determined that her best approach to dealing with this situation would be to find solace through her piano playing, Fay enthusiastically immersed herself into playing the instrument. Her immediate next-door neighbour was incensed at this. Nevertheless, Fay continued to practice her piano playing, with care to keep the volume as low as possible. In time, another neighbour heard Fay playing and she asked her to tutor her three children. Fay agreed and this decision turned out to be most beneficial. The word that she was a piano tutor radiated throughout the neighbourhood and in a short time Fay had a flourishing business teaching some fifteen students at different levels. She entered them into piano competitions like the annual Kiwanis music festival and had great success. Her endeavors changed the neighbours' perception of Fay in a dramatic manner. She was no longer seen as someone who did not belong; on the contrary, she became a most popular person within her neighbourhood. Fay continued with her piano tutoring for several years until her own children became more self-sufficient.

She then began to re-build her career, starting with the completion of a Certificate in Librarianship at Algonquin College that yielded a job at the National Library of Canada. This was her entry to a long-term career as a Librarian in the Federal Government. Fay then went to work at Revenue Canada and then at the Canadian Security Intelligence Service (CISIS). During this phase Fay secured a Bachelor of Arts in Literature from Carleton University and later on went to the University of Western Ontario to obtain a Master's Degree in Library & Information Science (MLIS).

In 1971, Fay's life would be upended once again. This time her husband was assigned to Singapore. The family of five moved to Singapore where they resided for the next three years. Fay said this was the most exciting period of her life. The family returned to Ottawa from their three-year sojourn in Singapore and began to re-integrate into the community. The Ottawa Caribbean community had gradually grown to the point where the need to disseminate information about Caribbean community events and activities had become a major concern. The communications media that were available for community-based information was limited to word-of-mouth, and posters or flyers that were either handed out at events or left at a few Caribbean retail outlets.

A technology shift in the broadcast industry provided an opening to rectify this problem.

"The year 1972 saw two events that would prove highly significant to the cable industry for decades. Telesat Canada, Canada's national satellite carrier, formed in 1969 by an Act of Parliament, launched Anik A1, the world's first domestic communications satellite operated in geostationary orbit by a commercial company. With CBC as its first customer, Telesat began satellite television transmission for Canadian broadcasters and launched Anik A2 the next year. Telesat's operations were the precursor to satellite television distribution coast-to-coast and the transmission foundation of Canadian national specialty television services."[179]

Television broadcast was now in the process of transitioning from antenna to Satellite/Cable technology. And Skyline Cable (now Rogers) led the way in Ottawa. One of the challenges for Skyline was to fill out their programming with sufficient content. And in this regard, two gentlemen from the Caribbean, **Carl Grey** and **Orville Adams** found an opportunity to bring Caribbean content to the local community. They introduced a Caribbean-content program slot in the Skyline Cable line-up. The Program initially called 'Data' was designed to disseminate Caribbean-related information to the community through interviews and general announcements. They asked Fay to be the host of this half-hour segment. She accepted this role after some reluctance and launched her long-lasting foray into the build-up of the Ottawa Caribbean Community.

Starting in 1975 Fay brought in leaders of Caribbean Community organizations to have them explain their roles and initiatives to the Caribbean community at large, and to any interested viewers for the community channel on the Skyline Television network. She also brought in others, people like Ingrid Jean-Baptiste of Trinidadian origin as a co-host to broaden viewership appeal. The 'Data' programming was later changed to what became the 'Caribbean Calendar'. Over time this became one of the primary sources for Caribbean cultural expression in the Ottawa community. It also served the broader role of educating the wider community on the positive aspects of the people from the Caribbean who lived in Ottawa.

Caribbean Calendar has continued to be a mainstay in the Ottawa Region under the Rogers Cable network. For over 30 years,

> "this magazine-style show has highlighted the social issues, politics, people, and cultural events which make up Ottawa's vibrant Caribbean community. Caribbean Calendar succeeds in giving a voice and a face to those who are often overlooked by the wider, mainstream media. A team of reporters covers a combination of on-location shoots and in-studio interviews, bringing you colourful and diverse features. Tune in every

---

179 Canadian Communications Foundation. History of Canadian Broadcasting. History of Cable Television. https://www.broadcasting-history.ca/industry-government/history-cable-television Accessed on November 25, 2022.

month as Caribbean Calendar brings the stories of the 'real Caribbean' into Ottawa's living rooms."[180]

Fay continued in this role for some 20 years, becoming in the process one of the Ottawa Caribbean community's most effective community builders.

A consummate artist, Fay continues to play the piano. She has written and published a number of articles, a collection of poems, skits and plays, including one of Ottawa's Jamaican community's favourites 'SAMMY DEAD'. Written and directed by Fay Jarrett and Lorna Townsend, this play takes a light-hearted Caribbean-style approach to funerals. She founded the multi-cultural performance group 'Niwewetu' (Swahili meaning "it's just you") that performs Gospel and cultural-oriented music as well as skits to raise funds for philanthropic endeavours. At the present time Fay, long since retired, is very comfortable with her life's achievements, especially where the focus of her endeavours was on Caribbean community development.

Dr. Junior Smith
CKCU Radio

Junior Smith came to Ottawa as a teenager under the auspices of his mother Hyacinth Redway. One of the primary objectives of the initial group of Caribbean immigrants was to have their family members join them in Canada. This was of great significance to women who had immigrated under the Domestic Scheme. Most of these women, some of whom were mothers, pursued this course of action immediately following their contracted period of domestic service. Once they obtained their Landed Immigrant Status, many mothers brought their children and other family members to Canada. In some cases, the domestic employee continued working as a domestic, and sometimes for the originally sponsoring family; however, having gained their Landed Immigrant Status, they were no longer contract bound, and were able to live and work wherever they found employment. Nevertheless, the family re-unification initiative was usually pursued immediately. And while prospective family members underwent the immigration sponsorship process, the Landed Immigrant

---

180 Rogers tv. Caribbean Calendar. https://rogerstv.com/show?lid=12&rid=4&sid=2732 Accessed on November 25, 2022.

sponsors worked tirelessly to establish themselves at satisfactory levels of economic self-sufficiency to provide for their families once they arrived.

"That's what my mom did," Junior Smith explained. "She left Jamaica in mid-1960s just before I started high school." Junior's mother came to Ottawa on the West Indies Domestic Scheme and after quite some time, she became a Landed Immigrant. Once she had established herself on a firm economic base, she sponsored her family members. Initially she reunified her daughters, and soon afterwards she sponsored a contingent of seven remaining family members. This included her mother and father, her son Junior and two of his cousins, all of whom traveled to Ottawa as a group, arriving in mid-1974. Junior had just completed high school at St. Georges College in Kingston Jamaica. It had taken some "10 to 15 years" for the family to be fully reunited with her.

It was summertime when he arrived, so the climate-related impact of making the transition was minimal, and he was especially excited to be re-united with the rest of his family. Junior's plan was to pursue post-secondary training at a University in Ottawa. Six months later he enrolled at Carleton University in the Chemistry program. Determined to be self-supporting while attending university, he worked with the Central Canada Exhibition as part of their cleaning crew; he worked as a dishwasher and at any job that could assist his goal of self-sufficiency.

He had some adjustment issues within the work environment, primarily cultural and linguistic. In the second year he secured a more stable job with the Royal Canadian Mint. No longer wanting to study chemistry, he switched over to the mathematics program, graduating in 1979 with a Bachelor of Science in Mathematics, majoring in statistics.

His part-time entry level job at the Royal Canadian Mint, within the Federal Government, enabled him to access internal job postings, and after graduation, he applied for a job with Statistics Canada. It proved to be a good match and he was hired. He found his entry into the workforce at Statistics Canada to be very pleasant: "They were welcoming, and apart from the limitations on what jobs you could apply for, because of the French language requirement, I felt included when I first started."

By this time, Junior Smith had already made his mark on Ottawa's Caribbean community by initiating and hosting the Carleton University radio program – Reggae in the Fields (RITF). (See Appendix I: An interview with Junior Smith documented by Catherine Clark[181].)

---

181 September 15, 2017 ~ Catherine Clark http://blog.catherineclark.ca/author/catherine/
Accessed on February 15, 2020. Interview reproduced with permission from Catherine Clark.

Law & Justice

Ottawa Police

Herbert (Herbie) Waugh broke the racial barrier in the Ottawa Police Services when the Ottawa Police force hired its first Black officer in 1970. Waugh worked as a police officer for several years in the early seventies until the organization hired a second Black officer, **Terry Friday**. Waugh soon resigned from the force for reasons he did not explain. Chris Harris who served as community liaison to the Ottawa Police organization indicated that the environment was extremely racially intolerant at that time. Terry Friday, the Ottawa Police's second Black officer, remained on the force throughout the 1970s and 1980s, and was eventually promoted to the rank of Staff Inspector.

The Royal Canadian Mounted Police (RCMP)

The thought of becoming a Royal Canadian Mounted Police (RCMP) officer had not entered his mind when **Trevor Edwards** arrived in Canada from Barbados in 1970.

> "The Royal Canadian Mounted Police (RCMP), or Gendarmerie royale du Canada (GRC), often known as *The Mounties*, are the federal and national police service of Canada, providing law enforcement at the federal level."[182]

Trevor Edward's two sisters had previously emigrated from Barbados to Canada under the West Indies Domestic Scheme. His elder sister **Lileith Edwards** arrived in 1966 and his second sister **Pam Edwards**, who arrived two years later in 1968, sponsored her brother Trevor. While in Barbados, Trevor worked as an Accounts Clerk in the Ministry of Education, and his objective in coming to Canada was to pursue formal studies in accounting.

Since Trevor already had family members with established residences in Ottawa, he was able to become immediately immersed in the Caribbean community. The people from the West Indies were extremely accommodating. "People knew each other" and everyone was helpful. His integration into the broader Canadian Society began with his first job in the Federal Government via an employment agency. And once he entered the Federal workforce as a contractor, he applied for internal postings and was accepted as a full-time

---

182 *Wikipedia*. Royal Canadian Mounted Police.
https://en.wikipedia.org/wiki/Royal_Canadian_Mounted_Police Accessed on August 17, 2018.

employee. He then enrolled at Algonquin College to study accounting. Shortly after he began studies in the Algonquin College Business Program, Trevor was approached by an RCMP Recruitment Officer inquiring if he knew anyone who was interested in joining the RCMP, and also if he might be interested. After discussing it with the Recruitment Officer, Trevor indicated that "he was so convincing that the RCMP was the place for me that I enrolled in the Recruitment program."

In 1973 Trevor was sent off to the RCMP Training Academy (Depot) in Regina, Saskatchewan. He completed his training in 1974. This "was the first time I was exposed to so many Canadians." However the rigorous training did not allow much time for social interactions outside the training facility. After graduating, Trevor was posted to an in-house job in Ottawa, and after a year he was posted to begin community policing work in Sydney, Nova Scotia. This was:

> "an experience that I will remember until I die. The Sydney community
> was predominantly European immigrants, but it was heavily interspersed
> with Blacks from the Caribbean islands of Barbados and Jamaica."

Trevor was pleasantly surprised to find himself amidst a unique Canadian community where a sizable segment of the population was from his home country. In 1976 Trevor married his fiancé Marcia Gittens, and returned to Ottawa with a new assignment within the RCMP Media Relations section. He was later assigned to the Prime Minister's protective detail. In this role, Trevor was required to provide proactive services to foreign dignitaries and had the privilege of meeting many Heads of State, including Nelson Mandela. He continued in this role until he retired from the RCMP in 2007 with over 30 years of service. Trevor Edwards was one of the first RCMP officers of Caribbean origin.

Hugh Fraser was born in Kingston, Jamaica on July 10, 1952. Two years later, in 1954, his father, **Cecil Fraser**, arrived at Queens University to pursue an undergraduate degree in economics with the intent of returning to Jamaica following his graduation. He had left his wife, Rose Fraser, and two young sons behind; the eldest being two-year old Hugh and a younger eight-month-old brother. Then in 1957, during his undergraduate studies, Queens University established a Law

The Honourable Justice Hugh L. Fraser, FCIArb. Senior Justice, Easter Ontario.

Hugh Fraser — Athletics Ontario
athleticsontario.ca

faculty. Encouraged by one of Cecil's professors, he applied and was accepted as a Law student. Having shelved his plans to obtain a degree in economics, Cecil decided that he would bring his family to Canada. But since he was on a student visa with minimal income this would be difficult. His wife successfully applied to migrate under the Domestic Scheme, thus gaining entry to Canada. This decision required her to leave their two young children in the care of other relatives in order to take advantage of the opportunity.

In 1957 **Mrs. Fraser** arrived in Canada to provide child-care services for a prominent family in Kingston, Ontario. She had been a schoolteacher in Jamaica but her teaching career was forfeited when she came to Canada. However, she retrained herself as a nursing assistant, and went to work in healthcare at the Ontario Psychiatric Hospital. Two years later, in 1959, after she settled into Canadian life, and five years after Mr. Fraser left Jamaica to study in Canada, the Fraser family was re-united when seven-year-old Hugh and his younger brother joined their parents in Canada. Hugh was enrolled in school, but he was placed in a grade one year behind his age group. His mother protested, and the school complied. Actually, after being tested to determine the appropriate level, the results concluded that he should be advanced one grade level above. In effect, Hugh skipped one grade in elementary school.

In the meantime, Cecil continued his law studies at Queens, completed his Law degree in 1961 and was called to the Bar in 1963. He then began a legal career as a corporate lawyer with Canada Mortgage and Housing Corporation (CMHC). The family moved to Ottawa, taking up residence on Henderson Avenue in Sandy Hill. At the time, the Fraser family did not know anyone in Ottawa, and soon discovered that there were only a handful of Black immigrant families that had made Ottawa their home. Cecil settled into his legal role at the CMHC. With expertise in Property Law, he provided legal counsel on projects such as the planning of a proposed International Airport in Pickering Ontario. He would later take up a new position with the Federal Department of Justice.

Hugh was eleven years old when his family moved to Ottawa. He and his younger brother were enrolled at the York Street Public School. Shortly after they started their first term at the school, they realized that there was only one other

Black student on the campus. Hugh completed grade 7 and 8, and then in 1966 enrolled at Lisgar Collegiate, one of Ottawa's premier high schools, to complete his high school studies. Some of Lisgar's Alumni include Adrienne Clarkson, noted broadcaster and 26th Governor-General of Canada; Lorry Greenberg, Former Ottawa Mayor; Peter Jennings, ABC News anchor; Rich Little – Impressionist; and Tom Cruise, actor, along with many other notable persons.[183]

For the first two years in high school, Hugh was the only Black student at Lisgar. There were also no other Blacks in the Sandy Hill neighbourhood where the Fraser family lived, but Hugh found it relatively easy to forge friendships with the other kids in his neighbourhood. During that period the Sandy Hill community had a large population of Jewish families, so most of Hugh's childhood friends were Jewish, with whom he played sports in the park or on the street. Hugh indicated that he did not experience any significant incidence of racism as a Black kid growing up in Sandy Hill during the mid-sixties.

During the time that Hugh lived in Kingston, Ontario, he recognized that he could run faster than other kids. Along with a bunch of other kids, he secured a 'job' with a minor league baseball team to retrieve foul balls for which he was paid fifty cents per game. It became obvious that he could outpace the other kids as they all chased down the baseballs. By the time he arrived in Ottawa, he was encouraged to sign up for one of the race competitions in the park. And while at Lisgar, he tried out for the track team several times, first in grade 9 and then again in grade 10, but did not make the cut on either tryout. Undaunted and against his parent's wishes, he settled on playing football. He again tried out when he was in grade 11 and this time, he made the team. While he did not accomplish much during this first year on the track team, his track talent came to the fore when he got to grade 12 at age sixteen.

> "By my Grade 12 year I had broken national high school records for the
> 100m and 200m sprints. I had a drawer in my bedroom full of athletic
> scholarship offers from various universities in the United States and I was
> on top of the world."

Although Hugh wanted to take advantage of the opportunity, his parents were concerned about the downside impact of the US environment. So, Hugh remained at Lisgar to complete his High School year, 1970.

---

183 *Wikipedia*. **Lisgar Collegiate Institute.** https://en.wikipedia.org/wiki/Lisgar_Collegiate_Institute
Accessed on June 2, 2018.

At the peak of his high school track performance, Hugh sustained a serious hamstring injury.

"In my final year of high school, in the first outdoor competition of the year, I was running a 200-meter race well ahead of the competition when I heard a loud sound like a gun shot. I jumped high in the air and suddenly felt a very sharp pain in my right thigh. I tried to continue running but the leg wasn't working, and the pain was unbearable. I limped across the finish line still in front, but I knew that something was drastically wrong."[184]

Hugh ultimately recovered from this injury and went on to become a premier Canadian sprinter. He competed in the men's 200 metres at the 1976 Summer Olympics."[185]

"But unfortunately, at the peak of his career, there was a boycott of the 1980 Moscow Olympics and thus denied, Hugh was unable to compete in what would have been his final Olympic games."

In 1970 after his High School graduation, Hugh considered going into teaching and enrolled at Queens University, his father's alma mater, for a Bachelor of Arts degree. But during his third undergraduate year, after continual encouragement from his father to pursue a career in Law, Hugh decided to take the LSAT (Law School Admission Test). In 1974 he completed an Honours BA and was accepted at the University of Ottawa Law School. Completing his Law Degree, he was called to the Bar in 1979. At first, he articled with a local Law firm. Then he opened his own General Law practice. He moved on to work in a number of other Legal capacities, including as a Corporate Lawyer with Digital Equipment, and then with Brazeau Seller when he was appointed as a Judge.

As a practicing lawyer Hugh made, advocated, and facilitated changes to the 'Power of Attorney' Act. While representing the Alzheimer's Society, Hugh made a proposal for changes to the Provincial Government. He indicated that the Act had a significant flaw, where

---

184 Christian Embassy. My Olympic Experience; Justice Hugh Fraser-February 12, 2014 https://christianembassy.ca/wp-content/uploads/2014/08/Justice-Hugh-Fraser-May-2014.pdf Accessed on June 2, 2018.
185 Fraser finished third in the 1975 Pan American Games 4 × 100 metres relay (with Marvin Nash, Albin Dukowski, and Bob Martin). Fraser also finished fifth in the 200 metres and sixth in the 100 metres at the 1975 Pan American Games. Wikipedia. Hugh Fraser. https://en.wikipedia.org/wiki/Hugh_Fraser_(athlete) Accessed on November 25, 2022.

"if you named someone as the Power of Attorney when you were of sound mind, but later on you got dementia, then the Power of Attorney would no longer be valid."

From Hugh's point of view this was technically wrong. According to the existing Act, if the Power of Attorney was set between a husband and wife, and later one became mentally incapacitated, then the agreement would no longer be valid. Hugh had the Province make the appropriate change to the Act, such that "as long as you were of sound mind when you appointed that person it cannot be revoked". This change has benefited many Ontarians over the years. Another of Hugh's major accomplishments came after hearing a Human Rights Tribunal case relating to an allegedly discriminatory clause in the Unemployment Insurance Act as it related to certain classes of women. Hugh ruled that indeed that aspect of the Act was in fact discriminatory and ordered that the Government make appropriate changes to the Act. This order was appealed up to the Supreme Court which allowed the lower court's ruling to stand. The government not only had to change the Act but it had to pay out millions of dollars to a group of women who were negatively impacted by the flawed statute.

It was during his part-time work as a judge on the Human Rights Commission that Julius Isaacs, the only Black Chief Justice of the Federal Court of Canada, asked Hugh if he had ever considered becoming a Judge.

Hugh was well aware that he was often the lone Black in the group, whether at school, university and Law School years, and did not consider this to be an impediment in his journey to achieve his objectives. But when he applied for articling positions, he ran into a number of situations that jolted him to recognize that racial attitudes were alive and well.

In one instance he was granted an interview on the basis of his resume. The interviewer, upon recognizing who he was, continued to make himself busy with phone calls and other administrative work, virtually ignoring Hugh's presence for a considerable period of time. Hugh politely acknowledged that he understood that the interviewer was very busy, terminated the meeting and made his exit. On a second articling interview, he was allowed to remain in the reception area for several hours. When it became obvious that the interview would not be happening, he left.

As a result of this experience Hugh decided to start his own practice in real estate law, later branching out into other areas. In time he worked in corporate law, and it was during this period that he was appointed to the Ontario Bench.

Shortly thereafter, he presided over the very sensitive and high-profile case in Ipperwash, Ontario. He ruled that:

> "Native protester Dudley George was unarmed when he was killed by a police bullet, and the officer who shot him knew it, only to lie about it in court later. ...
>
> Judge Hugh Fraser said that acting Ontario Provincial Police Sergeant Kenneth Deane's testimony about the events just before and after he shot Mr. George at the gates of Ipperwash Provincial Park on September 6, 1995, was false, as was the testimony given by at least two of his fellow officers."[186]

Most of his later work focused on arbitration at international games including Olympic events. Hugh saw this as a culmination of his career where he was able to integrate his two main interests, Law with Track and Field. From 1988-1990 Hugh was a member of the Dubin Commission of Inquiry into the use of anabolic steroids and other banned substances in sport. The recommendations from that Commission provided the impetus for a new drug testing regime for sport in Canada.

> Summary Biography: "The Honourable Justice Hugh L. Fraser (Ret.), FCIArb joins JAMS after an accomplished career as a justice of the Ontario Court of Justice (Ottawa). He was appointed as a judge of the Ontario Court in 1993 and became regional senior justice for the East Region of Ontario in 2013, a position in which he managed and advised more than 70 judges and justices of the peace. During his 25-year tenure on the bench, Justice Fraser conducted thousands of trials and directly mediated countless settlements in cases involving complex business/commercial, professional liability, torts, family, criminal, and personal injury matters.
>
> Justice Fraser is an Olympian and a recognized international expert in sports law. As an arbitrator for the Court of Arbitration for Sport (CAS), he was appointed to CAS's first ad hoc court and has served as either sole or panel arbitrator in dozens of sports-related disputes. He is a member of several ADR panels in North America and Europe and has conducted arbitrations throughout the United States and Canada, as well as in Australia, Brazil, Malaysia and Switzerland.

---

186 Officer Guilty in Ipperwash Killing. The Globe and Mail. https://www.theglobeandmail.com/news/national/officer-guilty-in-ipperwash-killing/article20397898 Accessed on June 2, 2018.

Prior to his appointment to the bench, Justice Fraser was also counsel to the Canadian Department of Justice. He also served on the Canadian Human Rights Tribunal. The Honourable Justice Hugh L. Fraser was named among the 135 appointments to the Order of Canada that was announced by Her Excellency the Right Honourable Mary Simon, Governor General of Canada, on December 29, 2021. Justice Fraser was awarded this honour "for his transformative contributions to Canadian sport as an internationally recognized expert in sports law and as a former Olympian."[187]

---

187 The Governor General of Canada. Governor General announces 135 new appointments to the Order of Canada. https://www.gg.ca/en/activities/2021/governor-general-announces-135-new-appointments-order-canada Accessed on November 27, 2022.

Science & Technology

Aerospace Medicine

Dr. Donald Holness

Donald Holness arrived in Canada in 1957 to attend McGill University in Montreal. His objective was to complete an Undergraduate Bachelor of Science Degree. Don had finished his high school studies, graduating from Cornwall College in Montego Bay in 1955, before working in the Quality Control department for a group of sugar estates in Jamaica. His parents, both of whom were teachers, insisted that he pursue post-secondary studies; Don's mother even held back half of his weekly salary to help finance his potential university studies. After working for two years, Don decided to get a university degree, despite that in 1957 there was no fully accredited University in Jamaica: "The University began at Mona, Jamaica, West Indies [was founded] in 1948 as a College of the University of London. It achieved full university status in 1962."[188]

Therefore, like his contemporaries, Don looked at other educational institutions abroad to pursue advance studies. He looked at US universities and found those to be "prohibitively expensive". Then investigating the Canadian Universities, he applied to McGill University in Montreal, Quebec which was a popular target for Jamaicans seeking higher education in Canada. The student venue was one of the few ways that people from the Caribbean could enter Canada during the late 1950s.

Don booked his flight to Montreal via Trans Canada Airlines (TCA), which "operated as TCA from 1937 to 1965, when it was renamed Air Canada."[189] The flight to Montreal "took about eleven and a half hours, because we had to make frequent stops."

188 The University of the West Indies Mona. https://www.mona.uwi.edu/about Accessed on May 14, 2020.
189 *Wikipedia.* Trans-Canada Air Lines. https://en.wikipedia.org/wiki/Trans-Canada_Air_Lines Accessed on May 14, 2020.

Don had no personal contacts in Montreal, but there were a number of other students on the same flight. Arriving in late evening, he and the other foreign student counterparts received a great welcome from the McGill student representatives who met them at the Dorval Airport to escort them to the campus. Don checked into the 'Y' (YMCA) for his first night's stay in Canada. "And the next morning was an eye opener, waking up to these strange surroundings and realizing that you were thousands of miles away from home."

Don graduated with a BSc Major in Biology in 1961 and went on to complete an MSc in Physiology in 1963. He then began to look for job opportunities in Montreal. However, the same year that Don completed his graduate degree, Quebec began to experience a period of social unrest. The Front de libération du Québec (FLQ) movement, founded in 1963, shook the social environment in Quebec, and more specifically the social environment in Montreal. Don recognized that not only was the Province of Quebec entering a period of social uncertainty, but an economic transition was underway, ushering a shift from a majority private enterprise driven economy to a public sector driven economy.[190] "The period from 1960 to 1980 was characterized by greater involvement of the public sector in economic activity, through the creation of government corporations."[191]

As a consequence, Don encountered difficulties in obtaining employment in Montreal. He had however sent out an application to the Defence Research Board (DRB) in Downsview Toronto, and he was hired.

> "The DRB's main focus was on niche fields where Canada either had
> expertise and experience (arctic research, ballistics, and chemical and
> biological warfare defence), an interest in mastering (aeronautics,
> computer science, and electronics), or the means to make contributions
> (atomic research)."[192]

Don, his wife **Marie** and Gregory their first child, moved to Toronto in August 1963 where Don commenced his employment at the DRB. The location was the Canadian Forces Base (CFB) Downsview, Medical Labs. Marie had arrived in Montreal in 1960 to study Nursing at the Royal Victoria Hospital. The couple met

---

190 Black in Canada. Donald Holness. http://www.blackincanada.com/2010/12/29/donald-holness Accessed on May 14, 2020.

191 Linteau et al., *1989 Special study: Economic history of Quebec over the past six decades.* https://fdocuments.in/document/special-study-economic-history-of-quebec-over-the-past-the-provinceas-economic.html?page=1 Accessed on August 14, 2020.

192 *The Canadian Encyclopedia.* Defence Research. https://www.thecanadianencyclopedia.ca/en/article/defence-research Accessed on May 14, 2020.

shortly after she arrived, and they married during Don's final year in university. After working at CFB for about two years, Don's supervisor encouraged him to apply for a scholarship that was being awarded by the Defence Research Board (DRB). His application accepted, he entered the University of Western Ontario where he completed a PhD in Physiology, graduating in 1968. He returned to DRB and worked there until 1980. Don said that "at that time the Peter Principle[193] came into effect, up until now I was doing research work, but they sent me to Ottawa to do administrative work."

Don benefited from an extensive research career:

> Highlights: Group Leader, research program in diving and aerospace medicine, Defence Research Lab (1978-82); was also Canadian Project Officer and Representative to NATO Advisory Group for Aerospace Research and Development (R&D), addressing issues in aerospace medical life support and nuclear, biological and chemical protection of aircrew. From 1982-88, Dr. Holness was Staff Officer at the Department of National Defence headquarters, responsible for monitoring the research programs, including occupational health, aerospace medicine, also analyzed and assessed Canadian participation in international defence R&D programs; became Scientific Liaison Officer at the Canadian Embassy in Washington, responsible for promoting interaction between U.S. and Canadian scientists in their respective defence departments (1988-92,). Returned to the Department of National Defence headquarters in 1992 and continued to analyze and assess Canadian participation in international defence R&D programs before retiring in 1996.

> Honours: Inclusion in Who's Who in Black Canada (1st & 2nd editions; 2002, 2006); James Bertram Collip medal for graduate studies in medical sciences, University of Western Ontario (1969).

> Works: Several scientific and technical articles in international journals, including Canadian Journal of Comparative Medicine & Veterinary Science; International Journal of Biometeorology; Ergonomics; Journal of Aviation, Space and Environmental Medicine.[194]

Donald's wife Marie had earlier abandoned her nursing career to pursue studies in Marketing while the family lived in Toronto. She then worked with Texas Instruments, a Dallas-based Information Technology Company. Her

---

193 *Wikipedia.* The Peter Principle. https://en.wikipedia.org/wiki/Peter_principle Accessed on November 28, 2022.
194 Black in Canada. Donald Holness. http://www.blackincanada.com/2010/12/29/donald-holness Accessed on May 14, 2020.

profession mandated frequent travel to the US where she met with clients, soon becoming aware of the stark cultural differences between Canada and the US. When the family moved to Ottawa, Marie joined Control Data Corporation (CDC), a mainframe and supercomputer firm headquartered in Minneapolis, MN. Entering as a Customer Service Representative, Marie rose to Account Manager whose primary responsibility was to manage Energy, Mines and Resources. She rapidly rose in the ranks at the CDC to become one of their top performers in North America. When the couple moved to Washington DC, Marie was effectively transferred to work with a branch of Control Data in Rockville, Maryland. Marie found herself battling the usual stereotypes while working in the US, much more so than when she was in Canada. In Don's case, his counterparts at the Pentagon were taken aback by the fact that a 'Person of Colour' was in fact the representative for the Canadian Government at the highest levels of the Military establishment. This faded to the background, once the Americans recognized that they were dealing with someone in position who had the expertise, knowledge and talent.

Satellite Communications

Victor Gooding, shortly after graduating from high school with Advanced Level certification, enrolled at the Caribbean Institute for Meteorology & Hydrology (CIMH) in Barbados to obtain certification as a Meteorologist.

Victor Gooding
Source: blackincanada.com

> "In 1951 the British Caribbean Meteorological Service was established to promote and co-ordinate regional activities in the fields of meteorology and allied sciences, to provide support and advice to governments in dealing with issues of an international nature affecting weather and climate and to represent the regional meteorological community's interests at the international level."[195]

Victor obtained his certification and began to

---

195 *Wikipedia.* Caribbean Institute for Meteorology and Hydrology https://en.wikipedia.org/wiki/Caribbean_Institute_for_Meteorology_and_Hydrology Accessed on March 4, 2020.

work as a Meteorologist in Barbados, but his goal was to become an engineer. That would entail either going to the University of the West Indies – Trinidad & Tobago Campus, or to another institution further afield. "I always wanted to go to Canada. I had a brother, Douglas, and a sister, Hazel, in Montreal." Given this connection, he headed to Montreal in 1969 to join his two siblings.

Victor promptly enrolled at Sir George Williams University (SGWU, Concordia) in Montreal just in the wake of the Caribbean students' protest at its Computer Centre.

> "The Sir George Williams affair (also known as the Sir George Williams riot) took place in winter 1969, when more than 200 students peacefully occupied the ninth floor of the university's Henry F. Hall Building. These students were protesting the university administration's decision regarding a complaint of racism that had been filed several months earlier by six Black students from the Caribbean against a Biology professor. On 11 February 1969, to dislodge the students occupying the building, the police intervened forcefully, and the situation deteriorated, resulting in over $2 million worth of damage and the arrest of 97 people. The Sir George Williams affair is regarded as the largest student uprising in Canadian history. For many observers and historians, it represents a key moment in the rebirth of Black militancy in Montréal."[196]

In September 1969 when Victor started his first class in Electrical Engineering, the acrimony was palpable. Caribbean students had elected to boycott all non-academic activities. Victor, an avid sprinter, was expecting to continue his athletic involvement in track and field; however, he was disappointed to learn that there was no longer a track team at Sir George Williams. Despite pushback from the Caribbean Students Association, he joined the soccer team along with two other Caribbean students and a Trinidadian coach. He graduated in 1973 with a Bachelor's Degree in Electrical Engineering (with distinction), and was also named Most Valuable Player (MVP) for the soccer team and Top Graduating Athlete. He was also awarded a scholarship to pursue a Master's Degree at Queen's University in Kingston, despite the fact that his initial intent was to return to Barbados immediately following the completion of his undergraduate degree. His Master's thesis provided new analysis and characterization of data communication via satellites, an area in its infancy. Upon achieving his Master's degree, he was awarded a prestigious and valuable

---

196 *The Canadian Encyclopedia*. Sir George Williams Affair.
https://www.thecanadianencyclopedia.ca/en/article/sir-george-williams-affair Accessed on March3 2020

scholarship from the Natural Sciences and Engineering Research Council of Canada (NSERC) to undertake a PhD in Electrical Engineering at Queen's University. Upon graduation, Victor taught Electrical Engineering at Queen's for nearly two years, before moving to Ottawa in 1980 to embark on a career in the Satellite Communications industry.

At Telesat, Victor held a wide range of positions. He was involved in some of the earliest satellite system analysis, and network design for voice, data, and video services for the Anik A satellites, the first domestic communications satellites in the world. Subsequently he helped plan new Anik satellite systems (Anik C, D, and E series) as well as MSAT, Canada's first mobile services satellite. From 1985, he undertook corporate strategic planning to identify potential opportunities and threats to Telesat's satellite business. In 1989, he became responsible for customer operating assignments on the Anik satellites. In 1994, he became an independent Telecommunications Consultant, undertaking a variety of engineering projects for Stentor, CANARIE, Industry Canada and ARABSAT. He joined TMI Communications in 1996 as Engineering Team Leader for a number of mobile satellite service development projects. He then re-joined Telesat in 1997 and became involved in R&D relating to advanced satellite systems and applications. This work included specification of new broadband satellite systems utilizing state-of-the-art technologies such as spot beams, on-board processing, and emerging coding/modulation schemes, as well as the introduction of the higher Ka-band and V-band frequencies of operation. Of note, Victor was Project Manager for the Canadian Space Agency-sponsored $80M development and implementation of the Ka-band payload of the Anik F2 satellite launched in 2004, at that time the largest satellite ever built. Subsequently, he was a key member of the team that pioneered direct-to-home satellite Internet service in Canada via Anik F2.[197]

Victor has always excelled in soccer and on the track, and in Barbados, he had been a top high school sprinter. He played varsity soccer for SGWU for 4 years, culminating in being named MVP and top graduating athlete in 1973. While at Queen's he competed in track at varsity, national and international levels. From 1973-76, he dominated the Ontario University sprints, setting three records in one day at the 1975 university championships. In Ottawa, Victor also coached competitive club soccer for 17 years. As a result of his performances, he was

---

197 Information gathered from the interview with Victor Gooding.

selected to the Barbados Olympic 4x400m relay team (1976). In 1994, he was elected to the Queen's University Track & Field Hall of Fame.

Victor continues to live in Ottawa and is currently Chairman of the Errol Barrow Memorial Trust, a charity that offers scholarships to Caribbean students. He also operates Music Doctor Labs, a multimedia business specializing in music production and digitization of analog audio and video.

Victor has been the recipient of many awards and accomplishments[198]:

Scholarships:
Quebec Government Graduate Scholarship (1973)
RS McLaughlin Graduate Fellowships, Queen's University (1973)
NSERC Graduate Scholarship (1974-76)
Business-related awards:
Telesat Award of Excellence (1985)
BCE First Invention Award (2006)
BBPA Technology & Innovation Award (2007)
Athletics awards:
J.G. Finnie Trophy, Soccer MVP, SGWU (1973)
Association of Alumni Award, Top Graduating Athlete, SGWU (1973)
Hec Phillips Trophy, Most Outstanding Track & Field Performer, OUAA (1975)
Jack Jarvis Trophy, Outstanding Individual Athlete, Queen's University (1975)
Track & Field Hall of Fame, Queen's University (1994)
Patents
Method to assess potential performance and capacity of spot beam satellite systems utilizing advanced coding & modulation (2005); System and method for satellite network capacity boost by frequency cross strapping (2014).
Education:
PhD, Applied Science, Queen's University (1977)
Master's, Applied Science, Queen's University (1974)
B.Eng., SGWU (1973).

---

198 Black in Canada. Victor E. Gooding. http://www.blackincanada.com/2010/09/15/victor-e-gooding Accessed on March 3, 2020.

Information Technology

The City of Ottawa emerged as one of North America's leading-edge cities at the onset of the Information Technology era, "introduced in 1948". The pioneering company,

> "Computing Devices was founded by two Polish engineers, Joe Norton and George Glenski with financial backing by a prominent Ottawa entrepreneur by the name of Peter Mahoney. Its early products were a digital trainer for the Canadian navy and an instrument known as a position and homing indicator (PHI) for the Canadian Air Force. The company grew very rapidly during the fifties and early sixties, supplying a wider variety of systems to the Canadian military."[199]

During this time the core device that drove electronic technology equipment was the vacuum tube. And just before the Computing Devices Company came into existence,

> "The first working device to be built was a point-contact transistor invented in 1947 by American physicists John Bardeen and Walter Brattain while working under William Shockley at Bell Labs. They shared the 1956 Nobel Prize in Physics for their achievement."[200]

It was the invention of the transistor that brought about the changes to the technology environment, leading the way to the development of the integrated circuit which ultimately projected humanity into the technology era that it's now experiencing.[201]

Just over a decade later,

> "In 1962, Northern Electric established a research laboratory on the western outskirts of the city. That laboratory was later called Bell Northern Research and it became the research arm of Nortel, which became the new corporate name for Northern Electric."

As the transistors transitioned into integrated devices Ottawa solidified its position as a leading-edge city in the micro-electronics technology.

> "Microsystems International Limited (MIL) was a telecommunications microelectronics company based in Ottawa, Ontario, Canada, founded in

---

199 Doyletech Corporation. http://doyletechcorp.com/exela-commodi-consequa/ Accessed on September 18, 2019.
200 *Wikipedia.* Transistor. https://en.wikipedia.org/wiki/Transistor Accessed on September 18, 2019.
201 *Wikipedia.* Microsystems International.
https://en.wikipedia.org/wiki/Microsystems_International Accessed on September 18, 2019.

1969. MIL was an early attempt to create a merchant semiconductor house by Nortel Networks (then Northern Electric)."[202]

This was a pioneering effort in the technology industry.

"Electronic manufacturers were at that time forced to create custom integrated circuits due to the lack of industry standard ICs. MIL was an attempt to create a merchant company that could supply such standard devices as well as custom devices for Northern Electric products. Northern Electric entered the field partly at the urging of the Canadian federal government even though it has strong doubts of the viability of the company."[203]

During the 1960s, a handful of information technology specialists of Caribbean heritage arrived in Ottawa. Most, if not all of these technology pioneers had initially immigrated to the UK from their home countries, and after having gained their technology credentials from a British institution, they later immigrated to Canada. This was during a period when Canada was recruiting technology talents primarily from Europe to meet the initial national demand for technical skills. At the same time, plans were being executed to develop domestic technology talent, thereby reducing the dependency on external sources. These plans were implemented in Eastern Ontario primarily via the institution currently known as Algonquin College.

"The Eastern Ontario Institute of Technology was founded in 1957 - Ontario's second tech training college. It later became the Ontario Vocational Centre, and finally Algonquin College."[204]

And on the heels of the Caribbean Heritage technology pioneers who came in from the UK, a second wave of Caribbean Technology-focused immigrants arrived in Ottawa. This second wave came to obtain technology training in post-secondary institutions. Most of these early students attended Algonquin College in the late 1960s to early 1970s. The following profiles focus on both these groups.

---

202 *Wikipedia.* Nortel. https://en.wikipedia.org/wiki/Nortel Accessed on September 18, 2019.
203 *Wikipedia.* Microsystems International.
https://en.wikipedia.org/wiki/Microsystems_International Accessed on September 18, 2019.
204 URBSITE. Eastern Ontario Institute of Technology (EOIT).
http://urbsite.blogspot.com/2009/07/eoit1963.html Accessed on September 18, 2019.

Avionic Systems

Christopher Harris was one of the early technology pioneers to arrive in Ottawa. Chris grew up in the parish of St. James, Jamaica. He attended the local school and then enrolled at the Mico Teacher's College in Kingston, Jamaica.[205]

Christopher (Chris) Harris

Following his graduation from Mico, Chris migrated to the UK where he attended a Technical College in Bristol England after which he began a technology career with the Hawker Siddeley Aircraft Company.[206]

Chris married and left the UK for Canada under the auspices of his employer who provided him with a letter of recommendation to join their Canadian Aircraft manufacturing operations, Bristol Aeroplane Company, in Montreal.[207] Upon his arrival, he was offered another position with Computing Devices of Canada (CDC) in Ottawa.

Chris and his family took up residence in Ottawa where he initially worked for CDC, and then moved to work for another technology company, Electronic Materials Inc. When this company went into bankruptcy, Chris went to work at the National Research Council (NRC) of Canada where he remained employed until his retirement.

Like many other early Caribbean immigrants, Chris immersed himself into volunteer activities that sought to build the foundational structures of the Ottawa Caribbean community, recognizing the issues being voiced by members of the

---

205 The Mico was founded in 1835 through the Lady Mico Charity, one of four teacher training institutions established during this period in the British colonies and the only one to survive until the present. The institution is thus the oldest teacher training institution in the Western Hemisphere and English-speaking world. Wikipedia. Mico University College. https://en.wikipedia.org/wiki/Mico_University_College Accessed on September 18, 2019.
206 Hawker Siddeley Aircraft was formed in 1935 as a result of the purchase by Hawker Aircraft of the companies of J. D. Siddeley, the automotive and engine builder Armstrong Siddeley and the aircraft manufacturer Armstrong Whitworth Aircraft. Wikipedia. Hawker Siddeley. https://en.wikipedia.org/wiki/Hawker_Siddeley Accessed on September 18, 2019.
207 Hawker Siddeley Canada was the Canadian unit of the Hawker Siddeley Group of the United Kingdom and manufactured railcars, subway cars, streetcars, aircraft engines and ships from the 1960s to 1980s. Wikipedia. Hawker Siddeley. September 19, 2019.

emerging Caribbean community. His first foray was to help the newly arrived Caribbean domestic workers deal with some of their concerns. As a result, he became one of the founders of Ottawa Community Immigrant Services Organization (OCISO) which has been providing comprehensive settlement and integration services to the Ottawa community since 1978. This organization is funded by the Federal Government and is now a firmly established organization with the stated mission:

> "OCISO supports immigrants through the journey of making Canada their home by providing creative and responsive programs that are culturally and linguistically appropriate, by building community through mutual respect and partnerships, and by fostering healthy and inclusive spaces for open dialogue and healing." [208]

Chris expanded his community volunteerism to address concerns and causes. He was a member of the advisory boards for the police services, Municipal and Provincial, and the RCMP. He was one of the founding members of the Jamaica-Ottawa Community Organization, and continues to involve himself in any cause where fellow immigrants were negatively impacted or where there were potential threats to the development of the Caribbean Community in Ottawa. Chris considers his major accomplishment to be his role in facilitating the racial integration of the Ottawa Police Force, a cause that he championed from the period when there were no Blacks on the force. He has received many awards for his community work: The BBPA Community Services Award, The City of Ottawa Award for promoting "Harmonious Racial Relations", The Order of Ontario and many others. And up to present day, Christopher Harris continues his tireless volunteer service to enable the on-going vibrancy of the mature Caribbean community in the Nation's capital city.

Telecommunications & Radar

Flight Lieutenant **Samuel (Sam) Estwick** "was born in Padmore Village, Barbados on 8 October 1915 to George and Josephine Estwick." [209]"He was always a Canadian first and Black second," said Eric Estwick, son of Samuel (Sam) Estwick. In 1940 when the coal miner from Glace Bay was rejected by the

---

208 OCISO. https://ociso.org/ Accessed on March 25, 2023.
209 Black Canadian Veterans. Estwick Samuel.
https://www.blackcanadianveterans.com/post/estwick-samuel Accessed on March 1, 2020.

Royal Canadian Air Force (RCAF) as fighter pilot material, he wrote his MP who brought the matter up in parliament.

In 1941 Mr. Estwick trained as a radar technician, graduating at the top of his class in radar school in Clinton, Ontario. In December 1942 he was sent overseas and saw active service in England, Africa and India on aircraft, ships, and air strips.

Sam Estwick
October 8th, 1915- February 13. 2007

His daughter Leslie Theodore noted, "He worked the radar for the planes on bombing runs and the crews would say, 'I want him onboard, in case anything goes wrong.'"

Mrs. Theodore also remembered her father's answer to her question, "why did he serve when they didn't want him?" Her father had heard about German U-boats cruising in Canada's waters and since his mother lived in Nova Scotia, there was no question—he would serve.

An amateur boxer from his youth, Sam honed his skills in matches with other officers on long ship journeys. Once he considered putting those skills into action when a bartender in Durban, South Africa tried to kick him out. Sam didn't need to fight, thanks to an English officer. The 5'7" tall Mr. Estwick later recalled the officer's words: "Hold on, Canada. He's too big. That guy's more my size. Let me do it. And he took the guy down."

Sam served in the RCAF until 1963 and then worked in telecommunications in Ottawa. He helped found the Ottawa Lions Track and Field Club and the Gloucester Senior Adults' Centre. He added his leadership skills to these two organizations as president and also served terms of leadership with the Ottawa Vanier Lions Club and the Society for Technical Communication.

Sam never forgot his Armed Forces past. He was a member of the RCAF's Dodo Bird Club, the Pre-War Club and the 410 Wing.

> "When Sam Estwick heard ... [that] his name had come up in his grandson's high school history class as part of a lesson on the Second World War, he simply chuckled."[210]

---

210 Reading and Remembrance. Flight Lieutenant Sam Estwick. http://readingandremembrance.ca Accessed on March 1, 2020.

As his family noted after his passing, Sam Estwick simply did what he felt was the right thing. He never intended to be in the history books.

Electronics Components R & D:

Darrell Brown

Darrell Brown was another early Technology professional who migrated to Canada from the UK. Darrell attended Manning's High School in Savanna-la-Mar, Jamaica, where he grew up.

"Savanna-la-Mar is the chief town and capital of the parish of Westmoreland, Jamaica. A coastal town, it contains an 18th-century fort constructed for colonial defence against pirates in the Caribbean."[211]

Darrell graduated in 1957 and had his eyes set on a career as a photographer. His father, however, was totally against him pursuing a career in photography; consequently, following his graduation he worked at the Jamaican Telephone Company (JTC). This was about the time that the Russians launched the Sputnik 1 satellite — October 4, 1957 at 7:28 p.m.[212], an event which piqued Darrell's interest in electronics. Introduced to electronics through his job at the JTC, Darrell set his sights on a career in the electronics field. He left Jamaica for London England to join his elder brother who had migrated to the UK several years earlier. Darrell's objective was to obtain post-secondary certification in the field of electronics technology with the intent on launching a career in that field.

On arriving in London, he realized that he was facing an uphill journey. "Life in London was difficult," Darrell said. While he was able to land a fulltime job that facilitated his economic welfare, it also became an obstacle to the achievement of his primary objective. In order to meet his goal, Darrell had to work fulltime during the day and then go to night school to study Telecommunications at the Southgate Technical College. He graduated in 1965 with City and Guilds Certificates in Telecommunications:

---

211 *Wikipedia.* Savanna la Mar. https://en.wikipedia.org/wiki/Savanna-la-Mar Accessed on March1 2020
212 Information gathered from Interview with Darrell Brown.

"The City and Guilds of London Institute was founded by the Corporation of the City of London (in 1876) and 16 livery companies (the Guilds), to protect and promote the standard of technical education."[213]

Ottawa Winterlude Canal Skaters – Photograph by Darrel Brown.

Darrell began working in his new career before he graduated, and continued working in the UK for about four years.

During the mid-1960s the technology industry began to emerge in most industrialized countries. Canada was home to several innovative companies, Northern Telecom being one of Canada's technology pioneers. There was an acute shortage of people with technology skills that caused Canadian companies to reach abroad with their recruitment efforts in search of technical talent. The Canadian Government partnered with technology companies in their overseas recruiting efforts. In order to encourage Technology graduates to come to Canada, the government offered interest free loans, payable in two years, to attract candidates with the appropriate skill set, and to facilitate their transition to Canada. Darrell took advantage of the government loan, arriving in Ottawa on July 2, 1966.

He had previously met an associate in the UK who had been living in Ottawa and had temporarily returned to the UK. Roy Mitchell not only encouraged Darrell to move to Ottawa, but also offered him temporary accommodation in his Ottawa apartment. Darrell, his wife Mildred, along with their two sons, three year-old Christopher and three month old Mark, headed off to Ottawa to begin their new life in Canada. Mildred and Darrell had met while they were in high school; she arrived in the UK a year after Darrell and the couple married in 1961.

The Brown family settled very quickly in Ottawa. "I was quite impressed with Ottawa. I found it more pleasing than London." And, within three weeks of his arrival he landed a job at Computing Devices of Canada:

"Computing Devices of Canada Limited was founded in 1948 by two Polish immigrants to Canada, George Glinski and Joe Norton. It got its start by manufacturing the Position and Homing Indicator (PHI), a device which kept track of an aircraft's position and indicated the return route to

---

213 City and Guilds. City & Guilds Our History and Patronage. https://www.cityandguilds.com/ Accessed on March 1, 2020.

its base. Other government contracts followed including one for the design and construction for the Royal Canadian Navy of a very large digital simulator which was never completed. One very large contract which had a significant influence on the company's growth was for the Kicksorter, a digital pulse counter designed at the Chalk River Laboratories of Atomic Energy of Canada Limited. If the Kicksorter had been slightly modified to do simple arithmetic, it would have been a rudimentary computer. A large number of these devices were purchased by AECL from 1957 until 1963 when they were replaced by one of the early models of the PDP series of computers produced by the Digital Equipment Corporation." [214]

Within a few weeks after Darrell began working, he found an apartment and moved his family to their new place at Parkway Park near Woodroffe Avenue. His next objective was to purchase a house since he did not like the idea of paying rent. The job at CDC provided him with as many hours as he could accommodate. Darrell was assigned to work on a military project with tight deliverable schedules. And for a period of time, he was able to work seven days per week averaging twelve hours per day. And before the end of his first year in Ottawa he was able to purchase a house at 124 Chesterton Drive in the Parkwood Hills area. Shortly after they settled in their new home, they were pleasantly surprised to meet another Black couple, Leslie and Pearl Ennis, who had earlier emigrated from Jamaica and had also purchased a house on the same street. Leslie was a teacher at Algonquin College and an R.A.F Veteran, and Pearl was a nurse.

Darrell worked at CDC for less than a year. His wife Mildred had secured a job at Bell Northern (Nortel) as an Electronics Component Assembler within the first year of their arrival in Canada. Shortly thereafter Darrell recognized that his job at CDC was becoming risky. The military project was coming to a close and the company began downsizing the project team. When Mildred told him that Nortel was hiring, he submitted his application, and was hired at Bell Northern (Nortel) initially as a Test Engineer Specialist. Mildred worked for approximately two years up to the birth of their third child Darrell (Jr.), and later he was followed by a fourth boy David.

Darrell was now fully established at Bell Northern (Nortel). He recalled that in the late 1960s there were very few Black technology professionals within the organization. In fact, apart from his wife, Darrell recalled just three others within the workforce — **Stan Xavier, Samuel Malcolm Estwick** and **Malcolm Lovell**.

214 *Wikipedia.* General Dynamics Mission Systems – Canada.
https://en.wikipedia.org/wiki/General_Dynamics_Mission_Systems - Canada Accessed on March 1, 2020.

Stan Xavier was from St Lucia, and Samuel Estwick was a WWII veteran who came to Canada from Barbados with his family when he was a four-year-old. He eventually became an Expert in Failure Analysis which is the "process of collecting and analyzing data to determine the cause of a failure, often with the goal of determining corrective actions or liability."[215] At that time this approach was non-existent at Bell Northern (Nortel). Darrell proposed that the company establish this area of expertise, obtain sponsorship, and initiated the Failure Analysis function within the organization.

Throughout his career at Bell Northern (Nortel), Darrell returned to his passion for photography. He spent his leisure time honing this craft and became well known within the Ottawa community for his photographic skills. He continued to work with Nortel for the remainder of his career. He took an early retirement in 1993, returned with his wife Mildred to his native Jamaica, and became a successful real estate development investor in the town of Savannah La Mar where he grew up.

Electronic Telecommunications

Stan Xavier began his career as a teacher in Dominica in the early 1960s, and completing his training program, he started as an Assistant Teacher. After a few years his desire to become a civil engineer prompted him to head to London England under the auspices of his uncle. Stan's objective was to attend Barking College in East London where his career adviser convinced him to enter into the emerging field of Electronic Telecommunications. He completed his program of study, graduating with top of class performance. During his job-hunting venture, he

Stan Xavier

sent a number of resumes and had very good responses for interviews. Stan accepted an offer from the Marconi Company which at that time was just entering the satellite communications industry.

"The Marconi Company was a British telecommunications and engineering company that did business under that name from 1963 to

215 *Wikipedia.* Failure Analysis. https://en.wikipedia.org/wiki/Failure_analysis Accessed on March 1, 2020.

1987. It was derived from earlier variations in the name and incorporation, spanning a period from its inception in 1897 until 2006, during which time it underwent numerous changes, mergers, and acquisitions. The company was founded by the Italian inventor Guglielmo Marconi and began as the Wireless Telegraph & Signal Company. The company was a pioneer of wireless long-distance communication and mass media broadcasting, eventually becoming one of the UK's most successful manufacturing companies."[216]

While at Marconi, Stan came across a recruitment advertisement for Northern Telecom in Canada. The attractive job offer came with an all-expenses paid relocation and interim accommodation. Stan packed up his belongings and headed for Ottawa. Being single, he made the transition quite easily. Upon arrival at work, he realized that there was only one other black employee at Northern Telecom. His predecessor was Sam Estwick (profiled earlier), another Caribbean immigrant from Barbados who was a manager at Northern Telecom when Stan arrived.

Stan had a 40 year career with Bell-Northern Research (BNR), the Northern Telecom R&D Division, rising up the ranks to Director of Advanced Telecommunications Technologies. During his tenure he was the Canadian representative on the International Electrotechnical Commission (IEC) a worldwide standards forum within the International Standards Organization (ISO).

"The International Electrotechnical Commission is an international standards organization that prepares and publishes international standards for all electrical, electronic and related technologies – collectively known as 'electrotechnology'. IEC standards cover a vast range of technologies from power generation, transmission and distribution to home appliances and office equipment, semiconductors, fibre optics, batteries, solar energy, nanotechnology and marine energy as well as many others."[217]

With this Canadian representation, Stan was elected Chair of the Working Group on Electromagnetic Compatibility (EMC). His work established standards governing Electromagnetic Emissions which is currently applied globally.

---

216 *Wikipedia*. Marconi Company. https://en.wikipedia.org/wiki/Marconi_Company Accessed on October 20, 2019.

217 *Wikipedia*. International Electrotechnical Commission. https://en.wikipedia.org/wiki/International_Electrotechnical_Commission Accessed on October 20, 2019.

Stan was one of the founding members of the Ottawa-Dominican Association. He is an avid cricketer and shortly after retiring from Nortel. Stan joined with another scientist to launch a new company 'inBay Technologies'.

"Stan is a co-founder of inBay Technologies, is a former Director of Advanced Technology at Nortel Networks. Throughout his career, he has managed major R&D and product commercialization initiatives, as well as university interaction programs in Canada, the US and UK. He has also served as CEO for early-stage companies."[218]

InBay Technologies Inc. is "an enterprise-focused cyber security start-up based in Ottawa, Canada. inBay pioneered the first truly 'passwordless' authentication solution and is leading a revolution in digital identity and cyber security."[219] Stan is currently working on other innovative projects to bring Distance Learning Technologies to students in his native Caribbean.

Communications Systems

Douglas (Doug) Prendergast arrived in Ottawa in the summer of 1970. His mission was to study Electronic Technology at Algonquin College, earn a three-year diploma and return to Kingston Jamaica to work in the Technology field. Having lost both his parents by the time he was six years old, Douglas, and his two brothers Gordon and Henry were brought up in a Christian Orphanage. By the time he was 12 years old, he and his brothers had to leave the orphanage, moving from one foster home to another. However, Douglas was able to attend high school by excelling at the Common Entrance examinations.

Douglas (Doug) Prendergast

218 Crunchbase. Stan Xavier. https://www.crunchbase.com/person/stan-xavier Accessed on October 20, 2019.
219 inBay Technologies Inc. https://www.inbaytech.com/about-us Accessed on December 1, 2022.

"Introduced to Jamaica in 1957, the first Common Entrance Examination (CEE) was conducted in 1958. The exam was widely welcomed because it created greater access to secondary schools for more Jamaican children." [220]

Douglas was admitted to Ardenne High School in Kingston Jamaica, founded in 1907:

"… just after the great earthquake that destroyed much of Kingston, the Rev. George and Nellie Olson came to Jamaica as Church of God Missionaries from Anderson, Indiana, U.S.A, where the Church of God has its headquarters. In 1927, they began the first school at Highholborn Street in Kingston with an enrolment of 5 students. In 1929 the Ardenne property of 12 acres was purchased through funds received from the Missionary Board of the Church of God in the U.S.A. and other private donors. The main block of buildings was erected."[221]

Doug completed high school just about the time that Jamaica made the transition from the British Pound (Sterling currency) to the Jamaican Dollar, which required the conversion of the cash registers to accept the new currency. He applied to the National Cash Register Company (NCRC) and was hired to convert cash machines. After working for about a year he realized that his inability to save added years to finance his planned post-secondary education. He investigated the feasibility of a scholarship to achieve this objective. He finally obtained a CIDA scholarship to attend Algonquin College in Ottawa, starting his course of study in the fall of 1970.

Doug completed his three-year diploma in Electronics Technology, and as planned he returned to Jamaica with the expectation that he would have no difficulties finding employment. To his dismay a year passed, and he was still unemployed. During the second year of his return, he was offered a position with the Jamaica Telephone Company (JTC).

"The Jamaica Telephone Company was incorporated in Kingston in 1892. But the first telephone in Jamaica was installed in Black River, St. Elizabeth, in 1883, just seven years after Alexander Graham Bell spoke the first words into his invention in 1876. Black River was also the first town in Jamaica to get electricity. The development of both the telephone and electricity were prompted by the town's rapid growth, which was

---

220 DIGJamaica. Primary Education in Jamaica: From Common Entrance to GSAT to PEP http://digjamaica.com/m/blog/from-common-entrance-nap-gsat-to-pep/ Accessed on March 25, 2023.
221 Ardenne High School. History.
http://www.ardennehighschool.edu.jm/aboutus.html#artlcleHistory Accessed on January 20, 2020

fuelled by European demand for the natural blue-black dye obtained from the region's logwood tree."[222]

Towards the latter part of the first year when Doug realized that his job search was a frustrating venture, he applied to return to Canada as a Landed Immigrant, and also applied to complete an engineering degree at both the University of Toronto and the University of Ottawa. He encountered many obstacles with his immigration application, but he was eventually granted Landed Immigrant Status and accepted by the University of Ottawa.

Doug believes that his application process turned positive when he explained to the immigration office some of the things that he did while he was studying in Ottawa; Doug had volunteered to work with Operation Beaver.

"Operation Beaver is an international program under the direction of Frontiers Foundation, a federally chartered non-profit organization, which supports the advancement of disadvantaged communities across Canada and the Third World. Sponsored by the Canadian Council of Churches, Operation Beaver began in 1964 as an ecumenical work program to provide assistance for the socially and economically deprived communities." [223]

During his summer holiday breaks he had worked with the Métis, and Indigenous peoples in Canada and parts of the United States who have mixed Indigenous and European ancestry, including Non-Status Indian communities in Northern Canada.[224] He volunteered to serve in Mud Lake-Labrador.

"Mud Lake is a small unincorporated community in central Labrador, Canada. It had a population of 50 as of 2016, a drop of 4 individuals from 2011. The town is not accessible by road. It is usually reached by crossing the Churchill River by boat (during summer) or snowmobile (during winter)."[225]

He also volunteered to work with native communities such as Goose Bay and Kenora. And it was this aspect of his resume that gained him re-entry into Canada after he appealed an initial failed attempt.

---

222 Jamaicans and Jamaica. https://jamaicans.com Accessed on January 20, 2020.
223 Aboriginal Multi-Media Society. Operation Beaver offers volunteers.
2020.https://ammsa.com/publications/windspeaker/operation-beaver-offers-volunteers Accessed on January 20.
224 *Wikipedia*. Metis. https://en.wikipedia.org/wiki/Metis Accessed on January 20, 2020.
225 *Wikipedia*. Mud Lake, Newfoundland and Labrador.
https://en.wikipedia.org/wiki/Mud_Lake,_Newfoundland_and_Labrador Accessed on January 20, 2020.

In 1978 Doug completed his undergraduate degree in Electrical Engineering, went on to complete a post-graduate engineering degree in 1980, and then in 1982 he completed the Master of Business Administration degree at the Telfer School of Business at the University of Ottawa. With the completion of this academic phase, Doug secured a job with Gandalf Technologies.

> "Gandalf was a Canadian data communications company based in Ottawa. It was best known for their modems and terminal adaptors that allowed computer terminals to connect to a number of host computers through a single interface. Gandalf also pioneered a radio-based mobile data terminal that was popular for many years in taxi dispatch systems."[226]

After a short stint at Gandalf, Doug returned to the University to do leading-edge research studies in Digital Satellite Communications. This pioneering research work has since translated into the normal everyday digital technologies that are used by mobile devices and in many other types of communications technologies.

His research work propelled him into the consultancy field where emerging communications companies, primarily in the USA had acute demands for Doug's expertise. He worked on one of the first digital radio devices, and was at the leading edge of the cellular phone revolution. He then initiated his own communications company Prendergast Communications Inc., and entered the commercial and industrial fields building microwave systems for large companies, and of installing and operating satellite dishes for businesses and residences across the greater Ottawa area. As a sideling, Doug entered the restaurant business with his first location in south-east Ottawa and later on Bank Street. Doug rounded out his career as a Research Engineer at Canada's Communications Security Establishment where he authored and co-authored several research publications in the field of digital technology systems.

---

226 *Wikipedia*. Gandalf Technologies. https://en.wikipedia.org/wiki/Gandalf_Technologies Accessed on January 20, 2020.

Computer Systems

After graduating in 1968 from Excelsior School in Kingston, Jamaica, **Dave Tulloch** started his first job as a junior auditor with Peat Marwick Mitchell & Co. (now KPMG). He enrolled at Jamaica's College of Arts Science and Technology (CAST) to pursue the Association of Chartered Certified Accountants (ACCA) accreditation, the ACCA being the global body for professional accountants. At that time the accounting firm had just implemented a minicomputer system to facilitate the processing of accounting records, and Dave noticed that a number of its clients were moving in a similar direction. He decided to switch his career

Dave Tulloch
Consulting Director

objective to learn about computers instead of accounting; however, there were no computer training programs offered in any regional institution at that time. Seeking to find training opportunities abroad, he applied to universities in the United States and, while investigating Canadian universities, he came across the CIDA scholarship program. He applied for a CIDA scholarship to study Electronics Technology, the closest match to his desired career goal.

Dave was successful with his CIDA application, and moved to Ottawa in August 1970 to begin his course of study at Algonquin Collage. He graduated in 1973 with the intention of returning to Jamaica to work in the computer or electronics field, but soon found that there were no jobs that matched the skills he had acquired. However, the technology industry in Ottawa was booming. Having spent his previous two summer breaks working at Bell Northern and Microsystems respectively, he turned his attention to the Ottawa industry and was immediately hired by Consolidated Computers Inc. (CCI), a company that pioneered the word processing system, with a product called 'Key-Edit'. By acquiring this job, he was able to secure Landed Immigrant Status.

Towards the end of the first year at Consolidated Computers Inc., Dave was hired by Digital Equipment Corporation (DEC), the company that made the mini-computers that were used in CCI's 'Key-Edit' systems.

"Digital Equipment Corporation (DEC), was a major American company in the computer industry from the 1960s to the 1990s. The company was co-founded by Ken Olsen and Harlan Anderson in 1957. Although the company produced many different product lines over their history, they are best known for their work in the minicomputer market starting in the mid-1960s. The company produced a series of machines known as the PDP line, with the PDP-8 and PDP-11 being among the most successful minis of all time. Their success was only surpassed by another DEC product, the late-1970s VAX 'supermini' systems that were designed to replace the PDP-11."[227]

Dave started his career at DEC as a Field Services Engineer, installing and maintaining computer systems in the Ottawa area. He rose up the ranks to take on Global responsibilities, allowing him to manage projects in over 30 countries, mainly in Asia and southern Pacific regions. During his tenure at Digital, Dave earned an undergraduate Business Administration and a Bachelor of Commerce Degree through part-time studies at the University of Ottawa, and later a Master of Business Administration Degree from Concordia University in Montreal. He ended his tenure at Digital as Canadian Computer Operations Manager and branched out to start a number of small businesses. In addition to his interest in 'Tropicks' the beauty and hair care retail outlet that he launched in 1982, he started a computerized 'Point-of-Sale' venture and then added the 'Take Five' jazz club to his small business portfolio. In 1996 the Ottawa BBPA chapter awarded Dave the Black Business and Professional Association's Award for his entrepreneurship endeavours.

Dave later re-entered the corporate world as a consultant, starting out as a Client Services Manager at SHL Systemhouse Inc. an Ottawa Outsourcing company. He then moved to KPMG as a Consulting Manager, and ultimately completed a 17-year tenure at Oracle Corporation, starting out as a Global Consulting Manager and ending his technology career as Director of Client Services in Oracle's Cloud Services business unit.

227 *Wikipedia*. Digital Equipment Corporation.
https://en.wikipedia.org/wiki/Digital_Equipment_Corporation Accessed on March 3, 2020.

Mobile Knowledge Systems

Dave Knibbs graduated from Kingston College, Jamaica at the end of the 1972 school year and moved to Ottawa under the sponsorship of his aunt, Olga Mullings, a Registered Nurse, who had immigrated to Ottawa from the UK several decades earlier.

Dave Knibbs
Information Technology Director

> "Kingston College was founded by Bishop Percival Gibson under the guidance of Dr. G.F.C. DeCarteret, Bishop of Jamaica. Bishop Gibson was the first headmaster. The school was envisioned as a remedy for the social deformity in which poor Black boys were allowed primary education only. K.C., as the school became known, admitted any boy who could satisfy the entrance requirements and pay the affordable fees. Indeed, Bishop Gibson sometimes arranged for fees to be paid for poor boys. The school was declared open on April 16, 1925 with forty-nine students."[228]

Shortly after arriving Dave applied to Algonquin College, Ottawa and was admitted for a diploma in Electronics Engineering Technology. His college program began in the fall of 1973, and in the interim he worked nights at the Taxation Data Center. After his graduation he started working with Gandalf, and in short time was hired by Gandalf Technologies.

> "Gandalf was originally formed by Desmond Cunningham and Colin Patterson in 1971 and started business from the lobby of the Skyline Hotel, on Albert Street in Ottawa. The company's first products were industrial-looking half-bridges for remote terminals which were supported by large terminal multiplexers on the 'computer end'. Gandalf referred to these systems as a 'PACX', in analogy to the telephony PABX which provided similar services in the voice field. These systems allowed the user to 'dial up' the Gandalf box and then instruct it what computer they wanted to connect to. In this fashion, large computer networks could be built in a single location using shared resources, as opposed to having to dedicate terminals to different machines. These systems were particularly

---

228 *Wikipedia.* Kingston College (Jamaica).
https://en.wikipedia.org/wiki/Kingston_College_(Jamaica) Accessed on February 5, 2020.

popular in large companies and universities. Gandalf also pioneered a radio-based mobile data terminal that was popular for many years in taxi dispatch systems."[229]

Dave started off testing modems, and after nine months on the job he was promoted into a supervisory role. The company then initiated the Automated Taxi Dispatch System, partnering with the Blue Line Taxi Company to launch and operate this service technology, and Dave moved into that division in another supervisory role. The Taxi Dispatch Services division was later spun off and after changing hands several times, the new company ultimately became today's iCabbi, a division of 'Mobile Knowledge Systems' that develops "innovative dispatch solutions to the For-Hire industry".[230] Dave continued his career progression to manager and ultimately to Director.

As an avid soccer player, he was a member of the first Algonquin College soccer team during the mid-1970s, and was the team's captain in its second year. He also played in the Ottawa and District soccer league for many years and then joined the Gloucester Hornets Soccer Organization as a coach. He continued to coach teen teams for several years, assisting a number of players to secure athletic scholarships to colleges in the United States. He then transitioned into the role of agent for international soccer players with the organization called 'Sports Management Worldwide', an international full-service sports agency with an extensive network of Agent Advisors serving athletes throughout the world.

229 *Wikipedia*. Gandalf Technologies. https://en.wikipedia.org/wiki/Gandalf_Technologies Accessed on January 20, 2020.
230 Mobile Knowledge. https://mobile-knowledge.com/ Accessed on February 5, 2020.

Transportation Services

The Ottawa-Carleton Transportation System (OC Transpo) was one of the accessible organizations employing Caribbean immigrant men as bus operators starting in the late 1960s. The following extract provides an insight into the social aspects of immigrant transit employees, as recorded on the web site established by a number of the earlier Transit workers.

"Welcome to the West Indian Transit Club Inc. web site. We are a club founded by West Indian employees of O.C Transpo in Ottawa, Ontario. The eight founding members saw the need for cultural and social activities for Visible Minority employees, a need that was not being met through the regular social activities of the workplace. From this beginning, the non-profit organization familiarly referred to as "The Bus Drivers" by the West Indian community, has grown into an active, viable organization, committed to working with diverse members of our society.

The West Indian Transit Club Inc. Founding Members. (left to right): Winston Joseph, Clyde Shaw, Lester Cranston, Alvin Bulgin, Roderick Harper, Nerval Mitchell, Knowlton Constance, & Othniel Morrison.

Through its annual fund raising events such as Spring Dance, Fall Dance and Boat Cruise, the 'Club' is able to generate funds which in turn allows it to greatly subsidize its annual summer community picnic. The event is eagerly anticipated by all. The emphasis is on family fun. A family Bowling Night has been held for the past four years on the Friday night before the Sunday summer picnic. This event is great fun and has been growing in popularity.

The Club has been an ambassador for multi-culturalism in the community, and has hosted two cultural shows. The most successful was entitled

'Dingolay', and brought together performers from the West Indian community as well as the African community in Ottawa. It was well attended by an audience of various ethnic backgrounds, and was an excellent showcase of local talent."[231]

Beauty & Aesthetics

The hairdresser provides one of the essential services to immigrant women. This need, for hairdressing skills that provide the special hair treatment required by black women, ranks very closely with the need for Caribbean foods by Caribbean immigrants. Generally speaking, the Black hair care service business operates as a 'cottage service' with many hairdressers operating from their homes. Beginning in the early 1970s a number of small Caribbean-focused hair salons opened in the City of Ottawa. One of the earliest on record was established on Sparks Street by **Ina Foster**, an immigrant woman from Jamaica. Later on, a number of other hairdressing salons, with a focus on Black women, sprang up around Ottawa. Archie and Yvonne Codett, Guyanese immigrants, operated one of the first Black-owned hair care businesses in Ottawa. The Nu Skin Boutique was initially opened on Sparks Street in 1973 and moved to a number of other locations until its closure at the Parkdale location in 1988. Other salons such as the Emerald Beauty salon on Kent Street operated by Katherine (Sue) Daley and Head-to-Toe, operated by Faye Campbell on McLaren Street are some of the earlier Black-Women focused salons in Ottawa.

---

231 The West Indian Transit Club Inc. https://witc-ottawa.tripod.com/index.htm Accessed on May 16, 2018.

Other Notables

As the nation's capital, the City of Ottawa is the seat of the Federal Government and the centre for diplomatic missions. With these two attributes, the City of Ottawa became a magnet for attracting a number of distinguished Caribbean immigrants who emerged at the pinnacle of their professional careers. In recognition of their important contributions, introduced here are some of these prominent Caribbean immigrants who lived temporarily in Ottawa.

Lincoln MacCauley Alexander, PC, CC OOnt, CD, QC (January 21, 1922 – October 19, 2012) "was a Canadian lawyer who became the first Black Member of Parliament in the House of Commons, the first Black federal Cabinet Minister (serving as federal Minister of Labour). He held the seat through four successive elections until resigning his seat on May 27, 1980. Alexander was also the first black Chair of the Worker's Compensation Board, and the 24th Lieutenant Governor of Ontario from 1985 to 1991. He was the first person to serve five terms as Chancellor of the University of Guelph, from 1991 to 2007. Alexander was also a governor of the Canadian Unity Council.

Lincoln MacCauley
Alexander
PC CC OOnt CD QC

Alexander was born on January 21, 1922, in a row house on Draper Street near Front Street and Spadina Avenue in Toronto, Ontario. He was the eldest son of Mae Rose (née Royale), who emigrated from Jamaica, and Lincoln MacCauley Alexander, Sr., a carpenter by trade who worked as a porter on the Canadian Pacific Railway, and who had come to Canada from St. Vincent and the Grenadines. Lincoln had a younger brother Hughie, born in 1924, and an older half-brother Ridley "Bunny" Wright, born to his mother in 1920 prior to her marriage to his father.

Alexander went to Earl Grey Public School where he was the only Black in his kindergarten class. He noted in his memoir that he "never raced home from school and cried" but earned the respect of his classmates, sometimes by fighting. This taught him "to always walk tall, and with a certain bearing, so people knew I meant business." In his 2006 memoir, "Go to School, You're a Little Black Boy," Alexander recalled: "Blacks at that time made up a sliver-thin portion of the city's population, and racial prejudice abounded." When the family moved to the east end of Toronto,

203

and he attended Riverdale Collegiate, Alexander knew only three Black families. "The scene in Toronto at that time wasn't violent, though you had to know your place and govern yourself accordingly." [232]

"Lincoln Alexander was a leading figure in the fight for racial equity in Canada. In provincial, federal, public, and private roles, he consistently advocated for the equal treatment of Black Canadians."[233]

Rosemary Brown
PC OC OBC

Rosemary (Wedderburn) Brown PC OC OBC "was born in Kingston, Jamaica in 1930 and moved to Canada in 1951 to study Social Work at McGill University in Montreal. She then earned a Master of Social Work at the University of British Columbia... She also helped to found the British Columbia Association for the Advancement of Coloured People (BCAACP) in 1956 to help advocate for housing, employment and human rights legislation.

Rosemarie Brown served as a Member of the Legislative Assembly (MLA) in the British Columbia legislature as a part of the New Democratic Party from 1972 to 1986, making her the first Black Canadian woman to be elected to a Canadian provincial legislature...

In 1975, she became the first Black woman to run for the leadership of a Canadian federal party (and only the second woman, after Mary Walker-Sawka), finishing a strong second (with 40.1% of the votes on the fourth and final ballot) to Ed Broadbent in that year's New Democratic Party leadership election.

After departing politics, she became a professor of women's studies at Simon Fraser University. In 1993, she was appointed Chief Commissioner of the Ontario Human Rights Commission and served until 1996. In 1995, she was awarded the Order of British Columbia and in 1996 was named an Officer of the Order of Canada.

---

232 *Wikipedia*. Lincoln Alexander. https://en.wikipedia.org/wiki/Lincoln_Alexander Accessed on February 27, 2020.

233 Ontario Ministry of Public and Business Service Delivery. The Honourable Lincoln Alexander (1922 – 2012). http://www.archives.gov.on.ca/en/explore/online/alexander/index.aspx Accessed on February 27, 2020.

Brown was sworn to the Queen's Privy Council for Canada as a member of the federal Security Intelligence Review Committee, responsible for overseeing the actions of the Canadian Security Intelligence Service, a role which she held from 1993 to 1998. She also served on the Order of Canada Advisory Committee from 1999 until her death in 2003.[234]

Honors and Awards

National Black Coalition Award, 1972.
United Nations Human Rights Fellowship, 1973.
YWCA Woman of Distinction Award, 1989.
Honorary doctorate degree from the University of British Columbia, 1995
Order of British Columbia, 1995
Order of Canada, 1996
Government of Jamaica Commander of the Order of Distinction, 2001
Canadian Congress Award for Outstanding Service to Humanity, 2002
Honorary doctorate degrees from various Canadian Universities. [235]

Glenda P. Simms, Ph.D., LL.D. (HONS.)

Glenda P. Simms "was born at Stanmore in the parish of St. Elizabeth in Jamaica and was raised by her great-grandmother who instilled in her that she could do anything that she set her mind to do. "And so when I went to St. Alban's Primary school in Stanmore, and they wanted me to do the things that girls are supposed to do. I wouldn't." Instead, Glenda spent her time reading and learning about those things that were not taught in school. She excelled in her classes starting at the St Albans primary school in Stanmore, continuing throughout her academic career. "After graduating from Bethlehem Teacher's College, she taught at Vauxhall Senior School, Vere Technical High and Cornwall College" [Montego Bay, Jamaica].[236]

"In 1966, she migrated to Canada, and there distinguished herself in the fields of Education and the Public Service. She received a Doctorate in

234 *Wikipedia*. Rosemary Brown (politician).
https://en.wikipedia.org/wiki/Rosemary_Brown_(politician) Accessed on February 27, 2020.
235 Idem.
236 Gender Equality – Cayman Islands. Keynote Speaker.
http://genderequality.gov.ky/resources/keynote-speaker Accessed on February 27, 2020.

Educational Psychology from the University of Alberta, and a Certificate in the Program for Leaders in Development from Harvard University, USA.

During her time in Canada, Dr. Simms received numerous accolades, including four honorary doctorates from the University of Alberta, Queens University, the University of Manitoba and The University of Western Ontario; the Black Achievement Award for contributions in public policy; the Inter Amicus Human Rights Award from McGill University; and a Citation for Citizenship from the Canadian Government."[237]

In 1990 Prime Minister Brian Mulroney appointed Dr. Simms to be President of the Canadian Advisory Council on the Status of Women, and in this role, she was selected as one of Canada's representatives to the Global Women's Conference held in Kenya. After serving for a period of six years, Dr. Simms returned to her native Jamaica to join "the Jamaican government services as Executive Director of the Bureau of Women's Affairs until August 2005."

"Dr. Simms is a staunch advocate for the elimination of discriminatory practices in society, and lectures extensively – locally and internationally – on a variety of feminist, educational, social, and political issues.

As an author of numerous publications, an advisor to governments, a gender specialist, researcher and projects leader, Dr. Simms has contributed immensely to the implementation of important social and political initiatives in Canada, the Philippines, the Turks and Caicos Islands and Jamaica. She has been an inspiration and a positive example for women, men, and minorities by the standards of her excellence, leadership, and achievements." Currently, Dr. Simms is working as a private consultant and gender specialist and has worked in the position of Senior Advisor to the Prime Minister of Jamaica on Gender Issues and Women's Affairs. She also was appointed as an expert on the Committee for the Elimination of all Forms of Discrimination Against Women at the United Nations for four years, from January 2005 to December 2008. This body of independent experts from around the world monitors implementation of the Convention on the Elimination of All Forms of Discrimination against Women.[238]

She is a founding member of both the Congress of Black Women of Canada and the National Organization of Immigrant and Visible Minority Women, through her tenure as the President of the Canadian Advisory Council on the Status of Women and the Executive Director of the Jamaican Bureau of Women's Affairs.

---

237 Gender Equality – Cayman Islands.
238 Gender Equality – Cayman Islands. Keynote Speaker.

Jean Augustine PC, CM, OOnt, CBE "was born in 1937 in Grenada and "immigrated to Canada in 1960 under the West Indian Domestic Scheme. She studied at the University of Toronto where she obtained a Bachelor of Arts and a Master of Education. After university she worked as an elementary school principal with the Metropolitan Separate School Board in Toronto. She was also actively involved in Toronto's Caribbean community, sitting on the first committee to organize the Caribana Festival in 1967.[239]

Jean Augustine
PC CM OOnt CBE

She has become engaged in numerous organizations for education and social justice, serving with the National Black Coalition of Canada, the Urban Alliance on Race Relations (UARR), the Board of Governors of York University, the Board of Trustees for The Hospital for Sick Children, the Board of Directors of the Donwood Institute, the Board of Harbourfront, and Chair of the Metro Toronto Housing Authority. She was also named National President of the Congress of Black Women of Canada in 1987.

In the 1993 federal election, Augustine became the first Black Canadian woman elected to the Parliament of Canada; she served three terms as Chair of the National Liberal Women's Caucus. In February 2002, Augustine was elected Chair of the Standing Committee on Foreign Affairs and International Trade. While in office, Jean Augustine was solely responsible for championing Federal legislation to recognize February as Black History Month in Canada with a unanimous vote of 305–0. This allowed Canadians to honour their Black history during the same month as the Americans.

Augustine also was the first Black Canadian woman in the Federal cabinet. On May 26, 2002, she was appointed Secretary of State for Multiculturalism and the Status of Women. In December 2003, she was re-appointed to the new Cabinet as Minister of State (Multiculturalism and Status of Women). In 2004 she was appointed to the position of Assistant Deputy Chair of Committees of the Whole, making her the first Black Canadian to occupy the Speaker's Chair in the Canadian House of Commons.

---

239 *Wikipedia*. Jean Augustine. https://en.wikipedia.org/wiki/Jean_Augustine Accessed on February 15, 2018.

Augustine was the founding chair of the Canadian Association of Parliamentarians on Population & Development, chair of the National Sugar Caucus, chair of the Micro-credit Summit Council of Canadian Parliamentarians, chair of the Canada-Slovenia Parliamentary Group, and chair of the Canada–Africa Parliamentary Group.

On November 28, 2005, Augustine announced her intention to retire from the House, saying that she would not be a candidate in the 2006 Canadian election. She endorsed Liberal Michael Ignatieff to succeed her.

In 2007, Augustine was nominated by the Government of Ontario to become the first Fairness Commissioner, a position created to advocate for Canadians with foreign professional credentials. Augustine retired from the position of Fairness Commissioner in March 2015.

In 2007, Augustine donated her personal records to the Clara Thomas Archives and Special Collections at York University. "Pushing buttons, pushing stories" is a digital exhibit of Augustine's personal political buttons.

In 2008, the Jean Augustine Chair in Education was established in the Faculty of Education at York University.

Augustine serves as the patron, visitor or honorary chair of a number of organizations, including the NATO Association of Canada."[240]

Honours and awards
- A documentary film on Jean Augustine's life and achievements (2022)
- Lifetime Achievement Award (2021) from Maclean's Magazine
- Awarded an Honorary Doctor of Laws from University of Toronto, Awarded an Honorary Doctor of Laws from McGill University (2009), Awarded an Honorary Doctor of Laws from Trent University (2017).
- YWCA Woman of Distinction Award, the Kay Livingstone Award, the Ontario Volunteer Award, an African Canadian Achievement Award (Pride News Magazine), the Rubena Willis Special Recognition Award, and the Toronto Lions' Club Onyx Award.
- Member of the Order of Canada "for her distinguished career as an educator, politician and advocate for social justice in Canada" (2009)
- Appointed Commander of the Order of the British Empire (CBE) in the 2014 Birthday Honours, Grenada.
- Canadian Immigrant Award (2011).

---

240 *Wikipedia.* Jean Augustine.

Ann Cools "was born and raised in Barbados, the daughter of pharmacist Lucius Unique Cools and homemaker Rosita Gordon Miller Cools. Both her grandfather and an uncle were politically active on the island. When she was four years old, two of her siblings died from peritonitis. Cools attended Queen's College Girls School in Barbados. In 1957, when she was 13 years old, her family migrated to Canada, where she studied at Thomas D'Arcy McGee High School in Montreal before going to McGill University for a B.A. degree in social sciences, sociology, and psychology. She is married to business consultant Rolf Calhoun. Her personal interests include classical music, playing the piano, reading, gardening and dogs.

Senator Ann Cools

In February 1969, Cools participated in a 13-day civil disobedience sit-in at Sir George Williams University (later Concordia University); where over 400 students occupied the computer center to protest the school's inadequate handling of complaints of racism against a professor. When the riot-police stormed the building, some floors were set on fire, computers were destroyed and computer cards and paper rained down from the 9th floor onto the street below where there was a counter-demonstration chanting "Let the Niggers burn." While Cools was nowhere near the 9th floor that day, she was one of 97 students arrested. Unlike most of them Cools refused to plead guilty to be set free instead of serving two months in jail. About the affair she has said "it took me a long time to recover it shocked me to my core." Several years later she was pardoned.

As a social worker, Cools was one of the pioneers in the protection of women from domestic abuse. In 1974, Cools moved to Toronto where she founded and served as the executive director for *Women in Transition Inc.*, one of the first shelters for domestic violence victims in Canada. With a high demand for its services, she obtained funding for and opened a second shelter in 1987. She was the co-organizer of Canada's first domestic violence conference, *Couples in Conflict*.

Cools has presented evidence that men and women are equally capable of domestic violence and aggression, which is not a gendered characteristic, but a human pathology of intimacy. In January 2016, in a Canadaland audio podcast interview with Desmond Cole, Cools supported and cited the work of the English domestic violence pioneer and expert Erin Pizzey, when she claimed that women are equally violent as men in domestic violence conflicts.

Cools is a strong advocate for children's rights. She believes they should have continuing relationships with both mothers and fathers after divorce, and the importance of fathers for the children's development. In the 1990s, Cools was instrumental in the creation of the Senate/House Special Joint Committee on Child Custody and Access, which in December 1998 issued its report, For the Sake of the Children, and she served on it. A principal recommendation of this report was that following a relationship breakdown, shared parenting should be presumed to be in the best interests of the child. She was candid in her criticism of the Liberal government of Prime Minister Jean Chrétien when legislation proposed to be introduced in the House of Commons was shelved after intense lobbying by women's groups.

While a strong advocate for women and domestic violence victims, she has also criticized certain aspects of the feminist movement, for instance stating that "this feminism that has grown up suddenly in the last few years, where all virtue and goodness are stacked up on the side of women, and all evil and violence is stacked up on the side of men — well, human nature doesn't work that way."

From 1980 to 1984, Cools served on the National Parole Board of Canada, which is the parole board for prisoners in the Federal system.

She caught the eye of Prime Minister Pierre Trudeau and twice sought election to the House of Commons of Canada as a candidate of the Liberal Party of Canada. She lost the Liberal nomination in a closely contested race against John Evans for the 1978 by-election in Rosedale. She ran again in 1979 and won the nomination but was defeated in both the 1979 and 1980 elections by Progressive Conservative candidate David Crombie.

But her electoral performance impressed Prime Minister Pierre Trudeau and in 1984 he arranged for her appointment to the Senate of Canada by Governor-General Edward Schreyer and she became the first Black Canadian Senator, designating herself as representing the Senate division of Toronto-Centre-York. Cools grew increasingly critical of the Liberal governments of Jean Chrétien and Paul Martin, and of same-sex marriage. On June 9, 2004, she announced that she was crossing the floor to join the Conservative Party of Canada.

In the fall of 2006, Cools was barred from her committee duties for the Conservative Party, after questioning a new government accountability bill. In 2007, Cools was ousted from the Conservative party group after accusing two fellow senators of having grabbed and assaulted her. She also mentioned that she had witnessed a Senator hitting a child. She sat as a non-affiliated Senator from 2007 until 2017 when she joined the Independent Senators Group.

From the retirement of Lowell Murray on September 26, 2011, until her own retirement on August 12, 2018, Cools was the longest-serving member of the Senate. She is the first female Black Senator in North America. With the retirement of Charlie Watt, Cools was the last Senator appointed by Pierre Trudeau remaining in the Senate.[241]

Hedy Madeleine Fry, PC MP "was born in San Fernando, Trinidad, and Tobago, of Indian, Chinese, Scottish and Spanish ancestry. After declining an English Literature scholarship to Oxford, Fry earned her equivalent of a BA in Science in one year and then went on to receive her medical training at the Royal College of Surgeons in Dublin, Ireland. She migrated to Canada in 1970 and established a practice in Vancouver.

Dr. Hedy Madeleine Fry
PC MP

Dr. Fry worked at St. Paul's Hospital (Vancouver) for 23 years. She served as president of the British Columbia Federation of Medical Women in 1977. She was president of the Vancouver Medical Association in 1988-89, the B.C. Medical Association in 1990-91, and chaired the Canadian Medical Association's Multiculturalism Committee in 1992-9. She volunteered as a Tawny Owl as a member of the Girl Guides of Canada, leading a Brownie group. Fry was also a host on the nationally televised CBC show *Doctor Doctor*.

Dr. Fry sought and won the Liberal Party nomination for Vancouver Centre for the 1993 federal election over lawyer David Varty and college lecturer John Lang in March 1993. She was elected to the House of Commons of Canada, defeating Progressive Conservative Prime Minister Kim Campbell. Fry was only the fifth person to unseat a sitting prime minister, and the first to do so on his or her first try for office. She has been re-elected in every subsequent election (1997, 2000, 2004, 2006, 2008, 2011, 2015 and 2019).

Dr. Fry served as Parliamentary Secretary to the Minister of National Health and Welfare from 1993 until 1996 when she was appointed to the

---

241 *Wikipedia.* Anne Cools. https://en.wikipedia.org/wiki/Anne_Cools Accessed on February 27, 2020.

Cabinet as Secretary of State for Multiculturalism and Status of Women. She did not remain a minister after cabinet was shuffled in 2002.

When Paul Martin became Prime Minister of Canada at the end of 2003, he made her Parliamentary Secretary to the Minister of Citizenship and Immigration with special emphasis on Foreign Credentials. After the 2004 election, she was named Parliamentary Secretary to the Minister of Citizenship and Immigration and the Minister of Human Resources and Skills Development with special emphasis on the Internationally Trained Workers Initiative.

In 2006 Dr. Fry beat high-profile NDP activist and former MP Svend Robinson and in 2008 she defeated high-profile Conservative Lorne Mayencourt. On May 4, 2006, she became the 11th person, third woman, and the only Westerner to officially enter the Liberal party leadership race. She launched her leadership campaign saying that Canada's diversity is its greatest competitive advantage, "our weapon of mass inclusion," and called for a "non-ideological" approach to problem solving. She withdrew from the contest on September 25 and announced her support for Bob Rae.

Re-elected in Vancouver Centre for a sixth term in 2008, Dr. Fry was appointed the Official Opposition Critic for Canadian Heritage. On November 21, 2008, Liberal leadership candidate Bob Rae announced that she would serve as his Campaign Co-Chair in British Columbia.

Dr. Fry was re-elected in 2011 by a margin of approximately 2,000 votes. When the Liberals lost power in 2006, she was named as Critic for Sport Canada in the Liberal shadow cabinet. In 2011, as the Liberals lost their designation as Official Opposition, she was named Liberal Critic for Health.

In the 2015 election, Dr. Fry won her riding once more, becoming the oldest Canadian MP and the longest serving female MP. During the 42nd Parliament, she was appointed to the National Security and Intelligence Committee of Parliamentarians, which provides oversight to Canada's security services and requires a Top-Secret security clearance.

In the 2019 Election, Dr. Fry once again won her riding – for a ninth consecutive term. She currently serves as the Special Representative for Gender Issues at the Organization for Security and Cooperation in Europe's Parliamentary Assembly, a role she has held since 2010. She is also a member of the Standing Committee on Foreign Affairs and International Development, and the Special Committee on the COVID-19 Pandemic."[242]

---

242 *Wikipedia*. Hedy Fry. https://en.wikipedia.org/wiki/Hedy_Fry Accessed on February 29, 2020.

Jennifer Hosten, born in St. George's Grenada, is "a radio announcer, development worker, diplomat, author, model, and beauty queen who won the 1970 Miss World Beauty Contest representing Grenada. She was the first woman from her country to win the title which she did at age 22. ... She studied in London and then worked for the BBC's Caribbean radio service before becoming a flight attendant.

Jennifer Hosten

The 1970 beauty contest was held in London, England Jennifer Hosten won, becoming the second Black woman to win Miss World after the Jamaican Carole Joan Crawford in 1963. The Black contestant from South Africa was placed second, and the BBC and newspapers received numerous protests about the result with accusations of racism being made on all sides. Four of the nine judges had given first-place votes to Miss Sweden, while Miss Grenada received only two firsts while receiving the most overall points. Miss Sweden, who was favored to win, finished fourth. After the contest Hosten joined Bob Hope on his annual tour to U.S. forces overseas and made numerous other personal appearances all over the world with quiet dignity despite the controversy surrounding her victory. ...Hosten then worked with Air Canada in customer relations, and married David Craig, an IT Manager with IBM. They lived in Bermuda until 1973, when they moved to Ontario, Canada. Hosten earned a Master of Arts in Political Science and International Relations from Carleton University, Ottawa. She has two children, a daughter, Sophia Craig, and son, Beau Craig. From 1978 to 1981 she was Grenada's High Commissioner to Canada.

Hosten meeting with former Prime Minister Pierre Elliott Trudeau while serving as High Commissioner for Grenada to Canada in 1978.

In 1998 she served as Technical Adviser on Trade to the Organization of Eastern Caribbean States (OECS) while living on the island of St. Lucia. More recently she worked as a Canadian diplomat (Aid Division) at the Canadian High Commission in Dhaka, Bangladesh before returning to the Caribbean."[243]

---

243 *Wikipedia.* Jennifer Horsten. https://wiki2.org/en/Jennifer_Hosten Accessed on February 27, 2020.

Trevor Stanton

Trevor Stanton always wanted to be an air force pilot. He saw a path to realize this dream with the Royal Canadian Air Force (RCAF). After his graduation from Kingston College Jamaica, he worked for a brief period in Kingston and then set off to Canada to join his sister and brother-in-law who lived in Montreal. Trevor arrived in Montreal in September of 1959 and within days of his arrival he went to the RCAF recruitment office intending to sign up to join the Air force. When the 6'6'' Stanton sat down and told the recruitment officer that his objective was to fly for the RCAF, to his chagrin, the officer responded "you're not gonna fly our airplanes". Trevor learned that at 6'6" he had outgrown the height requirements; RCAF pilots could be no taller than 5'10'' in order to be seated comfortably in the aircraft. Automatically rejected as a potential air force pilot, he nonetheless was still set on joining the air force and settled for a role as a member of the RCAF ground crew. This was the start of a 10-year RCAF career.

He started initial Basic training in St. Jean, Quebec, and then was posted to Gimli, Manitoba where he served for 18 months. There he learned to play the saxophone. His next posting, a 10-month stint in Goose Bay, turned out to be his worst experience in the RCAF. However, it was during this period that he received in-depth training to become an aircraft mechanic, which turned out to be a pivotal point in his RCAF career. Trevor was then posted to the northernmost RCAF base in Resolute Bay on Ellesmere Island (Resolute Bay is an Inuit hamlet on Cornwallis Island in Nunavut, Canada. It is situated at the northern end of Resolute Bay and the Northwest Passage and is part of the Qikiqtaaluk Region. Resolute is one of Canada's northernmost communities and is second only to Grise Fiord on Ellesmere Island.[244]) The likelihood that in 1959 a young Jamaican man would be seen in Resolute Bay was as remote as the place itself. But Trevor felt completely at ease this close to the North Pole.

At that time the majority population was comprised of military personnel. However, there was a small Inuit village a few kilometers south of the RCAF

---

244 *Wikipedia*. Resolute Bay.
https://en.wikipedia.org/wiki/Resolute,_Nunavut#:~:text=Resolute%20or%20Resolute%20Bay%20(Inuktitut,part%20of%20the%20Qikiqtaaluk%20Region Accessed on March 16, 2020.

base.[245] Trevor spent two years at the Resolute Bay camp. "It was great" he said. "When I went there they had a defunct radio station on the base which had the call letters CFRB." The Air force decided to re-furbish the radio station shortly after he arrived since it was the only mode of mass communication with the base community. He decided to join the station staff because music was a component of their programming, and that was of interest to him. This became a launching pad for his career in radio. His audience ranged from about 25 in the winter up to about 100 in the summer. By the end of his posting at Resolute Bay, Trevor had honed a solid set of radio broadcasting skills that would serve him well in later years. He served at a number of other RCAF bases in Canada. His next posting was at St. Hubert in Quebec. His buddy who was a guitarist often dragged him along on his outings to hear live bands, and it was during one of these outings that he was attracted to the saxophone. He enrolled in the RCAF band training program, and was given a clarinet to start. The band leader told him that if he mastered the clarinet, he would be able to play any other reed instrument. He worked diligently to master the clarinet and once he was comfortable, he moved on to play the tenor sax. His next posting was the Northern Armstrong Ontario base, and shortly thereafter, he was posted overseas at a Canadian base in Baden, Germany. (Canadian Forces Base Baden–Soellingen or CFB Baden–Soellingen, formerly known as RCAF Station Baden–Soellingen, was a Canadian Forces base located near the farming community of Söllingen, part of the municipality of Rheinmünster in the West German state of Baden-Württemberg).[246]

Just prior to his posting in Germany, Trevor married his fiancée Ruth Starratt whom he had met while in St. Hubert. The couple headed off to Germany where Trevor completed his RCAF tenure. They returned to Canada and after his honourable discharge from the RCAF, he launched his second career by applying his radio broadcasting skills. He applied for a position at a small station in Peterborough and became a broadcaster. He also worked with one of his counterparts at the station who hosted a Jazz segment. and thoroughly immersed himself in Jazz music. Having learned to play the sax while in the RCAF, he focused his saxophone talents at playing Jazz.

Trevor moved to Ottawa from Peterborough to work as a Broadcaster at the CFMO radio station in Ottawa. After several years when CFMO went out of

---

245 Travel Nunavut. Resolute. https://travelnunavut.ca/regions-of-nunavut/communities/resolute/ Accessed on July 29, 2019.
246 *Wikipedia.* CFB Baden. https://en.wikipedia.org/wiki/CFB_Baden%E2%80%93Soellingen Accessed on July 29, 2019.

business, he moved back to Montreal to work at CKO an all-news station in Montreal. Unfortunately CKO also went out of business, signalling the end of his life as a broadcaster, so he returned to work in the aircraft industry, firstly with Canadair and then with Bombardier, Inc. from which he later retired with his wife Ruth to an idyllic area near Alexandria, Ontario. At the time of my interview with Trevor, he was leading a Jazz band in Alexandria.

CONCLUSION
Seeds of Multiculturalism

In January 1962 Ellen Fairclough, Canada's Minister of Citizenship and Immigration dismantled Canada's discriminatory Immigration Policy. With this act, Canada in effect declared an end to formalized racial discrimination in Canadian migration. The glacially slow rate of change in Canada's racial demographics started to increase. Canada implemented the new immigration policy by ushering in people from the Caribbean as its first officially sanctioned group of non-white immigrants, and this started to prepare the nation for what was now proclaimed to be a multicultural society.

Within the next decade, as these new immigrants from predominantly Caribbean islands settled into their new home country, they did not discard their birthright customs and inherent culture. Instead, they looked for various ways to express who they were at the core of their humanity. And with actions of cultural expression, they began to till the multicultural soil. It was most appropriate that in seeking a way to express their passion for cricket in a group of their peer West Indian comrades, and in the face of institutional racism expressed by four words "No Blacks, no Cricket", Governor General Roland Michener started to sow the seeds for a Multicultural Canada that we now enjoy to the envy of the world.

The majority of profiled subjects entered Canada either under the Domestic Scheme, as a CIDA student or under the Points System. Either strategically or unwittingly, by instituting these immigration programs in the '50s and '60s, Canada began to sow the seeds of Multiculturalism. The domestic workers were immediately woven into the inner circle of the Canadian families that they served. The students were integrated into classrooms with Canadian students making many lasting friendships, and the Points System brought in job-ready professionals who began to contribute to economic development without being burdensome to society. The long-term effect of each of these early immigrant groups, and of those who followed later is obvious as one travels around Ottawa or anywhere else in Canada.

"In a statement to the House of Commons on October 8, 1971, Prime Minister Pierre Trudeau announced Multiculturalism as an official government policy. Based on the recommendations of the Royal Commission on Bilingualism and Biculturalism, the policy of multiculturalism was intended to be a social leveller, preserving the cultural freedom of all individuals, and recognizing the contributions of diverse ethnic groups to Canadian society. The Commission was appointed in 1963 to examine the existing state of bilingualism and biculturalism in Canada and to work towards developing an equal partnership between the British and French elements within the country. Commissioners were additionally instructed to consider the cultural contributions of other ethnic groups, but many cultural groups throughout Canada expressed concern that the latter part of the mandate was being ignored."[247]

The commission addressed these concerns in their fourth and final report, recommending that minority groups be given greater recognition and support in preserving their cultures. "The recommendations of the commission were adapted to become the government's official policy of multiculturalism."[248]

The publications by Freda Hawkins and Michael Temelini[249], Critical Years in Immigration: Canada and Australia Compared and "Multicultural Rights, Multicultural Virtues: A History of Multiculturalism in Canada", respectively provide in-depth analysis on the evolution of Canada's Multicultural Policy and the move to establishing the concept of a "Just Society". Trudeau defined the Just Society before becoming the Prime Minister of Canada:

> "The Just Society will be one in which the rights of minorities will be safe from the whims of intolerant majorities. The Just Society will be one in which those regions and groups which have not fully shared in the country's affluence will be given a better opportunity. The Just Society will be one where such urban problems as housing and pollution will be attacked through the application of new knowledge and new techniques. The Just Society will be one in which our Indian and Inuit populations will be encouraged to assume the full rights of citizenship through policies which will give them both greater responsibility for their own future and more meaningful equality of opportunity. The Just Society will be a united Canada, united because all of its citizens will be actively involved in the development of a country where equality of opportunity is ensured and individuals are permitted to fulfill themselves in the fashion they judge best."[250]

---

247 Canadian Museum of Immigration at Pier 21. Canadian Multicultural Policy, 1971. https://pier21.ca/research/immigration-history/canadian-multiculturalism-policy-1971. Accessed on March 16, 2020.
248 Sarah V. Wayland, "Immigration, Multiculturalism and National Identity in Canada," *International Journal of Group Rights* 5, no. 1 (1997): 46-47.
249 Freda Hawkins, Critical Years in Immigration: Canada and Australia Compared, 2nd ed. Montreal: McGill-Queen's University Press, 1991, 218; Michael Temelini, "Multicultural Rights, Multicultural Virtues: A History of Multiculturalism in Canada." in Multiculturalism.
250 Cecil Foster (2007). Blackness and Modernity: The Colour of Humanity and the Quest for Freedom. McGill-Queen's Press. p. 329.

Canada has irrefutably maintained its enviable role as world leader in its humanitarian domestic and foreign policy. It continues to evolve in its role in the world as a nation that follows the chosen path of "Peace, order and good government", words used in section 91 of the British North America Act of 1867 (now Constitution Act, 1867).[251]

Domestic Immigrants

Either unwittingly or by strategic design, Canada may have set the stage for the current social construct of a multi-cultural society. It is clear that there are many people in Canadian society who are not favourable to Canada's multicultural policies. But there is also a growing tolerance of the racial diversity that is inherent in Canadian society. The initial policy changes admitting domestic workers from the Caribbean as its first group of non-white immigrants could be viewed as the catalyst for the current make-up of the Canadian society. The work of the domestic services provider which mandated having a Black person living within a white household, and being entrusted with caring for their children, sensitized a generation of Canadian children to racial diversity.

In effect, the Canadian family had a contract with their Black helper. The Caribbean domestic services providers were literally integrated with the Canadian family and their primary role was to care for the most precious and vulnerable family members — the babies, toddlers and infants who were in the charge of the domestic helper. Their Canadian family had to trust the stranger from the Caribbean. And this trust had to be maintained throughout the minimum tenure period of one year. The infants within the family also underwent an intense cultural experience. Considering that even seeing a Black face would have been a novel experience for most of these infants, living with one who took care of you could be tantamount to culture shock. But children, especially very young children, are resilient. Most would adapt to this experience as if it was a natural event. Through this forced integration of Blacks and Whites on a relatively micro-sociological scale, many of those Canadian families would have lived a positive experience with what would have most likely been their first encounter with a Black person.

---

251 *The Canadian Encyclopedia.* Peace, Order and Good Government's Evolution.
https://www.thecanadianencyclopedia.ca/en/article/peace-order-and-good-government's evolution
Accessed on March 16, 2020.

Ultimately, the children's views of Blacks would have been positively fashioned, and this would likely remain with them throughout their lifetime. While this may not fully explain the growing propensity of Canadian society towards racial tolerance, it is arguable that many of the children who were raised in part by Caribbean domestics grew up to be more tolerant of other races than those who were not. These children would also be from middle to upper-income families and hence would most likely succeed in academics and ultimately be leaders and policymakers in the Canadian society. While no data exists to support the effect of the Caribbean domestic worker on Canadian society, one can certainly argue that they played a very positive role in shaping the minds of many Canadians to have an amicable disposition towards non-whites.

In contrast to their southern neighbors, whose experiences were often portrayed in the stereotypical movie of the black maid in the American household, for the most part, the American maid came to work in the morning and went back home in the evening. There were cases where some household help lived with the families, but these were mainly the minority situations. For the Canadian family, this would turn out to be a different experience.

The lasting impact of the Canadian Domestic Scheme in fashioning Canada's social ecosystem cannot be underestimated. Some of the earliest ethnic Canadian immigrants, post Immigration policy liberation, were domestic caregivers from the Caribbean. They were trusted mother-substitutes who took care of infant children at home while their parents were at the office. The children in their care would have been at the trailing end of the Baby Boom generation. These are the children from mostly middle-class families, those who were economically able to sponsor a domestic helper.

Many of these families had never previously encountered a Black person prior to this experience. But now, their newborn and toddlers would be left in the care of a total stranger from a foreign land. Many Canadian families were willing to take that risk. And today, Canada, despite its flaws in racial relationships, is still recognized as the world's beacon with regards to racial tolerance.

> "Recent rankings name Canada the world's most tolerant society, and suggest its openness to immigrants and ethnic minorities may be very good for business."[252]

---

252 Canada Named Most Tolerant Country in the World. CTV News. https://www.ctvnews.ca/canada/canada-named-most-tolerant-country-in-the-world-1.2640276 Accessed on March 16, 2020.

Indeed some of those baby boomers who received care from their Caribbean caregivers, may have become policy makers within the Government institution. It would be fair to assume that infants are conditioned by their environment. The "Nature vs. Nurture" debate contests the predominant determinant between our genetic composition and our developmental environment as to who we are.

> "Nature refers to all of the genes and hereditary factors that influence who we are — from our physical appearance to our personality characteristics. Nurture refers to all the environmental variables that impact who we are."[253]

Regardless of what factor predominates, there is no denying that both are influential. The fact remains that Caribbean domestic caregivers were positively influential in the development of a number of Canadian children.

What is now irrefutable are the social and economic contributions delivered to Canadian society by the follow-on entrants through family reunification and later the children of domestic workers. Family reunion brought Canada additional labour resources, many of whom had professional skills that were immediately utilized to increase economic activity. Others entered training and higher education institutions to build up their skills and ultimately make their own contribution to the Canadian society. The domestic workers whose primary motive to migrate to Canada was to "better themselves" ensured that their own children continued to fulfill that goal through their own lives. The results are consistent with that motive. Children of domestic workers include MDs, PhDs, professional engineers, and broadcasters. They are embedded in just about every professional area across the employment spectrum, and in many areas of entrepreneurial activities. As in any cohort, some children have been less successful; unfortunately, media coverage tends to focus on those cases. Ultimately,

> "Canada is successful as a nation because it has always been a country founded and built by people who came here by choice, who immigrated for a chance at a new life and who have worked hard, generation after generation, to build a tolerant society."[254]

---

253 Very Well Mind. What Is Nature Versus Nurture. https://www.verywellmind.com/what-is-nature-versus-nurture-2795392# Accessed on March 16, 2020.
254 Surjit Singh Flora. Huffington Post. https://www.huffingtonpost.ca/surjit-singh-flora/canada-is-my-home-now_b_17077942.html Accessed on March 16, 2020.

Student Immigrants

After my interviews with a number of immigrant students from the Caribbean, I saw a pattern emerge. Most of the student immigrants intended to obtain higher academic credentials from Canadian educational institutions before returning to their home country to pursue their chosen careers. But very few did this. Many of those who graduated from Canadian institutions and returned to the Caribbean with college diplomas, undergraduate and post-graduate degrees ultimately came back to Canada as Landed Immigrants, and then became Canadian citizens.

With very few exceptions, the professionals that have been profiled came to Ottawa to study. And for a variety of reasons, even the few who went back home, returned to Ottawa to work at their chosen field of endeavour. Many of those students who were sponsored by CIDA with the condition that they return to their home countries are also now Canadian citizens. The earlier groups of student immigrants started their own families in Canada, and now their children who were born in Canada have, in many cases, attained higher levels of academic achievements than their parents.

Many of these first-generation Canadians of immigrant student parents are approaching middle age. They are solidly established in the spectrum of professional, social, and entrepreneurial disciplines where they continue to provide significant and positive contributions to Canadian society.

Professional Immigrant Class

The Caribbean immigrants who entered Canada under the "Points System" were selected on the basis that they begin immediately to make a contribution to Canada's economic development. The objective of this program was to augment Canada's labour force with specific skills in those areas where there were acute shortages. The "Professional Immigrants" were able to fill Canada's labour needs in a broad spectrum of economic areas. The top three "human factors" in the selection criteria applied by the points system was based on the individual's age, level of education, and official languages proficiency. These were additional hurdles for many Caribbean professionals to surmount.

From Canada's perspective, the country was gaining the necessary skills that it needed to support its own economic growth. And from the Caribbean nations' perspective this was largely seen as a "brain drain" of its most important resource. Those individuals who chose to immigrate to Canada viewed it as an opportunity to improve their own lives and the lives of their family members. So many of the professionals who immigrated to Canada in the late 1960s onwards, initially secured employment in their professional areas of expertise, but they continued their personal development, upgraded their skills and academic growth by enrolling in educational institutions. Canada's labour force continued to grow with the additional expertise brought by the entry of the Caribbean professionals. And this trend continues with a new generation as the children of these immigrants continued to outperform their parents in skills and expertise.

The Next Generation – Fast Forward 2020

The first generation of Caribbean immigrant children has made its presence evident in many facets of Canadian society. In just about every city, across the vast Canadian landscape, you can encounter professionals in almost every discipline, whose parents immigrated to Canada from one of the island nations in the Caribbean, sometime between 1955 and 1980. The offspring of the immigrant residents in Ottawa can be seen on local and national television, and can be heard on radio airwaves. They have assumed leadership roles in medicine, in academia, in social services, in Government and in the broad spectrum of enterprises within the Canadian professional entity. And despite the pigmentation differences in many cases, they see themselves as Canadians.

Canadians of colour and children of immigrants tend to be far more educated than Canadian whites and aboriginals, according to two studies. "Canada's white males are the least likely to hold university degrees in the knowledge economy," says a report by Jack Jedwab, president of the Canadian Institute for Identities and Migration. Only 24 per cent of white Canadian men between ages 35 and 44 have university degrees, according to Jedwab's research. That is less than half the university-educated rate of Canadians of South Asian, Chinese, and Korean background.[255]

An internal federal Immigration Department report by Garnett Picot confirms a related trend. The 2016 census shows that 36 per cent of the children of

---

255 Douglas Todd. 'Privileged' white males tend to be less educated – that's among education complications uncovered by census. The London Free Press. February16, 2018

immigrants aged 25 to 35 hold university degrees, compared to just 24 per cent of people in that age bracket with Canadian-born parents. Picot said in his report, titled *The Educational and Market Outcomes of the Children of Immigrants: A Success to be Preserved*: [256]

> "Canada fortunately has among the best educational and economic outcomes for the children of immigrants in the western world. This success sets Canada apart from most European nations, and to some extent, the U.S."

And now, the second generation is emerging, marching across the graduation stage at many institutions of higher learning and moving into the next phase of professional careers. Many of the first generation had become familiar with their backgrounds because they were directly connected with their parents and learned this first-hand. But this history is lesser known by the grandchildren of the Caribbean Immigrants, because as with any population, the knowledge of their history becomes more diluted as time ensues.

While it is not an exhaustive historical account of the Caribbean immigrants in Ottawa, it should provide readers, especially those of Caribbean heritage, with a reasonable solid grasp of the evolution of the Ottawa Caribbean community and how they factor into the Ottawa and Canadian experience. And hopefully, this publication will also provide future generations of people with Caribbean heritage with a reference to their history.

The focus of this publication was on the initial twenty-five years following the beginning of formalized Caribbean immigration to Canada. And at the time of this writing some sixty-five years has ensued following the arrival of the first large group of predominantly Black faces in Canada as a whole and Ottawa as a microcosm of the nation. During this period, Canada has evolved to become a multicultural and racially diverse society. And most, if not all of those profiled, came to the conclusion that Canada is a great country and that they have little or no regrets regarding their decision to migrate to Canada and make it their home. At the same time they recognize that some of the attitudes that they experienced in their initial years continue to persist. These were described under the heading "Racial Attitudes". The incidences cited by a number of the profiled respondents would clearly be classified as incidents of racism today. It would be instructive to

---

256 Douglas Todd: "Who are the most and least educated in Canada?" Vancouver Sun. https://vancouversun.com/opinion/columnists/douglas-todd-immigrants-children-and-canadians-of-colour-most-educated. Accessed on March 16, 2020.

understand if these attitudes still hold or have dissipated. Some answers on this social phenomenon of 'diversity and inclusion' can be found in the following account as related by a first generation Canadian of Caribbean immigrant parents.

The Epilogue that follows was written by my youngest daughter Melanie Tulloch who was born in Canada. It presents us with collaborative evidence of the matters revealed in the main text by the lives of Black migrants.

Epilogue

Canadian Black History *and Me*

by Melanie Tulloch

This is me in junior kindergarten. I was a cute kid. If you haven't figured it out yet, I'm the one in the middle row sitting next to the teacher. Shy and quiet at times but for the most part outgoing around those I felt comfortable with. As a child I wasn't taught the value of embracing differences. Like every kid I always wanted to fit in. It didn't help that while everyone else was eating "fruit roll-ups" and "lunchables," I was bringing the food that my Jamaican immigrant parents packed for lunch for me that day. I didn't always feel like an outsider, but I can't say I always felt a sense of belonging.

From an early age, I didn't see Black representation in my day to day. It wasn't in many of the books at school, on TV, or with the Barbies I played with or even my friends at school. My sister had a black Cabbage Patch doll which I believe my parents had purchased in the U.S., and that was the coolest thing ever to me. When you are a young person and you don't see yourself represented in the world, which to you are your books, TV shows, toys, and friends, then it makes you feel as though you don't belong. It can be difficult to see through your own eyes the endless possibilities of what you can ever aspire to be. This is why representation matters.

I never learned much about Black history as a young person at school. But thankfully I had fantastic parents who read me books on Black history throughout my childhood to fill in the missing gap that was there. My mom brought us to the library every week, ensuring that my school bag was filled with diverse books. I remember once my dad encouraged me to write a speech about Jackie Robinson, the first Black major league baseball player who withstood a lot of racism throughout his career. The speech I gave on Jackie Robinson at school was used to not only educate myself but my classmates. My bedtime stories at times consisted of great black leaders of past and present day. Every February my parents filled my schedule with community events, library outings and concerts celebrating Black History Month. This was so special to me. Eventually I started getting involved in Black History Month activities as a teenager. It was a month

Our Lady of Wisdom School Junior Kindergarten Class of 1985

that I looked forward to. That is where I began to learn of the Black excellence and pioneers who have paved the way for me today.

It's so important to learn about Black History because Canadian children of all backgrounds often grow up not knowing how instrumental Black pioneers were in shaping Canada. We know that as demonstrated by the Ontario curriculum today, the contributions and achievements of Black Canadians are often excluded. Even today, while there are references to Black Canadian history in the curriculum documents, it is not included in the 12 "overall expectations" that Ontario teachers must teach and assess. It is up to the teacher's discretion if he/she wants to cover topics related to Black History. Many Ontario educators and parents are currently advocating that Black History is a mandatory learning requirement from K-12. But until this happens, we can all do our part and continue to self-educate because chances are you and the generations after you wouldn't have learned much about Black History without an intentional effort.

Lessons in Black Canadian History

So, if I as a Black person was not taught Black History in Canada and it required an intentional effort by my parents; I can only assume that it requires even more of an intentional effort for non-Blacks to learn about Black History beyond the few short stories in the history books.

When I was in Grade 10 in high school, we had a mandatory Canadian history course focused on the First and Second World Wars and the Great Depression. However, I don't recall learning about Black segregated schools in Canada. In fact, Ontario was one of two provinces that segregated schools up until the 1960s. Harrow Ontario, which is 375 km southwest of Toronto, is where the last school in Ontario was finally closed in 1964. These schools were not in the best of conditions. Imagine going into an elementary class in a dark, dingy poorly lit basement. I can't imagine learning in cramped, dirty spaces full of rats.

In areas with segregated schools, courts denied Black students access to white schools. In communities without segregated schools, Black students were segregated inside the classroom and teachers could be fired for advocating for the integration of classrooms. Although chattel slavery was abolished in Canada, in 1834, the segregation of Black people in Canada was justified for many years afterwards by perpetuating ideas that Blacks were inferior. In fact, one of the last segregated schools in Nova Scotia, the Lincolnville School, closed in 1984, 150 years after slavery was abolished.

Another history lesson I received beyond my high school curriculum was the history of Blacks in Nova Scotia and the story of Africville. You may have heard of race riots in the U.S. such as Tulsa in 1921, Rosewood in 1923, and the LA Riots in 1992. But it's also important to note that the first race riot in North America actually happened in Shelburne, Nova Scotia in 1784, which at the time had the largest community of free Blacks anywhere in North America.

I learned that Blacks in the Atlantic Provinces have a history dating back several centuries. But, because of racism, Black settlers were pushed to the margins of society and forced to live on harsh lands. Despite these difficulties, Blacks established communities throughout Nova Scotia as a way to maintain their culture and to resist poor treatment by non-blacks. Africville was a predominantly Black community established on the outskirts of Halifax. The first records of Blacks in Africville date back to 1848.

Africville was formed by Black families. Blacks who settled in Halifax more than 200 years ago were promised food, clothing, shelter, and land grants, but experienced horrific living conditions instead. The City of Halifax refused to provide basic services that other non-Black residents took for granted, such as sewage, access to clean water, and garbage disposal. Africville residents who paid taxes and took pride in their homes, asked the city to provide these basic services on numerous occasions, but no action was taken. Even further, the city worsened the problem by building many undesirable developments in and around Africville, including an infectious disease hospital, a prison, a slaughterhouse, and a garbage dump.

Instead of providing proper municipal services to the community, the City of Halifax eventually decided to relocate the residents of Africville, stating that it wanted to build industry and infrastructure in the area. As a result, the residents of Africville were forcibly relocated into public housing. This meant many Black community members lost their homes and became renters. The last remaining Africville home was destroyed in January of 1970 and today all that remains is a monument to Africville that stands in a park where the community once was. Nor is the promised infrastructure evident. Although this clearly isn't the greatest moment in our Canadian History it is an important one to learn as a young Canadian regardless of your race, ethnicity, and culture. Africville is a story that has shaped Canadian history and I realized as an adult that not only do omissions and distortions from our history books contribute to the development of prejudice, but it also contributes to that lack of understanding of some as to the root causes to the systemic issues that persist today.

It is important to note Black people's struggles but also their perseverance. There are many of examples of Black excellence and current trailblazers. Leonard Austin Braithwaite is one example. He was a U of T graduate, a lawyer, and a politician. Leonard was the first Black Canadian elected to a provincial legislature. In the Ontario Legislature, he spoke out against the Separate Schools Act, a law that allowed for the segregated schools in Ontario schools. One month later, a bill was introduced that amended the Act, legally ending school segregation in Ontario. Had it not been for his efforts, I could have easily been a student in the Black segregated schools that closed only a few years before I started elementary school.

Jean Augustine is a second example of Black Canadian excellence, as she is the first elected Black female Member of Parliament and first Black woman appointed to Cabinet. She petitioned the Ontario government to celebrate Black History Month in February. She also played a critical role in the Federal declaration of February as Black History Month in Canada. Had it not been for her persistence, I might have missed out on a critical aspect of my upbringing – the celebrating Black Excellence and the pioneers who shaped the path for me today.

Canada has a history of Black pioneers who have pushed for better outcomes for Black communities. Despite being the recipients of injustice, discrimination and hate, history has shown that it is often Black community members who have advocated for change on their own behalf. Therefore, it's so important to learn about Black History because Canadian children of all backgrounds often grow up not knowing how instrumental Black pioneers were in shaping Canada. It is also equally important to tell both sides of the story – that is our struggle, but also the amazing accomplishments we've had.

Fast Forward to Blacks in Canada Today

Today, Blacks represent 3.5% of the total Canadian population, as per the 2016 census; there are close to 1.2 million Black Canadians with more than 4 in 10 Black Canadians born in Nova Scotia. Most of the Black immigrants who came to Canada before 1981 were born in Jamaica and Haiti. Today the top birth countries of Black newcomers (2011 to 2016): are Haiti, Nigeria, Jamaica, Cameroon, and the Democratic Republic of Congo.

I often get asked "where are you really from?" which is a micro aggression because this person's first thought upon meeting me is that I'm not Canadian, even when I say I am. I then have to explain that I was born here and that my parents were immigrants. Sometimes it's not enough to say I'm Canadian.

Now in my adulthood, as it forced me to take inventory of the prejudice, discrimination, unfairness, injustices, offenses, and micro-aggressions you start to realize that non-blacks who have not done the work to understand their own biases, don't see you as you see yourself. As an individual, it's alarming that despite my credentials and experience, I've been subject to inferior treatment in many situations from childhood to my adulthood — many more than I would like to admit. At the end of the day, to me, racism is how you are treated. I feel the deep mistrust almost immediately when meeting someone who suffers from this invisible disease called racism.

It saddens me that there is controversy over the statement, Black Lives Matter; a statement that for some is a difficult thing to say out loud. In my opinion, it's important to note that standing in solidarity with Blacks and saying Black Lives Matter truly means that "we matter". Our world tells us that all lives matter, but the problem is in reality, we as a society don't treat all lives as though they matter equally. To me it is much greater than this worldwide movement. It is a personal call to action. I want my kids and their generation to live out the ideals we want for ourselves. I'm driven to change hearts and minds and through my work bring more attention to anti-Black racism. I want to leave the next generation with more inclusive spaces where everyone can thrive.

Facts:

- First Black in Canada: The first recorded Black person to arrive in Canada was an African named Mathieu de Costa who arrived in 1608 to serve as interpreter of the Mi'kmaq language to the governor of Acadia
- Slavery in Canada: Date 1689 to 1834
- Slavery ended in the US in 1863 (Emancipation Proclamation signed by Abraham Lincoln)
- Over 30,000 slaves came to Canada via the Underground Railroad until the end of the American Civil War in 1865

Shonda Rimes has a great quote for this: "When you are an F.O.D. or First, Only, Different," she writes, "you are saddled with that burden of extra responsibility — whether you want it or not."

Very early in life I developed a passion for creating inclusive spaces where everyone feels a sense of belonging, safety and can be their authentic selves – understandable after being the only Black female in many spaces. I got along with most people at school and can confidently say I had the most diverse group of friends throughout my childhood. I know now as an adult that that sense of inclusion, belonging and a feeling of safety is something that each person should experience in every space, but it doesn't always happen that way.

Sources:

https://www.tvo.org/article/the-story-of-ontarios-last-segregated-black-school

https://www.thecanadianencyclopedia.ca/en/article/racial-segregation-of-black-people-in-canada

https://www.canada.ca/en/canadian-heritage/campaigns/black-history-month/historic-black-communities.html

https://www.thecanadianencyclopedia.ca/en/article/jean-augustine

https://www.jeanaugustine.ca/jean-augustine-bio/

https://www.thecanadianencyclopedia.ca/en/article/leonard-braithwaite

https://www.cbc.ca/kidscbc2/the-feed/all-about-black-history-month

https://www.thecanadianencyclopedia.ca/en/article/the-shelburne-race-riots

Summary

Note 1: Maroons from the Caribbean

"On June 26, 1796, Jamaican Maroons, numbering 543 men, women and children, were deported on board the three ships Dover, Mary and Anne from Jamaica after being defeated in an uprising against the British colonial government. Their initial destination was Lower Canada, but on 21 and 23 July, the ships arrived in Nova Scotia. At this time Halifax was undergoing a major construction boom initiated by Prince Edward, Duke of Kent and Strathearn's efforts to modernize the city's defences. The many building projects had created a shortage. Edward was impressed by the Maroons and immediately put them to work at the Citadel in Halifax, Government House, and other defence works throughout the city.

Funds had been provided by the Government of Jamaica to aid in the resettlement of the Maroons in Canada. Five thousand acres were purchased at Preston, Nova Scotia, at a cost of £3000. Small farm lots were provided to the Maroons and they attempted to farm the infertile land. Like the former tenants, they found the land at Preston to be unproductive and they had little success as a result. The Maroons also found farming in Nova Scotia difficult because the climate would not allow cultivation of familiar food crops, such as bananas, yams, pineapples, or cocoa. Small numbers of Maroons relocated from Preston to Boydville for better farming land. The British Lieutenant Governor Sir John Wentworth made an effort to change the Maroons' culture and beliefs by introducing them to Christianity. From the monies provided by the Jamaican Government, Wentworth procured an annual stipend of £240 for the support of a school and religious education." The Maroons were not interested in converting from their own religion to Christianity. Strong-willed and opinionated people, they refused to work for less money than was paid to white workers.

"After suffering through the harsh winter of 1796–97, Wentworth reported the Maroons expressed a desire that "they wish to be sent to India or somewhere in the east, to be landed with arms in some country with a climate like that they left, where they may take possession with a strong hand.""[257]

---

257 *Wikipedia.* Black Canadian, Maroons from the Caribbean.
https://www.wikiwand.com/en/Black_Canadian Accessed on February 8, 2023.

Note 2: Key reforms to Canada's immigration policy

"The 1960s, however, saw several key reforms to Canada's immigration policy. In 1962, the government tabled regulations virtually eliminating racial discrimination as a major feature of immigration policy. As such, prospective immigrants could no longer be denied entry to Canada on the basis of colour, race, or nationality. In 1966, the federal government tabled a White Paper on immigration, recognizing immigration as a major contributor to the national goals of population and economic growth. Nevertheless, to prevent high levels of unskilled immigration to Canada, the paper recommended a preference for immigrants with skills that would be valuable in the Canadian workforce.

The shift to an emphasis on skilled immigrants continued with the introduction of a Points System in 1967. Under this system, there were no quotas or restrictions on the number of people who could immigrate to Canada. Instead, prospective immigrants were required to pass a points test based on a number of qualities. These included whether they knew English or French (Canada's two official languages); had arranged for employment in Canada; had a relative or family member in Canada; had proper education or training; and were immigrating to an area of Canada with high employment."[258]

Note 3: History of Jamaican Immigration to Canada[259]

"As of 2011, there were 256,915 Jamaican-Canadians, both citizens and permanent residents. This group makes up nearly a third of all Black Canadians, who are Canada's third largest Visible Minority. Also, Canada has long been a destination for Jamaicans seeking a better life and Jamaica has been the largest source of migrants to Canada from the West Indies.

Though a few Jamaicans came to Canada as slaves before the abolition of slavery in the British Empire, and a few more came prior to 1900, very few Jamaicans migrated to Canada before the 20th century. And in the early decades of the 20th century, when Canada deliberately discouraged non-white immigrants, even fewer came. In the first decades of the 20th century, the West Indian population of Canada actually decreased.

However, after World War II, Canada needed cheap and began trying to lure foreign workers from the British colonies. Jamaican men came here to

---

258 Immigration Policy in Canada: History, Administration and Debates. Feature by Jay Makarenko Society, Culture & Communities August 12, 2010.
https://repolitics.com/features/immigration-policy-in-canada/ Accessed on: February 8, 2023.
259 IMMIGROUP History of Jamaican Immigration to Canada.
https://www.immigroup.com/topics/jamaican-immigration-canada/ Accessed on February 8, 2023.

work. They were actively recruited to help fuel the growing Canadian post-war economy. Women were also attracted through the Domestic Scheme of 1955, and sought to do the same thing. Once here, Jamaican women and other foreign domestic workers began to sponsor their husbands and children so that they could join them in Canada.

So many West Indians came to Canada that, four years after the Canadian government introduced the plan to attract foreign workers, it imposed strict limitations on immigration specifically directed at people from the West Indies.

But in 1962 Canada removed official racial discrimination from immigration policy and this is when emigration began in earnest. In 1967, Canada introduced a points system – a version of which is still in place today – and middle class Jamaicans soon migrated to Canada in large numbers. There were only a few thousand Jamaican Canadians in the 1960s but the population exploded and there were nearly 190,000 by 1996. In the last twenty years, the population of Jamaican-Canadians has increased by over a third.

Most Jamaican Canadians can be found in the Greater Toronto Area (GTA). Fully one third of self-identifying Jamaican-Canadians live in the city of Toronto. Large communities can be found throughout Toronto's suburbs, particularly in Brampton, where nearly 1/8th of all Jamaican-Canadians live. Other major Jamaican-Canadian centres include most of the many of the major cities in Canada: Vancouver, Montreal, Edmonton, Winnipeg, Regina, Ottawa and Halifax."

APPENDICES

Appendix A

Interview Questionnaire

When did you arrive in Ottawa?

Why did you choose to come to Ottawa?

Who did you know in Ottawa at that time?

What were you doing in your home country immediately before you came to
Ottawa?

Was your trip to Ottawa your first foreign travel?

What was the trip like?

What was your first impression; environment, people, culture?

What do you recall about your first week in Ottawa?

How did you go about developing friendships shortly after your arrival?

What did you do for the first 12 months after your arrival?

How did you set about doing this?

What obstacles did you encounter?

How did you deal with these obstacles?

Who would you say was instrumental in assisting you during this period?

When did you start to do <Career>?

How did you decide on doing this?

How did things turn out?

How do you feel about this life-changing decision at this time?

What would you consider to be your major accomplishment since coming to
Canada?

What regrets do you have?

Appendix B

10 Fast Facts about
Caribbean Immigrants in Canada [260]

By NewsAmericas Staff Writer
April 24, 2016

"News Americas, TORONTO, Canada, Mon. April 25, 2016: Starting May 2, 2016, Statistics Canada will begin sending census letters and packages to all Canadian households, including Caribbean nationals or West Indians who call the country home, to ensure there is an accurate count of the population. Canadians and residents of Canada will be allowed to complete their census questionnaire online or on paper. While the 2016 count may return a different data set, here are 10 facts about Caribbean Canadians based on the 2011 census:

1. Canadians of Caribbean origin belong to one of the largest non-European ethnic groups in Canada.

2. Caribbean nationals presence in Canada dates back to 1796 when a group of 556 Jamaicans arrived in Canada after an unsuccessful British attempt to enslave them in Jamaica. Between 1800 and 1920 a small number of Jamaicans and Barbadians immigrated as labourers to work in the Cape Breton and Sydney mines but immigration from the Caribbean to Canada really began in the 1960s, and by 1973 accounted for almost 13 per cent of all immigration to Canada.

3. According to data from the 2011 National Household Survey, the majority of the Caribbean population living in Canada were born outside the country and are largely concentrated in Ontario and Quebec. The vast majority of Canadians of Caribbean origin lives in either Toronto or Montreal.

4. They are put at an estimated half a million or almost 2% of the total population of Canada.

---

260 NewsAmericasNow. 10 Fast Facts about Caribbean Immigrants in Canada. https://www.newsamericasnow.com/10-fast-facts-about-caribbean-immigrants-in-canada/ Accessed on February 8, 2023.

5. The largest group of Canadians of Caribbean origin is Jamaicans. Of all those who reported they had Caribbean origins in 2001, 42% said they were Jamaican, while 16% were Haitian, 12% said they were West Indian, 10% were Guyanese, 10% came from Trinidad and Tobago and 5% were from Barbados.

6. The Caribbean community in Canada is relatively young. Children under the age of 15 make up some 27% of all those who reported Caribbean origin, compared with 19% of the overall population. At the same time, 17% of people of Caribbean origin were between the ages of 15 and 24, versus 13% of the overall population. The large majority of Canadians of Caribbean origin report they belong to a Christian religious group. Women make up the majority of Canadians of Caribbean origin with some 54% o compared with 51% of the overall population.

7. Canadians of Caribbean origin are generally less likely than other adults to be married but are less likely than other adults to live alone. On the other hand, Canadians of Caribbean origin are much more likely than the rest of the population to be lone parents.

8. To the east of Toronto in Durham Region, the largest group of immigrants (besides those from the UK) come from Jamaica. Although the Eglinton West neighbourhood in Toronto has come to be known as Little Jamaica (along with additional West Indies influence from Barbadian, Guyanese, and Trinidadian residents), towns like Pickering, Ajax and Oshawa in Durham Region feature vibrant Jamaican communities that maintain strong bonds with their cultural heritage.

9. Haitian immigration to Quebec has skyrocketed in the past 10 years, particularly after the devastating 2010 earthquake which sent thousands of Haitians to search for new homes outside of their native land. Haitians are put at 13.9 percent of the total black population in Canada.

10. According to the Ethnic Diversity Survey, a majority of Canadians of Caribbean origin have a strong sense of belonging to Canada and are also involved in Canadian society. At the same time, though, many Canadians of Caribbean descent report they have experienced discrimination based on their ethnicity, race, religion, language, or accent in the past five years, or since they arrived in Canada while many felt it was based on their race or skin colour."

Appendix C

Canadian Multiculturalism Act
R.S.C., 1985, c. 24
(4th Supp.)[261]

Preamble

WHEREAS the Constitution of Canada provides that every individual is equal before and under the law and has the right to the equal protection and benefit of the law without discrimination and that everyone has the freedom of conscience, religion, thought, belief, opinion, expression, peaceful assembly and association and guarantees those rights and freedoms equally to male and female persons;

AND WHEREAS the Constitution of Canada recognizes the importance of preserving and enhancing the multicultural heritage of Canadians;

AND WHEREAS the Constitution of Canada recognizes rights of the aboriginal peoples of Canada;

AND WHEREAS the Constitution of Canada and the Official Languages Act provide that English and French are the official languages of Canada and neither abrogates nor derogates from any rights or privileges acquired or enjoyed with respect to any other language;

AND WHEREAS the Citizenship Act provides that all Canadians, whether by birth or by choice, enjoy equal status, are entitled to the same rights, powers and privileges and are subject to the same obligations, duties and liabilities;

AND WHEREAS the Canadian Human Rights Act provides that every individual should have an equal opportunity with other individuals to make the life that the individual is able and wishes to

---

261 *Wikipedia.* Canadian Multiculturalism Act.
https://en.wikiedia.org/wiki/Canadian_Multiculturalism_ Act. Accessed on April 27, 2018.

have, consistent with the duties and obligations of that individual as a member of society, and, in order to secure that opportunity, establishes the Canadian Human Rights Commission to redress any proscribed discrimination, including discrimination on the basis of race, national or ethnic origin or colour;

AND WHEREAS Canada is a party to the International Convention on the Elimination of All Forms of Racial Discrimination, which Convention recognizes that all human beings are equal before the law and are entitled to equal protection of the law against any discrimination and against any incitement to discrimination, and to the International Covenant on Civil and Political Rights, which Covenant provides that persons belonging to ethnic, religious or linguistic minorities shall not be denied the right to enjoy their own culture, to profess and practise their own religion or to use their own language;

AND WHEREAS the Government of Canada recognizes the diversity of Canadians as regards race, national or ethnic origin, colour and religion as a fundamental characteristic of Canadian society and is committed to a policy of multiculturalism designed to preserve and enhance the multicultural heritage of Canadians while working to achieve the equality of all Canadians in the economic, social, cultural and political life of Canada;

NOW, THEREFORE, Her Majesty, by and with the advice and consent of the Senate and House of Commons of Canada, enacts as follows:

Short Title, Marginal note:

1 This Act may be cited as the Canadian Multiculturalism Act.

Appendix D

'A Tribute to the Third World Players'[262]
Provided by C. Lloyd Stanford

The theatre group Third World Players / Le Théâtre du Tiers Monde was founded in November 1978 to stimulate interest in the cultural heritage of immigrants from the Third World. The founders were Lloyd Stanford, Karl Gordon, Jennifer Hosten-Craig, who had 'floated' the idea to Lloyd Stanford, Ricardo Smith, and David Craig.

The first production, **Slices of Life** was mounted with the assistance of the Penguin Theatre in April 1979 and set the tone of the multi-lingual and multicultural repertoire that has been characteristic of the group. The selections made by Karl Gordon included works in French, Haitian Creole, Standard English, and Jamaican patois. This was followed, that summer, by a one-hour TV special based, in part, on that material, entitled **Accents Shakespeare Never Knew.** The 1980 **Salute to Jamaica**, presented in collaboration with the University of Ottawa's Department of Community Affairs, was also multi-lingual and included a memorable production of Karl Gordon's one-act play **Uncle George.**

Other notable productions over the ensuing years included: the world première of Roderick Walcott's **Cul de Sac,** directed by the playwright and presented in collaboration with Carleton University's Faculty of Arts; **A Multi-Cultural Theatre Festival,** featuring **La Repeticion** by Anton Arrufat, **Red Oleanders** by **Rabindranath** Tagore and **L'anglais tel qu'on le parle** by Tristan Bernard, staged at Carleton University, in mid-July 1984; another production of "L'anglais tel qu'on le parle" for the Festival of the Arts put on by Celebration Arts Ottawa; a repeat presentation of "Red Oleanders", in October 1984, this time in collaboration with the university's Asian Studies Committee; a week-long run in summer 1983 of Karl Gordon's **Old Man of the Village** at the Great Canadian Theatre Company's 'space', reprised in September 1987 at the Ottawa Technical High School; the August 1986 production of Gordon's **Sometimes It Does** (in which the renowned Canadian actor/playwright and director Andrew Moodie

---

262 Flo's Seniors. C. Lloyd Stanford. A Tribute to the Third World Players. https://floseniors.com/event/1285/ Accessed on February 15, 2023.

made his stage début); **Marcus Garvey: The Power of his Words**, staged at the National Library, on February 28, 1995.

Since November 1980, in addition to its stage work, the group has broadcast, on CKCU-FM, a regular programme called **Third World Players Present** featuring rehearsed readings from Third World literature as well as interviews with writers and literary critics from the Global South, including those residents in Canada. These broadcasts have included: a series of 'literary portraits' of Argentina, the Bahamas, Barbados, Brazil, Chile, Columbia, Cuba, Guyana, Haiti, India, Jamaica, Pakistan, Sri Lanka & Trinidad and Tobago; seasonal themes like summer and autumn; festive or religious occasions like Easter, Thanksgiving and Christmas; special topics like " stories for the young", "women in Third World literature", "female writers of the Third World", "great Black writers"; important literary events like the presentations of the "Poetry of the Americas" made by the embassies and high commissions of the countries of the Americas, the Canadian Commission for UNESCO and Library and Archives Canada in 2003 and 2006 to mark international poetry day. The programme has often served as the radio launch or preview of works by many a writer as well as ground-breaking anthologies like Cyril Dabydeen's "A Shapely Fire: Changing the Literary Landscape of 1987", Luciano Diaz's 1992 intercultural anthology of poetry "Symbiosis", and Eddy Garnier's pioneering bilingual (French/Créole) 2006 haiku collection "Gerbe en germes : Pake Grenn".

It is significant that through these broadcasts and its stage presentations, Third World Players has introduced the radio audience and the public to the work of four Nobel Prize winners from the Global South before they became laureates, namely, Chinua Achebe, Wole Soyinka, Gabriela Marquez, and Derek Walcott, as well as Michael Ondaatje, long before his Booker and the Governor General's awards. The programming has included some African radio plays, aired with the permission of Germany's Deutsche Welle, as well as several programmes produced in collaboration with Radio Mona at the University of the West Indies in Kingston, Jamaica. Some of the local writers featured over the years include members of the group of Chilean writers in exile. Third World Players was invited to contribute to the collection that was made of the literary output of those writers in Canada as part of "Project Adrienne", the exchange programme between the National Library of Canada and the National Library instigated by then Governor General Rt. Hon. Adrienne Clarkson. One of the most distinguished of these writers, Jorge Etcheverry, has been a member of Third World Players from the early 1980s.

Third World Players have participated in cultural evenings and other special presentations by several organizations including the Ottawa Branch of the Royal Commonwealth Society, the Jamaica (Ottawa) Community Association Inc., CUSO, Focus on Black Women, NCARR, as well as groups or government departments observing special occasions like Martin Luther King Jr Day or Black History Month in the National Capital Region. The troupe has also been guest readers of the writers' groups Sasquatch and El Dorado and has appeared on a community Christmas TV special.

Given the aim fixed at the group's founding, Third World Players have been particularly pleased to help introduce outstanding writers to schools and to the public. These initiatives include: the invitation, extended jointly with the Ottawa Branch of the Royal Commonwealth Society, The National Library and the Commonwealth Society, , in 1989, to Derek Walcott to conduct workshops for the Ottawa School Board and to read at the National Library and the Commonwealth Club; an invitation to Jamaica's Mervyn Morris, in 1991, to conduct workshops for the Carleton Board and to read at the Ottawa Library; and collaborating with publishers to present an Ottawa stage launch of Olive Senior's "Discerner of Hearts", at the National Library, in 1995. The latter two endeavours resulted in memorable broadcasts as well. The impact of the appearances on the students— manifesting evident pride in cultural heritage – and members of the public of Third World origins in these instances was visible.

The theatre group has staged solo or collaborated in significant book launches at Library and Archives Canada, notably Jennifer Hosten's "Beyond Miss World", in October 2008, and Rachel Manley's memoir of her grandmother Edna Manley entitled "Horses in Her Hair", in November 2008, in collaboration with the Jamaica High Commission. Moreover, in September 2012, TWP took part in the Canadian celebration of Jamaica's 50th anniversary of independence with the presentation "Celebrating Jamaican Literary Excellence", which featured readings by prize-winning authors Olive Senior (winner of the 1987 Commonwealth Writers' Prize), and Rachel Manley (winner of the 1997 Governor General's Award for Non-Fiction).

Three other 'catalytic' effects of TWP's stage and broadcasting efforts are worth mentioning: very early, the troupe encouraged Caribbean Voices through joint presentations, supported the 'inter-cultural' drive of groups like El Dorado, and provided opportunities for several talented actors, directors and producers to 'showcase' their skills on stage, radio and, in some cases, on film.

Appendix E

Bel-Air Cricket Club 263

by Ewart Walters, CD, MJ, Order of Ottawa

Long before the late Pierre Trudeau made multiculturalism the official policy of Canada, the Bel-Air Cricket Club had already embodied it. It was a West Indian club with members from various countries, yes but isn't that what the West Indies, with all its mixtures and fusion is all about? There was even an Italian, Sam Trucino and a New Zealander, Robert Thurling, among its members in its earliest years. True, Sam was really just a friend of the team, but he actually played one match! Since then, the organisation of cricket lovers which began life as the Coral Reef Cricket Club has included Australians and Sri Lankans, while remaining a West Indian Club at core.

The moving spirit behind the formation of the club was Ivo DeSouza, the Counsellor at the Jamaica High Commission (JHC). George Girard (St. Lucia), Larry Davis, and Bert Tertullian (Bahamas) were the first leaders. They used to meet at the Coral Reef Club on Friday and Saturday nights. When the Jamaica High Commission was established in August 1962 in Ottawa, propelled by Ivo DeSouza, the idea came up to form a cricket club and DeSouza sent his accountant, Donald White, to the planning meeting in October 1962. Present were Larry Davis, George Tertullian, Clarence King, a man named Hutchinson, along with Don White who became Treasurer and served in that position for most of the life of the club.

The first captain was Rufus McCommon of Guyana. He was related to Angela who George Girard used to date. His deputy was Allan Marson Mayers (Barbados) the Vice-Captain at the time. McCommon left shortly afterwards and Mayers acted as captain. One day, a friendly game was scheduled at Rideau Hall II, but Mayers' team-mates saw him playing in a match at Rideau Hall I, so they selected a new captain in the person of Ivor Mitchell (Jamaica) who was on staff at the JHC. Mayers then turned his back on the club and told new West Indian

---

263 Bel-Air Cricket Club. History of Bel-Air https://www.belaircricketclub.com/about-bel-air/history-of-bel-air Accessed on September 2, 2018.

immigrants not to join Coral Reef. The next year, Mitchell gave way to Jeff Stevens, a Trinidadian, who took over the captaincy.

Early members included Ian Douglas, Thelston Nelson (Trinidad), Ivor Mitchell, Hugh Bonnick, Don White, Eric Samuels (Jamaica), George Girard, Allan Mayers, Ellsworth Samuels (Antigua), Larry Davis, Clarence King, Chuck Edwards, and Laynes Alphonse (St. Lucia).

In 1964 there were Ramsaji, Jeff Stephens, Bobby Scotland Michael Bankay, and Eddie Cadogan.

The year 1965 brought about Willesley (Wes) Smith, Eddie Decoteau, Carlyle Mitchell, Ewart Walters, Claude Robinson, Willie Morrison, George Assing, Henry Cadogan, Ivan McFarlane, L. Campbell, Vincent Edwards, Neville Grant, Lester Belgrave, Martin Howard, Carl Evelyn, Dr. Lawson Douglas, Dr. Vincent Crawford, Eddie Walter, Guy Dixon, Ralston Briscoe, Bernie Hibbert, Cyril Joseph, Guy Dixon, Ron Brown, Wally Bayne, and Tony Jarrett into the club. Later members included Dennis Awang, Fred Blades, Edmund Napoleon, Oakley Brereton, Wally Bayne, Patrick Waterman, Keith Woleston, Lesroy George, Waldo Burrowes, "Doc" Bayne, Arthur Moore, Dennis Rajkumar, Noel Foster, and Tyrone Collins.

Outstanding captains of the club include Neville Grant (Barbados), Noel Foster (Jamaica), Fred Blades (Barbados), Dennis Waithe (Guyana), and Tony Russell (Jamaica).

West Indians playing on other teams at the time included the superb and stylish Guyanese opening batsman Rudy Collins who played for Canadian Forces, Jamaican leg-spinner Egbert Mair, and pace bowlers Lloyd Stanford and Rudy Gordon who played for Ottawa; Birch Mayers of Barbados who played for New Edinburgh; and Herbie Waugh of Jamaica who played for New Edinburgh, Jimmy Siew of Trinidad, and Clinton Calixte of St. Lucia who played for the Canadian Forces.

An opening bat for most of my life, I also played competitively as a middle-order bat for the Canadian Forces. Nevertheless, I always played for Coral Reef as an opening batsman and part time leg-spinner. Along with Eric Samuels, I spearheaded the drive in 1967, first to secure a place in the league and when that was done, to get our own grounds.

Eric Samuels was a trailblazer and a sportsman. His presidency of the Bel-Air Cricket Club from the early 1960s to the early 1980s saw him shepherd a special period in the life and times of Ottawa. It was a time of high emigration from the Caribbean region and the cricket Club became an instrument with which he could help to usher scores of new Canadians easily into the Ottawa society without many of the usually attendant difficulties.

In most places in the world, cricket is played on a clay pitch. Here in Ottawa, we played on a coconut matting roughly 22 yards long by three yards wide and one inch thick. When the club was admitted to the league, it had to purchase its own matting. After the game we would roll the matting up but there was nowhere to leave it. Eric soon solved that problem. He took it home in his car trunk with more than half of it sticking out.

We would then help him push it through the window of his basement at Bellamy Street. To this day we are not quite sure what his wife, Nye, thought of this, but we were always welcome at their home after a game.

Modern day cricket playing immigrants, mostly from the south Asian sub-continent and who have joined teams that play at the Governor-General's grounds at Rideau Hall, do not have a clue as to why they play there. They take for granted a hard-won legacy they don't know was left for them by Eric Samuels.

At the time, individual black players were able to play on existing teams but Coral Reef, the "Black team" was barred from playing in the league as a team because, as the Ottawa Valley Cricket Council of the day said, "We don't want any team in the league from any one racial group." Of course, they were ignoring that they themselves were from one identifiable racial group.

While some of us raged at the prejudice and stubborn resistance of the leadership of the Ottawa Valley Cricket Council to admitting a Black team into what was a white league. Eric Samuels remained calm and applied the strategic negotiating strategies that led the Governor-General of the day, to throw down the gauntlet to the league with the famous statement: "No Blacks, no cricket."

Needless to say, that Vice-Regal statement opened the doors. But it was Eric Samuels who turned the key. Samuels and Ewart Walters negotiated with the city and the NCC to find a suitable ground because, although the league was forced to admit the club, they said there was not enough space for it to be one of the Rideau Hall clubs. However, Coral Reef's demand for entry to the league could not have come at a more opportune time.

Appointed to replace Georges Vanier who died in March 1967, the new Governor-General was the Rt. Hon. Daniel Roland Michener. An avid sportsman and athlete who followed a daily exercise regime, he could be seen jogging every morning. His encouragement to engage in daily exercise has been credited with having a lasting effect on the physical well-being of many Canadians. Many people still remember his support of the 'Participaction Program' – a campaign aimed at increasing the fitness of all Canadians. He further encouraged sport by establishing the Roland Michener Trophy for the Juvenile "AAA" championship in Ontario as well as a championship trophy for sport fishing, called the Michener Tuna Trophy.

Mr. Michener was a great motivator of Canadian youth and he encouraged them to be part of Canada's great future by achieving their full potential. He believed that his role as Governor General put him in a unique position to inspire Canadians by applauding their best efforts. His encouragement of excellence extended to journalism with the creation of the Michener Awards for Journalism in 1970.

During their stay at Rideau Hall, Roland Michener and his wife Norah relaxed protocol in a number of ways – the most well-known example was the dropping of the curtsey. The Micheners frequently visited abroad, and they instituted periodic meetings with provincial Lieutenant-Governors, which started in 1973.

It was this man to whom Jamaican High Commissioner Vincent McFarlane turned for help with the Coral Reef Cricket team. His answer was brief and to the point and it cut the ground out from under the racism that had discriminated against Coral Reef. "No Blacks, no cricket!" he informed the Rideau Hall cricket clubs.

In the face of this terse statement, the objectors had no option. Wearily they formed themselves into the Rideau Hall Cricket Association and summoned us to a meeting at the pavilion. Representing Coral Reef were Eric Samuels, Hugh Bonnick and I.

To my absolute shock the first thing they said was, "OK gentlemen, what do you have to say?" They had quite blithely dismissed our request up to the last time we met, and here they were now – having been rapped sharply on the knuckles and in danger of losing their playing facilities – here they were asking us what we had to say. Fuming, I quickly pointed out to them the absurdity of the situation and told them the ball was in their court; they had to tell us something, I declared angrily, with both Bonnick and Eric touching me under the table and saying, "Take it easy Ewart."

So, the OVCC was forced to admit a (mostly) Black team into the league, but they then dropped bombshell. We had to find our own playing field since the facilities at Rideau Hall were taken up by the four clubs already there and there was no space at Rideau Hall for an additional club. All right, we said and left the meeting determined to find a suitable facility.

Really, it was a daunting task. Bonnick, the diplomat, preferred to stay out of any negotiations we arranged. I was a student and would only be in Ottawa a short time. The only person with two feet on the ground so to speak was Eric, an agricultural scientist who worked full-time with the Federal Government. We arranged meetings with the NCC and the City of Ottawa in an attempt to find playing facilities. Eric began these meetings but then had to travel to Rome and it was left to me, a student, to continue the negotiations.

Eventually, a suitable area at Woodroffe and Baseline Avenues was found. The ground bordered a street named Bel-Air and at that point we agreed to change the name of the club from Coral Reef to Bel-Air. That is where we prepared our first wicket and played our first season of league cricket in 1968. However, at the end of the season the city said it would find another field for the permanent use of the cricketers. From 1968 until 1976, Carlington Park was devoted to cricket for the use of the Bel-Air cricketers. At the time, this ground was ideal for cricket in terms of location, storage, water supply, shelter and so on. But in 1977, when the cricketers began preparations for their season, they found the ground sub-divided into playing areas for baseball. It was now completely unsuitable for cricket.

Hastily, the city arranged for the use of a field at the corner of Pinecrest and Dumaurier. It was a small ground without any facilities at all. The cricketers endured, but the city readily agreed that the facilities here were far from adequate. When this ground also fell to the apparent burgeoning need for baseball facilities, we were offered Balena Park and did play a few games there, but it was an even smaller ground. And so, in 1985, arrangements were made to prepare a second field at Lynda Lane for the use of Bel-Air CC (another club was already using the portion of that ground nearest to Lynda Lane).

A few residents put up strenuous objection. It was so bad that the contractor who was levelling the field had his bulldozer vandalized. There was a great deal of publicity and controversy in the press and radio. City Council was determined to provide some facilities for the Club and in 1986, the Bel-Air CC joined Canterbury Cricket Club in using the land at Lynda Lane, an area the city said was to be devoted entirely to cricket.

Facilities here were again below the requirements. And again, the city recognized this and eventually, a makeshift clubhouse on Billings Avenue was made available on a shared basis with two other organizations and this reduced the difficulties but did not solve the entire problem. In 1992, following an argument between a visiting cricketer and a resident of the houses on the southern side of Lynda Lane, two things happened. One was that police arbitrarily began harassing club members about parking their cars on the field. Secondly, city authorities suddenly placed boulders and other barriers between the fields and

Lynda Lane to prevent motorized access. The Bel-Air Cricket Club objected to this on the following grounds:

CUSTOM: While the club is aware that, strictly speaking, there is a by-law prohibiting parking on the grounds, it is also aware that it has never been subjected to any harassment from police for parking on this ground until after the argument in May when the resident threatened to call the police. In other words, the city has been fully aware of the limitations of the facilities at the site and has been quite willing to turn a blind eye to the few cars that park there. (The cars are almost out of sight, parked close to the hedge at the far end of the field between the cricket and baseball facilities). The Club has been allowed to park there since it began using the field and should not arbitrarily lose this facility.

RACIAL DISCRIMINATION: The entire history of the club has been one where it has had to identify and fight discrimination based on race or colour. In this case, while police harassed Bel-Air Club members about parking on the grounds, (white) people parking on the other side of the hedge at the baseball diamonds were not similarly harassed. Indeed the city itself was content to place boulders outside the cricket field only until it heard that the cricketers were complaining about the discriminatory treatment with regard to the fact that the people on the other side of the hedge were not being treated in the same way. It was only then that boulders were placed to prevent access to the baseball field.

The game of cricket takes six hours or more. The rules provide for water breaks during which players refresh themselves with water. The 30-plus degree temperatures of the last few summers have made the ready availability of water much more necessary. Because there is no water facility at the ground, the club has usually brought water coolers in players' car trunks. The rules also include specific guidelines about what is to be done by players and officials in the event of rain during a match. The city regrets it is unable to provide "permanent" pavilion facilities on the land "because it is owned by the NCC." The facility at Billings Avenue does not readily meet the requirement of shelter from rain during a match. This is another reason why players park their cars on the side of the field near the hedge. It is disruptive and undesirable for cricketers, officials, and spectators to dash off from the field to the Billings Avenue clubhouse a quarter of a mile away every time it rains. Or for the officials to walk up and back for the required inspection of the playing conditions during breaks in rainfall. Nor is this the culture of cricket. Only cultural insensitivity would dictate such action as a satisfactory *modus operandum*.

TAXPAYERS: The cricketers are taxpayers like anyone else. The city recognizes this and wants to provide facilities for the playing of cricket like any other sport. Sadly, it has been unable to do this, but, for the most part, the cricketers have been willing to accept the makeshift arrangements that have greeted them everywhere else except at Carlington.

INTEGRATION: Cricket has been an inexpensive and easy way to integrate new Canadians into the Ottawa area. Cricket is a gentleman's game with rules and culture that imbue the game's participants with high principles of sportsmanship, deportment, and character. In the national capital region, which is characterized by a mosaic of cultures, races and colours, cricket has done well in its mission of breaking down resistance to easy race relations. Cricket has been supported by the City of Ottawa and the city would do well not only to continue that support but to extend it wherever possible."

Appendix F

Harry Jerome Business Award acceptance speech

by Carlton Braithwaite; Toronto, March 17. 1990 [264]

I think success depends essentially on two things:

i) The way we think. It is important that we think we can achieve any goals we set ourselves and that there are no limits to the number of goals we can set; that we believe in ourselves and think positively at all times.

ii) What we are willing to do. To be successful it is absolutely necessary that we be willing to do whatever it takes to achieve the results we want: mentally, psychologically and physically, provided that in so doing we do not compromise our sense of values.

I know there are people who will immediately question this simple claim. They will ask: "Do you really expect us to believe this after the failures we have experienced?"

My answer is that I am convinced that when you know your own mind and live your own life, you can wipe out a record of unsuccessful experiences just as you can erase a message on a tape recorder, and leave a wonderfully receptive mind – or tape – to receive new and positive impressions. While some people have been able to do this for themselves – the ones who are most likely to accept my claim – others need help before they can believe it and experience the success they seek.

Let me tell you a story about a man I helped to find the success mode or consciousness to which I am referring. Once I got him started he was able to do the rest for himself.

This man came to my office to find out whether I could help him to find a job. He was in rough shape. He looked thin and hungry and was willing to accept any job and any sum of money that I could give him to purchase a meal. As I listened to him, I could not help but ask myself: "Why is this man, with a respectable level of education in a country filled with opportunity, in such a state?"

---

264 Acceptance Speech provided by Carleton Brathwaite.

I asked him: "Why are you willing to settle for so little? How would you like to become a millionaire?" He looked at me with tears in his eyes and said, "Mr. Braithwaite, please don't make a joke at me." I told him that I was serious. I told him that every man has some kind of assets which, if used correctly, he could turn into a million or many millions of dollars. He got irritated: "What do you mean by assets? I don't even have a dime in my pocket!"

"Get your mind to look at the positive side," I told him, "and you will have the most important asset you will ever have. Let us work on that now. Tell me: "What are your skills? What are you good at?"

I learned that before he came to Canada, he was a salesman but in his last few jobs he had been cleaning houses and shampooing rugs, etc. He said that he was quite good at it, but the cleaning company went broke. At first, I got the impression that he did not believe he could again become a good salesman. Clearly, he did know something about selling and in talking to him I discovered he still wanted to sell. However, the memory of past failures inhibited him and I had to help break those self-imposed mental blocks and help him see, not what he had recently been, but what he could become.

As we continued talking, my own mind was busy. I knew of a company which had just developed a whole new line of household cleaning equipment and other materials that would be useful to housewives. Bingo!, I said to myself. Here was a potentially winning combination, a company with good new products and with need for sales people and a man who had experience both as a cleaner and as a salesman.

I asked him how he felt about representing a company and selling its cleaning products, many of which could practically sell themselves. I told him any housewife to whom he could give some free samples would be glad to invite her neighbours to witness a demonstration, after which he could take orders from the ladies present. Some of them would be glad to run similar cleaning parties in their own homes and the business could become self-perpetuating.

"Sounds good," he said. "But how am I going to get money to buy some food in the meantime? And where am I going to get some money to buy an appropriate outfit, etc. for this job?" Such questions were understandable in a mind focused on obstacles rather than on opportunities.

I told him that if he got himself in the right frame of mind he would either find the things he needed, or find a way to do without those things and still achieve the goal. When your mind can truly picture a desired goal and feel success consciousness driving it towards that goal, you can attain the goal. Knowing this, I wanted to help him but I had to further investigate his frame of mind.

Encouragingly, he was very close to having the desired positive state of mind. I waited until I was sure that he had it and, assuming he was a good risk, I gave him money to buy food, and access to a charge account so that he could buy what was necessary to get him started.

By the end of the first month he had made a thousand dollars, and had doubled that by the end of the second. After some time he was put in charge of training other people. Most of all, he instilled in them the positive success attitude which now had full hold of his mind and as they prospered, so did he.

After three years, this man who had such limited expectations of himself is relatively comfortable and has perfected a home demonstration plan which nets him a good annual income.

Now, I believe that my company Uniprop has been able to achieve business success because we understand and apply the principles that are necessary to achieve success.

In our view, the way to succeed is to have clear goals, suitable strategies to achieve these goals, the ability to evaluate the results obtained in applying these strategies, and the willingness to be sufficiently flexible, to keep on modifying these goals and strategies until the desired results are obtained. Great emphasis is placed on ensuring that these goals are realistic and that belief in their attainment is shared by all members of our organisation. In developing the strategies required to achieve these goals, the most important and relevant strategic areas of knowledge and ability must be identified. For our company, which is involved mainly in real estate investment, we have identified the following four key areas, the order and significance of which might vary depending on the situation:

i) Knowledge of the industries and of the entire economic environment within which we operate, and of the analytical tools needed to assess the investment opportunities in these industries. This knowledge has to be accurate and timely, for it is a critical input for the analysis and ranking of the opportunities.
ii) Knowledge of negotiating and financing techniques together with the ability to negotiate skillfully. These include preparing carefully, using win-win techniques, arranging financing creatively and using leveraging intelligently. When leveraging to a very high level, one should be careful to ensure that there are adequate cash flows to deal with recurring expenses and emergencies as well as clearly defined plans for repaying debt and reducing debt equity ratios to manageable levels until the loans are repaid.
iii) Managerial ability: every attempt is made to attract managers who can communicate positively and motivate people to get the desired results.
iv) Marketing ability: this is a most important area of our business since the ability of the organization, to identify and penetrate its markets successfully, determines the revenues, profits and cash flows it must generate not only to stay in business but to grow to its desired level. of particular importance to Uniprop is the way the organization "sells" itself and the image that it portrays in the community.

To make good decisions in these four areas, it is critical to have an excellent database and to have the technology necessary to process the data required, for example to produce good financial statements and reports on a timely basis. Thus, the database and technology contribute in an important way to the development and evaluation of strategies. The results obtained on evaluating these strategies will indicate whether the strategies have been successful or need modification. It follows that as long as there is flexibility and willingness to keep on making modifications until the desired goals are achieved, success is virtually guaranteed.

It should be clear, however, that successful results depend on all individuals in the organization, the managers as well as those they lead; both groups need to be highly skilled and motivated. In summary, everyone has to be so positive and willing to do whatever it takes to get the results i.e. so empowered, that they believe that they can do virtually anything they want. Until they get precisely the results they want, they view other unsuccessful outcomes not as failures but as learning experiences!

To encourage our members to produce as well as to share in these successful results, individually and as a team, Uniprop has implemented a four-part compensation package which rewards results and which includes the opportunity to participate in profits and ownership. There is an ongoing staff development program and a generous benefits package which includes membership in one of Ottawa's leading health clubs.

Ladies and gentlemen, I strongly believe that economic success is perhaps one of the most powerful ways of dealing with the many obstacles and injustices that have been experienced by Blacks and others in this country. I believe that those who succeed should teach others how to do it, and should share it with them, if we are to fulfill the dream. This explains why, in addition to achieving the goals set for the Uniprop organization, I am committed to helping my people to gain economic power. But I would like to add that a very important way in which we can help ourselves increase our rate of achieving economic power is to develop bonding power and to learn to love one another much more than we do now. In doing this, however, I strongly believe we should work with others. There are many people in this Canadian society who are capable and willing to help us fulfil the dream.

As we work with these people we should gradually expand the number of believers, and free ourselves of myths and misconceptions, until the dream is fulfilled.

With this in mind, I shall continue to work with, and to share my success with my fellow Canadians not only in business but in such organizations as the Commonwealth Club of Ottawa – an international non-profit organization which helps people of all races to become wealthier, healthier and happier by participating in a series of networks which facilitate the achievement of these goals, and which encourages them to put back into the community, some of what they gained.

Appendix G

Meteoric Rise to Public Service Commissioner

by Gilbert Scott

I was working at the Jamaica Public Service Company for a period of six months when I ran into a school mate who told me that the Met (Meteorology) office had a number of open positions, and they were looking to fill these openings. I was receptive to this and before I had the opportunity to submit an application, the Director at the Met office showed up at my house, interviewed me in his car and I started working as a Meteorological Technician on the next Monday. I was engaged in Meteorology in Jamaica for eight years, advancing from a Meteorological Technician to a Forecaster. But the shift work, especially the night shift had become a problem. At the point that I decided to leave, I was offered a scholarship to complete a BSc degree in Meteorology in the UK. But I declined this offer, given that I would still be working under the same conditions when I returned to Jamaica. And I had already decided that this shiftwork was untenable.

I went to Canada as a professional. I went to Toronto in August 1968. It is by chance that I ended up in Ottawa. Shortly after I arrived in Toronto I realized that the only marketable skills that I had were in the field of Meteorology. I applied to the Canadian Meteorological Services (Canadian Atmospheric Advisory Services) and was offered a position which I accepted.

Within a few months after I started working at the Canadian Atmospheric Advisory Services the results of my eight years of meteorological work experience became obvious to my manager. He sent me off to Ottawa for a six-week training course. And within weeks after I started this training program, having received frequent feedback on my performance, my manager called and acknowledged that he had received positive reports on my performance. He also indicated that based on the feedback he received I might want to consider a position that was open in Ottawa that was two levels above my current job level. I did the math and I accepted the Ottawa job starting the first Monday in January 1969, following the completion of my training in December 1968.

My tenure with the Canadian Atmospheric Services would last until 1975. But during this period a number of very significant events, separate and apart from my work activities, would set the course for my subsequent career in the Federal Government. Shortly after I settled in Ottawa, I began to make contact with other Jamaicans and people from other Caribbean countries in Ottawa. A Jamaican organization that had started in the sixties was in decline but there was also a loose gathering that was emerging as a result of a group of Jamaicans who met socially from time to time. One of the first people I met within this group was Herbert Chambers aka Brutus. I knew Brutus from Jamaica. He worked with me at the Jamaican Met office. In fact, I trained him on the Job. But I had lost contact with him and did not know that he was living in Ottawa.

Our first meeting happened about three months after I had arrived in Ottawa, in early spring of 1969. At that time my wife, Jackie, who was working as a Temp in one of the Government offices ran into another Jamaican who worked in the same office. This person invited Jackie to a party at the GEM Club. So we went and within the first half an hour after arriving I ran into Brutus. Brutus had already built a network made up of other Jamaican immigrants in Ottawa, and these people, Owen (Bill) Stewart, Clyde Shaw, Milton (Robbie) Robinson and others, rapidly became my network of contacts as well.

But the significant incident that triggered the formation of the re-organized Jamaican Association in Ottawa was the call to action in support of one of our compatriots who had an encounter with the legal system. One member of our Jamaican community had been charged with a crime and the community organized a meeting to see how it could support this member. The call to action was issued by Clyde Shaw. I attended this meeting. And the majority of those who attended became the core and founding members of the Jamaican Ottawa Canadian Association (JOCA). I was elected President of the Association at the first formal meeting which was called to elect officers. This would turn out to be a pivotal determinant of my career in the Federal Government.

My assimilation into the Canadian society happened with little difficulty. It was not difficult for me to integrate into the Canadian work environment. My prior eight-year tenure in the Meteorology field had prepared me well to adapt to the professional rigors of the job. My work associates and managers recognized my abilities and also knew that it would take them several years to ramp up someone else to the level at which I was able to operate from day one. So I developed congenial relationships with my work colleagues and continued to become very active in the Black community in Ottawa, and more specifically with the Jamaican community.

In 1970 I enrolled at the Algonquin College (Woodroffe) Campus to pursue a three-year Diploma in Computer programming. This was my original reason for leaving Jamaica. I graduated in 1973, although I never took a job in this field because another community organization called Impact Heritage was initiated with a mission to expose young people to Caribbean culture. Shortly thereafter in October 1973, the Federal Government announced its Multiculturalism Policy and Program. And as a result of my involvement with the Jamaican Community Association, I was now coming into contact with the officers who were charged with implementing the Multicultural Program.

One of these officers eventually approached me in my capacity as the President of the Jamaican Association and invited me to apply for a federal grant.

But after carefully assessing what this entailed, I declined this offer. One of the determining factors was that the funding was project specific and by this time our association had already been carrying out activities relating to the type of projects that were being funded. In addition, there was also a concern that once Federal funds were being used, there could be potential allegations of misuse that our association wanted to avoid.

Shortly after this initial proposal from the Multicultural Program Director was resolved, the Program Manager responsible for administering the program that focussed on the Black Diaspora across Canada resigned his post. He was from Nigeria. I knew this because of the contacts that I had now established within the Multicultural Program organization. I dismissed any notion of applying for this type of position, thinking that it was outside my scope. Besides, the Jamaican Association was now in full operational mode, and we would often host various social events. I routinely invited my work colleagues from the Met office to attend these events. So, my Canadian counterparts were becoming more and more familiar with the Jamaican culture. One of these co-workers noticed the job advertisement for the vacant Multicultural Program Manager position in the newspaper. He clipped it out, attached a note that read "this is right up your street" and set the non-attached ad copy on my desk where it could not be missed when I arrived at work. When I saw it, I made a mental note, but I set it aside without intending to act on it. I had a number of days off, and when I returned to work, the job ad was repositioned more prominently on my desk with an added note stating, "This one is for you." I thought about it and reflected that my objective was to exit the Meteorology field some seven years later, and I was still deeply involved. So, I mused, what do I have to lose? And I submitted an application for the Multicultural Program Management Job. Lo and behold, I received a job offer which I accepted.

In August 1975 I started this new job with the Federal Government as a Program Manager in the Multiculturalism Division within the Department of Secretary of State. My responsibilities included the Canada-wide coordination of program activities that were primarily targeted at Black Communities across the country. And one of the key tasks was to review grant submissions from the various communities once these arrived in Ottawa for approval. In essence, I was the Ottawa liaison for the Black and African Communities vis-à-vis the Multicultural Program. This was my first Public Sector assignment.

After being on the job for a few months, it occurred to me that if I was going to be successful at this job, I would have to go out to the field offices to find out what was happening on the ground. I made a proposal to my boss to carry out a number of field visits. He was very receptive. His response was "Great idea, why didn't we think about this before?" He approved. And I set out to visit the local offices across Canada. This gave me the opportunity not only to meet the Multicultural operatives at these offices but also to meet with local community leaders and gain understanding relating to their local issues and concerns. With this additional knowledge, I was able to perform the job with a greater degree of effectiveness. And as a result, by 1978 I was promoted from the Program Liaison Manager to Senior Manager of the Ethnic Liaison Division, from Level 4 to Level 6, while continuing to maintain my previous responsibilities. The Program Manager Level 6 role expanded my responsibilities, such that the Multicultural Liaison Officers across Canada became my direct reports. I held this position until 1982 when another significant career change occurred.

I received a call from Marc Rochon, the Assistant Deputy Minister (ADM) responsible for Regional Operations within the department of Secretary of State. Marc informed me that he had a vacancy in Nova Scotia for a Regional Director and that he saw me as the right man for the job. I moved to Nova Scotia to take up the position as the Regional Director for the department, with oversight responsibilities for New Brunswick. The responsibilities that came with this new assignment included all matters relating to Department of Secretary of State in Nova Scotia and New Brunswick. And I would also have oversight for the Offices in Prince Edward Island (PEI) and Newfoundland from time to time. My new role continued to include responsibility for the Multicultural Program in these Provinces and was now expanded to include oversite of the Official Languages Program, the programs relating to the Status of Women as well as Citizenship. These programs fell within the portfolio of Gerald Regan who was the Minister responsible for the Secretary of State. During my tenure, I was appointed as a Notary Public for the Province of Nova Scotia.

I continued in this role up until 1985 when I received a call, again from Marc Rochon the Assistant Deputy Minister. When I answered the phone, his voice was stern. "Scott, I think it's time you get out of there, you've done everything you had to do and I have a man here who wants to talk to you." By this time the Multiculturalism Division had been upgraded to a Branch with its own Assistant Deputy Minister, Douglas Bowie, had been fully implemented, and Multiculturalism was now a department within the Federal Government. Marc Rochon, my current ADM had now moved on to Privy Council. The Privy Council would now have the responsibility for the newly established Multiculturalism Department.

I met with Douglas Bowie after I arrived in Ottawa and learned that he was looking for a Director-General to head up the Multicultural Department. This was an executive level position and after we discussed this role for a while, he told me to go back and pack for a return to Ottawa. So after three years in Nova Scotia, I was now heading back to Ottawa as the DG of the Multicultural Branch within the Federal Government.

My tenure as Director-General of the Multicultural Branch went from 1985-1988. The Conservatives had just taken power with Brian Mulroney as Prime Minister and a new Deputy Minister (DM) had been appointed to oversee the

Department of Secretary of State. For whatever reason, my relationship with the DM was shaky from the start and continued to be that way. And in the course of time, Douglas Bowie, the ADM who hired me left his job and a new ADM, Shirley Serafini was appointed to this position. Ms. Serafina immediately recognized that I was a great asset to her, and we established a very strong working relationship. But my relationship with her manager, now Deputy Minister, remained tepid. One day he summoned me to his office, told me that I had been on this job for too long and that it was time for me to get out of it. No exit timing was established and neither did he provide me with further insight as to what was being planned. I started to look around for other opportunities. I made contact with the network of colleagues that I had established over the years and had discussions with a former Deputy Minister, Huguette Labelle, about my career interests. I had previously indicated my interest in serving at the Privy Council. She discouraged me from proceeding down this path. However, she later went to work at the Privy Council and at this time she had moved over to become the Chair of the Public Service Commission.

Now that I was back in Ottawa, I re-engaged with the local Black community and since I was heading the Multiculturalism Branch I was invited to and attended as many of the community functions as I was able. The Harry Jerome Awards, an annual event hosted by the Black Business and Professional Association (BBPA) in Toronto, is one of these functions that I attend each year.[265]

I was scheduled to attend this event on the following weekend and also scheduled to attend a conference in British Columbia on the next Monday. I went into the office on Monday morning to make final preparations for this trip for which I would be leaving on Monday afternoon. Shortly after arriving my phone rang. When I answered, it was Marc, my previous ADM who had moved me to and from Nova Scotia. He was now the Deputy Clerk of the Privy Council and was not in my chain of command. With his signature terse voice, he said; "Scott, what are you doing?" I responded that I was preparing to leave for the BC conference in the afternoon. "Whatever you are doing, drop it and come see me right away," he said. So, I dropped everything and went across to the Privy Council office to meet with him.

Without much hesitation, he said "There is a vacancy at the Public Service Commission for a Commissioner. I think you'd be the right man for the job.

---

265 "The BBPA Harry Jerome Awards is recognized as the most prestigious national awards gala in the African-Canadian community and a coveted symbol of achievement. Winners receive awards in the following categories: Academics, Arts, Athletics, Business, Community Service, Diversity, Entertainment, Health Sciences, Leadership, Lifetime Achievement, Media, President's, Professional Excellence, Trailblazer and Young Entrepreneur." Black Business and Professional Association Facebook.
https://www.facebook.com/thebbpa/photos/a.483683705005136/2476511759055644/?type=3 Accessed on March 23,2023.

I talked to Jack Manion (the hiring ADM and Clerk of the Privy Council) already. Are you interested?" I had not met Jack before, so he took me to meet him, and we had an interview discussion. I returned to my office to continue on with my day's agenda. On the Thursday following my meeting with Marc and Jack, Marc called me. "You lucky ***, the PM bought it." I'm taken aback. I'm speechless. Marc sensed this and said, "You don't know what to say?" And before I could respond, he interjected, "you've got the Job as Public Service Commissioner. The PM bought it."

As it turned out, Prime Minister Brian Mulroney was slated to address the BBPA Harry Jerome Awards on the upcoming Saturday – an event I would also be attending. In my current role as the Director-General of the Multicultural Department, I was tasked with preparing notes for the PM's address, given that he would be addressing a multicultural audience. And in the rarest of coincidences, the PM would use this occasion to make the announcement regarding my new position as Public Service Commissioner. Marc (my manager-to-be) told me to get my security clearance for the new role and begin the transition process. I hustled to get things moving so that I could head off to Toronto for the weekend event. My current manager, Shirley Serafini was also scheduled to attend the Harry Jerome awards, but I was sworn to secrecy about the job change and could only divulge this information to my wife, Jackie.

The venue for the Harry Jerome Awards event was the Toronto Harbour Front Hotel. I had also made reservations to stay at the Harbour Front and invited a number of my social friends who were also attending the Awards to join me for cocktails immediately prior to the start of the Awards Dinner. While I'm in the bathroom getting ready for the Awards Dinner the phone rings. Jackie answers. She runs to me and whispers, "The Prime Minister is on the line." I grabbed the phone and as soon as I started the conversation, my friends showed up, none of whom knew anything about what I was going through. Jackie tried frantically to get them to keep quiet.

I continued to converse with the Prime Minister who said he had reviewed the recommendations regarding my suitability for the Job as Public Service Commissioner and was satisfied that I was the right person. Shortly afterward we headed off to the awards venue and I immediately sought out Shirley my current manager, because she had no idea what was pending and I thought that I should not allow her to be caught off guard. When I gave her the details, she broke down emotionally. And later, as planned, the Prime Minister made the announcement during his address at the Harry Jerome Awards."

Appendix H
Articles from *The Spectrum* [266]

Caribbean Voices in Action. Source: *The Spectrum*, November 15, 1989

---

266 Ewart and Merle Walters launched 'The Spectrum', a monthly community newspaper with the mission to "Making Minorities Visible".

Black Media Gala has plenty to celebrate

More than 30 years ago, one of the first television programs showcasing the activities of Ottawa's black community was *Data*, broadcast on what was then Ottawa Cablevision.

The program underwent a name change in the early 1980s to *Caribbean Calendar* to better reflect the growing Jamaican community in the city. And since then, Ottawa's black community has been well served by other media outlets including newspapers, radio shows and television programs.

Tomorrow night, leaders from Ottawa's African and Caribbean community present a Black Media Gala at the National Arts Centre, recognizing those media outlets and their hosts.

The dinner gala will feature guest speaker Dr. Robert Moore, former high commissioner of Guyana, and include details about the Black Media project, a City of Ottawa-funded program that is producing a history of the city's black media.

"We've been asking ourselves how important are we, how relevant are we now that there are so many more people in the black and Caribbean community," said Ingrid John-Baptiste, co-host of *Caribbean Calendar*.

"It's not as if they're living in their own little vacuum because they're absolutely integrated into the wider community and they do listen and read the mainstream media," added Ms. John-Baptiste.

She said the relevance has been in bringing the "positives of our culture" to the wider community on a regular basis through the different media. Ms. John-Baptiste said *Caribbean Calendar* has its loyal viewers, including non-blacks interested in learning about different cultures.

Some of the programs that will be recognized at the gala include *Caribbean Calendar*, which is broadcast on Rogers Cable; *The Spectrum* newspaper; *Reggae in the Fields*, which airs on CKCU-FM and *Black on Black*, which airs on CHUO-FM.

CITIZEN STAFF

the Spectrum

MAKING MINORITIES VISIBLE

EASTER STORY

"...and with his stripes we are healed."

Page 8

Nunziata blasts what passes for multiculturalism

NOT GOOD ENOUGH

Rosemary, Mairuth and Glenda

Glendamania

Immigrants' incomes declining

Black Man's Burden

page 4

Fashion For Literacy

page 9

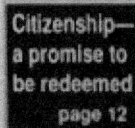

Citizenship— a promise to be redeemed

page 12

Appendix I

An interview with Junior Smith

Documented by Catherine Clark [267]

"Junior Smith has been giving Ottawa radio audiences a reason to sing and dance since 1976, the year he began hosting his popular local show "Reggae in the Fields" on CKCU FM. The show hit a chord with listeners – literally – and has gone on to become Canada's longest running Reggae program.

Junior has used the show not just as an avenue to share his love of Reggae music, but also as an opportunity to discuss social justice issues – particularly those which impact Ottawa's Black community – and to promote diversity. For his work using music and conversation to encourage dialogue and unity, Junior Smith is one of #150 Great People in Ottawa. Here he answers the questionnaire:

[Q] What makes Ottawa special to you?

Ottawa is the only city that I have lived in since I immigrated to Canada almost 45 years ago. I have lived in Ottawa longer than I have lived in Jamaica, my country of birth. I therefore call Ottawa my home, a place which has defined my growth throughout my adult life.

[Q] What do you love about living and working in Ottawa?

The blossoming of Ottawa's diverse cultural communities intrigues me because of my interest and work in achieving an atmosphere of "unity with diversity" across social groups.

[Q] The work that you do helps to make Ottawa a better place – why is this important to you?

In 1976, I started a radio program at Carleton University for strictly personal reasons. During my early years as an immigrant in Canada, I could not find any public radio stations in Ottawa that reflected my culture in the form of music. After my complaint to mainline radio stations went

---

267 September 15, 2017 ~ Catherine Clark http://blog.catherineclark.ca/author/catherine/ Accessed on February 15, 2020. Interview reproduced with permission from Catherine Clark.

unanswered, I decided to start my own radio program on CKCU FM 93.1. For me, the importance of RITF lies in its objective to promote various Black cultures in the form of music and spoken word. RITF not only reflects similar programming content that one would hear in Jamaica, but the program also adopts the country's motto, "Out of Many, One People." This is the hope – that Ottawa will become a city which fully embraces the diversity yet oneness of its citizens.

[Q] You give back to the Ottawa community in various ways – is there one Ottawa related achievement of which you are most proud?

RITF is now celebrating 41 years as Canada's longest running Reggae radio program. I am proud that this volunteer activity has become a "cornerstone" in the history of the city and has given the Black community a medium to express themselves in a diverse and changing social environment.

[Q] What do you hope for Ottawa in the future?

In 2016, I graduated from a Doctor of Ministry program at Saint Paul University with a focus towards understanding the immigrant cultural diversity in the Churches in Canada. The question of belonging to a community and a sense of wanting to feel welcomed regardless of race, colour or ethnicity, has been an ongoing concern for me. My hope for Ottawa is that our various stratified communities, including the churches, will continue to explore ways that would allow immigrants to feel welcomed; and to promote equal dialogue between cultural groups, given their varying human experiences. In doing so, Ottawa will move towards being the best city on the face of the planet!

Junior further explained that his first reggae program was a 30-minute test program aired on a Sunday afternoon, following a proposal he made to the Program Director. Nothing happened for almost a year. But during this time Junior was learning the fundamentals of radio broadcasting behind the scenes and when a slot came up within which a full live program could become part of the regular scheduling he grabbed it."

Junior now holds degrees in Mathematics, Statistics and Economics. He also has a Bachelor of Commerce, a Master of Business Administration, a Master of Pastoral Theology and a Doctorate in Ministry. These achievements explain the pre-eminent motivation for Caribbean immigrants. "Like many folks in the Caribbean in general, and in Jamaica in particular, they wanted to better themselves and they are always seeking to go abroad" to make this happen.

Dave Tulloch, author

Dave Tulloch was born in Jamaica. He immigrated to Canada in 1970 to pursue post-secondary education. He earned a diploma in electronics engineering technology from Algonquin College, a Bachelor of Admin and Bachelor of Commerce (Hon) from the University of Ottawa, and a Master of Business Administration from Concordia University. He has an extensive career in information technology and in IT consulting with Systemhouse, KPMG, and Oracle Corporation where he retired as a director. Dave taught IT and business courses at CEGEP (Hull) and tutored at Wake Tech College in North Carolina.

He wrote articles for the Ottawa Spectrum publication that focused on Ottawa's Visible Minorities community and currently writes articles for blackottawascene.com

The Caribbean. Images of white sandy beaches, blue skies, palm trees, warm temperatures year-round, places of leisure and fun, and pulsating rhythms of reggae and soca music, radiate throughout each island in the Caribbean Sea. Contrast this with Canada, more specifically Ottawa, one of the coldest cities in the world.

Why would anyone wish to uproot themselves to resettle there? Many native Caribbean people accepted this challenge and in this collection tell their stories of life in Canada.

A Caribbean Islet, north coast of Montego Bay, Jamaica. Photo by Dave Tulloch, 2022

"While the Canadian Government had specific reasons for admitting immigrants, the immigrants themselves had their own reasons for wanting to migrate to Canada ... By the time they had completed their set goals, they had established themselves inside new communities, made new friends, established new families and had been assimilated into the Canadian culture."
— Dave Tulloch, page 43

"Tell me and I will forget; show me and I may remember; involve me and I will understand."
— Dr. Garth Taylor

"A people without the knowledge of their past, history, origin and culture are like a tree without roots."
— Marcus Garvey (1887-1940)

Front: Rideau Canal in Ottawa, Canada. Oil painting by Shirley Van Dusen.

978 1989048740

Petra Books
petrabooks.ca

ISBN 978-1-989048-74-0
90000
9 781989 048740